PEOPLE'S WAR

PEOPLE'S WAR

CONDITIONS AND CONSEQUENCES IN CHINA AND SOUTH EAST ASIA

J. L. S. GIRLING

FREDERICK A. PRAEGER, *Publishers*
New York · Washington

BOOKS THAT MATTER

Published in the United States of America in 1969
by Frederick A. Praeger, Inc., Publishers
111 Fourth Avenue, New York, N.Y. 10003

Library of Congress Catalog Card Number: 69–19552

Printed in The United States of America

CONTENTS

MAPS

APOLOGIA

Despite the subtitle of this book I have not discussed the aftermath of people's war in China (the 'consequences' refer to Peking's policy on people's war and to US counter-measures; and the effect of these in South East Asia). But it is relevant to point out that, on the whole, China under Communism (even during the Cultural Revolution) is a better place for the *majority of people*—that is what I am concerned with: which democrats *should* be concerned with—than it was under the Kuomintang. In any case there was no real alternative; and the choice was made. Similarly with Vietnam: the choice was between Vietminh and French rule—Bao Dai offered no real alternative. It is true that once in power the Communists have revealed far less attractive features than they did as leaders of popular revolt: ruthlessness, dogmatism and exploitation among them (particularly in their treatment of the peasantry—the very people whose support was needed to win the revolution). But again it should be pointed out that, while there were evident cruelties in 'land reform' in North Vietnam, Ho Chi Minh did backtrack and admit his mistake—something that Ngo Dinh Diem, also led into error with his 'strategic hamlet' programme, could not bring himself to do. None of this can excuse condonation of injustice or oppression wherever it may occur; but at least for the period—and the problem—I am dealing with the balance was tilted clearly one way.

J.L.S.G.

'The guerrilla movement is only the result, not the cause of the problem.'

A. H. Nasution

INTRODUCTION

Insurrection, according to the Concise Oxford Dictionary, is a 'rising in open resistance to established authority' or an 'incipient rebellion', which is defined in similar terms. Thus insurrection on any scale—which is what matters—can also be considered a civil war, except in the case of a purely national uprising against foreign domination. Insurgency, rebellion, civil war, local conflict, people's war, are more or less interchangeable terms, irrespective of the type of 'established government' whose authority is being contested, regardless of the rights or wrongs of either side. (The Hungarian uprising of 1956 was as much a 'people's war' as the Vietminh campaign in Indo-China.)

Insurgency indicates prolonged resistance and thus differs from a *coup d'état*, either civil or military, which is a sudden seizure of power; though the result—if successful—may be the same, that is the overthrow of the established authority. (*Coups* often effect only a change of leaders, not a change of policies; the latter is more likely to be the case with a long and widespread and destructive war.) Insurgency also differs from 'aggression', which denotes an armed attack across frontiers. But insurgents may be assisted verbally, diplomatically, economically or militarily from outside to a varying extent, which tends to blur the distinction. However, such aid can only be supplementary and not decisive, for otherwise there would no longer be an insurgency.

Both *coups* and insurgencies are the products of unstable situations, and this is likely to be a continuing feature of the developing world. Little can be done to prevent *coups* taking place—except to broaden the basis of government—but there are ways of remedying popular discontent to prevent it taking the form of mass resistance or insurgency.

The successful outcome of insurgency in developing countries—to judge from the experience of China, Indo-China and South Vietnam; and from the 'negative' experience of Malaya, Greece and the Philippines—depends on the combination of six conditions, which are partly economic, partly military and partly political. (If only some of these conditions are realized an insurgency may still break out, though it is unlikely to succeed.) These conditions are:

1. Peasant support.
2. Ability to sustain 'protracted war'.
3. National appeal.
4. Leadership.
5. Organization.
6. Breakdown, or severe incapacity, of the opposing régime.

The first three are 'motivating' factors; the last three, factors of 'achievement'. Serious economic conditions in the countryside usually provide the underlying motive for taking up arms. 'Protracted war'—a complex of factors, notably the 'survival and growth' of insurgent forces based on 'liberated areas', gradually extending from remote jungle or mountainous regions, employing guerrilla tactics to wear down the enemy and thus gradually changing the balance of forces—this is the way for a weak and ill-equipped movement to carry on the war against a more powerful enemy. And a nation-wide appeal helps to crown it with success.

In more detail: 1. A peasant uprising is more likely to be the result of over-population, inexorably reducing the limited amount of cultivable land available to farm families (in the absence of other forms of employment), than of traditional 'feudal' abuses; though the two are usually combined. This was the case in China under the Kuomintang, which failed to carry out Sun Yat-sen's policy of 'land to the tiller' largely from fear of upsetting its conservative, landowning supporters; it was left to the Communists to do this instead (and thus to rally peasant support against the régime).

2. 'Protracted war' flows from Mao's recognition that a struggling revolutionary movement cannot expect to overcome a government at one blow by Soviet-style urban insurrection, nation-wide general strike, etc. Ho Chi Minh and Vo Nguyen Giap in turn emphasized that immediate victory over France was wishful thinking. Instead the war would be long and hard. In the beginning, the chief need for inexperienced, poorly organized guerrillas is security: a secure base in which to train, equip and build up a 'main force' without which the insurgents cannot go beyond the guerrilla stage and therefore cannot seriously threaten the centres of power. Security can be positive—if guerrilla areas are sufficiently remote from (as in China) or inaccessible to (because of mountain and jungle, as in Indo-China) the effective authority of government. Negatively, there is security if the government is prevented from concentrating its forces against the insurgents because of external distractions or internal splits or 'contradictions'. (It is significant that insurgent bases are often located on or near provincial boundaries. This is partly because rugged country or mountain ranges serve as natural boundaries or frontiers, partly because opposing forces are for this reason often

divided, since they come under separate provincial authorities or separate, possibly hostile, governments.) Divisions within the government—or just lack of co-ordination—and unity of the insurgents: these are two sides of the same coin. And the reverse applies.

3. An appeal that is nation-wide both in area and social coverage. The Chinese Communists started with a narrow class appeal—chiefly to landless tenants and poor peasants (after the suppression of the workers' movement) in a limited area, the south-east of China. It was the Japanese invasion which transformed the Communists from class warriors into vigorous and effective patriots, over an extensive and quite different area—north and central China. France's attempt to reassert its authority over Indo-China in 1945-46 did the same for the Vietminh. Moreover, the latter had no effective nationalist rival in Vietnam. This was because the French had wiped out most non-Communist nationalists in the 1930s (the Communists being better trained in conspiratorial methods were more successful in going underground). The Vietminh remained without rivals, because the French refused to grant real powers of independence to the Bao Dai régime, which never acquired the status of a truly national alternative. (This was also because of its own shortcomings.)

Factors of 'achievement':

4. History points to the importance of leadership both to revolutionaries and to governments. The mere roll-call of outstanding Communist leaders—from Lenin, Trotsky and Stalin to Mao Tse-tung, Ho Chi Minh and Tito—belies theoretical Marxist insistence on the exclusively determining role of economic conditions. Moreover the failings of leaders like Chiang Kai-shek, Ngo Dinh Diem and General Phoumi Nosavan, and conversely the success of President Magsaysay of the Philippines, were clearly important in the ability or otherwise of their governments to cope with insurgencies.

5. Organization is strongly emphasized both by Communists and by theorists of counter-insurgency. To Mao it marked the difference between the 'roving guerrilla bands' of Chinese history and his disciplined and dedicated revolutionary movement. Mao's aim was the organization of a State within the State. 'In these base areas,' as Lin Piao put it, 'we built the Party, ran the organs of State power, built the people's armed forces and set up mass organizations.' He went on: 'Our base areas were in fact a State in miniature . . . a grand rehearsal in preparation for a nation-wide victory.' This shows the importance of an organized basis for insurgency. Guerrillas are not merely destructive forces; the task of armed insurgents is as much to establish, expand and defend their own 'parallel hierarchies' of

administration (or 'infra-structure') as it is to destroy those of the government.

6. The effect of the breakdown or incapacity of the existing régime hardly needs emphasizing. This is often the result of war, which upsets or ruins living conditions, social and political institutions and the administrative framework. Without the instability or devastation caused by war an initially weak insurgent movement is unlikely to extend beyond the remote areas to threaten the centres of population and power. The havoc caused by the Japanese in China and by their overthrow of the French colonial régime in Indo-China played into the hands of the Communists. Elsewhere in South East Asia, non-Communist nationalists were strong enough—though in some countries only just—to seize the advantage of the wartime overthrow of colonial rule for themselves.

* * *

The *presence* of factors favouring the insurgents in any revolutionary situation—peasant support, national appeal, effective leadership and organization—usually indicates the *absence* of these factors as far as the government is concerned. In many developing countries there is no adequate 'third force' to provide a democratic alternative to a reactionary government or to an extreme revolutionary movement. Thus the problem in coping with an insurgency is how to get a 'reactionary' government—since it is usually a reactionary government which 'provokes' insurgency—to adopt democratic measures; that is, to win popular support away from the rebels, who depend on this for their security. Such governments, or rather their leaders, genuinely dislike democratic reforms, firstly because they consider the 'people'—that is, in large part the peasants—an inferior species, and secondly because any measure of reform threatens the vested interests on which they (the leaders) depend for support. Personal loyalty to the leader—whether it is Chiang Kai-shek or Ngo Dinh Diem—comes before the security or the welfare of the nation. In such cases, a change of leaders is the only way to ensure a change of policies; and this is not only difficult to achieve, but it may come too late to have any effect.

* * *

Similar situations of unstable societies and poor leadership are likely to continue. Moreover the motive force of peasant unrest will probably become even more important as rapid increases of population outgrow natural resources. India, Pakistan and Java, with extremely low standards of living and densely populated areas, may well become danger spots in Asia. Localized peasant uprisings have already taken place in India and Indonesia. It does not take much foresight to imagine—in the event of governmental incapacity—a fourth Communist insurrection in Indonesia: this time better prepared and more effectively based on the villages. And it is perhaps surprising that India in the face of such dissension in society and such depths of rural degradation should have gone so long virtually unscathed. The present vulnerability of Congress may mark the end of this phase. Regional and language conflicts may become more threatening, the civil service may crack under growing pressure, peasant passivity may change to violence. . . .

This is even more likely to happen in Latin America, where in a number of countries a largely Indian rural proletariat is oppressed by what is almost a caricature of the Marxist picture of a corrupt, selfish and ruthless absentee landlord class. Hitherto, the wretched Hindu outcast and the landless labourer of Latin America have probably been too cowed by poverty to revolt. But should they become affected by some slight improvement of conditions—by 'rising expectations'—then revolution may well break out. (It is the young men and the more active and enterprising of the villagers, rather than the very poor and downtrodden, who become revolutionaries.)

As for Africa, there is even more disorganization there than in Latin America as newly independent governments grapple with tribal and economic problems; but perhaps for this reason (fluidity rather than rigidity) there is less possibility of violent explosion. Moreover Africa is further removed from world power-centres and therefore internal confusion—as in the Congo situation—is less likely to generate outside intervention than in the case of Asia or Latin America.

Thus, conditions for revolutionary uprisings not only exist but are likely to become more widespread. They will not necessarily be Communist uprisings. In the next decade or two, 'Communist'—assuming the existence of a variety of national-Communist régimes—may have lost international significance. But this does not exclude the possibility of outside intervention in civil war situations, though this would no longer need to be justified on Communist or anti-Communist grounds. A change in the internal situation of a large country like India or Brazil or Indonesia would affect any 'balance of forces' outside it, if there were such, and this could provoke external intervention on one side or the other. But at least smaller countries of little or no strategic significance to world powers should be spared this fate. And these countries might avoid the risk altogether if they took care—by judicious measures—to prevent insurgencies from breaking out in the first place.

South East Asia and Southern China: Peoples, Places, Features

I THE SCENE

Revolution and Intervention in South East Asia

History repeats itself, Marx observed, 'the first time as tragedy, the second as farce'.[1] In South East Asia the tragedy is the involvement of the great powers, resulting successively in colonial rule, Japanese occupation, Communist insurrection and American intervention. The 'farce' is not so much that the great powers pursue different interests (for so do the countries of the area) but that individual countries' interests may change over a short period of time and even contradict themselves. What seems reasonable and straightforward at one time or from one point of view may, on another occasion or merely by a shift in perspective, take on an entirely different character—cloudy, complex and ominous.

Nowhere is this more apparent than in Vietnam—the cause of such profound concern throughout the world. One of the ironies of this tragic situation is that President de Gaulle should now favour the independence and unity of a people whose aspirations he thwarted, with such lamentable results, in the past. Though prepared to negotiate with Ho Chi Minh's 'Democratic Republic of Vietnam' in 1945-46, de Gaulle and his immediate successors refused to concede the principle of independence or to accept the historic unity of Vietnam. In face of the growing power and influence of Ho's government in Hanoi, the colonial administrators and French settlers were determined not to yield control of the commercial network, the rubber estates and the rice fields of Cochin-China—now the heart of South Vietnam.[2]

The war which started at the end of 1946 ended eight years later in France's defeat and ignominious withdrawal from Indo-China. (The present conflict in Vietnam is essentially a continuation of that struggle.) The Americans, who began by criticizing the French in Indo-China, ended by paying eighty per cent of the cost of the war.[3] In the present conflict in Vietnam, the French have reversed the procedure. Starting from a position of neutrality or support for American policy, they have moved to one of criticism and even outright opposition. One reason for French behaviour, it is suggested, is the desire that America should not succeed where France had failed. A better one is the belief that a neutral Vietnam within a neutral South East Asia—guaranteed by the agreement of the great powers, including China—is the only way to insulate the area from the disastrous consequences of the cold war.

The French have not only proposed neutrality, they have opted out of responsibility for a western military presence—to check 'Communist aggression'. In Washington it is believed that the French no longer care what happens to South East Asia: it does not matter to France (whose basic interests, in Europe, are in fact protected by American nuclear power) whether South Vietnam goes Communist or not. Even if it does, the French argue, it might be an advantage. It would accord with the 'natural' tendency—artificially obstructed by American 'interference'—for the more forceful North Vietnamese to dominate the South, the more active and industrious Vietnamese (altogether) to dominate the rest of Indo-China, and indeed, for the Chinese to dominate the area as a whole. Now whether this view is correct or not—and no doubt if South East Asia were left to itself this would occur—it is a far cry from de Gaulle's original conception of Indo-China under effective foreign—i.e. French—control.

Is foreign interference the cause (as the French now consider) or the consequence (as the Americans claim) of the successive crises in South East Asia? In other words, is outside intervention necessary (as the French once argued) to protect a defenceless area—to fill the 'vacuum' resulting from the wartime withdrawal of the colonial powers, for example—or does this merely (as the Americans used to think) provoke national unrest and stimulate Communist uprisings? Ironically, the Americans, during and immediately after the Second World War, helped to arm the Vietminh and looked askance at the colonial powers' attempts to regain control of territories lost to the Japanese and to national independence movements.

Curiously, the Russians were then on the opposite tack. Soviet post-war policy sought to restrain nationalist movements (supported by local Communists) in Indonesia and Indo-China, in the hope of exerting more influence in Western Europe, an area of far greater importance to Russia. Thus French Communists in Saigon were reported to have warned their Vietnamese comrades in 1945 against 'prematurely' seeking independence, since this might 'not be in line with Soviet perspectives' regarding France as a potential ally of the USSR.[4] As for the French Communist Party, then taking part in a coalition government in France, it was more concerned to 'make a nationalist appeal to the French electorate than to give overt support to the Ho Chi Minh Government'. Communist members of the French Cabinet actually voted early in 1947 in support of the fight against the Vietminh.[5]

But the outbreak of the cold war was to change all that.

COMMUNIST REVOLTS: 1948

South East Asia, with its natural resources, discordant nationalisms and unstable régimes, has long served as a lure for outside intervention and intrigue. There is no doubt that Stalin considered it, in the early stages of the cold war, as ripe for revolt—whether under colonial rule or where 'bourgeois national' leaders had obtained 'independence'. By the time the Cominform had been established in September 1947, proclaiming that the countries of 'new democracy' and the workers of all countries must unite with the USSR—'the bulwark of anti-imperialism'—against the imperialist camp, the Vietminh had been fighting for almost a year against the French. The Communist-led Huk guerrillas were enlarging their operations in the Philippines. In 1946 and 1947 Malaya and Singapore had seen massive strike activities by Communist trade unions, Indonesia lay torn between nationalists (aided at that time by influential Communists) and the Dutch, and Burmese nationalists (despite the misgivings of ethnic minorities) were demanding independence from the British.

Already a trial of strength between Communists and nationalists had begun in Burma. One group of Communists—the fanatical 'Red Flags'—wanted war against Britain, another and larger group ('White Flags') planned to work for Communism within the ranks of the future ruling party, the Anti-Fascist People's Freedom League: but it was expelled in 1946. In July 1947 the founder of the A.F.P.F.L., General Aung San, was assassinated and his para-military force—the People's Volunteer Organization—was left leaderless. The main group of Communists, led by Thakin Than Tun, denounced the independence treaty signed by U Nu in January 1948 and called for the overthrow of the Nu Government as 'tools of the British imperialists'.[6] Than Tun, with Chinese, Vietnamese, Indonesian and other Communists, attended the Conference of the Youth and Students of South East Asia Fighting for Freedom and Independence, held in Calcutta in February 1948, and a month later led his party into armed revolt.

Palme Dutt, the veteran British Communist, summed up the situation in his message to the Calcutta Conference. 'The whole region of South East Asia,' he wrote, 'is today the central arena of the struggle for national liberation against imperialism. The approaching victory of democratic China heralds a new era in Asia. . . .' The Chinese delegation, echoing the Manifesto of the newly formed Cominform, spoke of the 'bitter struggle' between the people's anti-imperialist front and the imperialist camp: 'The people of South East Asia, who have been enslaved by imperialism for many years, should take advantage of the present moment and strive for complete liberation. . . . [The Chinese struggle] requires the assistance of and association with the liberation campaign of the peoples of South East Asia.'[7]

The Second Congress of the Communist Party of India was held in Calcutta immediately after the Youth Conference. The Indian Communists accused bourgeois governments of 'betraying' the freedom struggle by striking a 'treacherous deal' with the imperialists and their allies.[8] The Indian Communists were reported to have discussed resorting to outright rebellion, but they recognized that it would be suicidal to attack the Nehru Government in view of the 'strong ties of loyalty that still bind the people to the Congress'.[9] Instead they hoped to undermine the Government by fomenting strikes and peasant disturbances (some of which, notably in the Telengana area, developed into local insurrections). To a certain extent the Burmese and Malayan Communists also sought to come to power by promoting chaos and confusion short of civil war; but when the two governments reacted and attempted to arrest the Communist leaders, the later found they were left with no alternative but to take up arms. In any case, the Burmese and Malayan Communists seemed to view their strikes and turbulence as a prelude to revolt rather than as an alternative to it.[10]

Certainly, the Malayan Communist Party, after two of its representatives had returned from the Calcutta meetings, rejected its former policy of 'peaceful' mass struggle. 'Our party has now already purged itself of the rightist policy of opportunism,' the Central Committee declared in a report captured later by government security forces, 'and has correctly established a firm and revolutionary standpoint to lead the revolutionary war.'[11] When the party launched its open insurrection in June 1948, it envisaged a protracted campaign in three stages: guerrilla raids on rubber plantations, tin mines and police outposts to sabotage the economy and the administration; increased military activities to deprive the government of effective control of all but the main towns and communications; and finally, 'liberated areas' to be established and gradually be extended throughout the country. This plan was set out in the party's *Strategic Problems of the Malayan Revolutionary War*, issued in December 1948, and clearly based on Mao Tse-tung's own *Strategic Problems of China's Revolutionary War*.[12]

Indonesian Communists, who had previously been associated with the Republican régime, were also influenced by the 'militant tone' of the Calcutta 'Youth Conference'. But it was not until July 1948 that they realized there was little hope of gaining power through political means and turned more and more to the idea of using military force.

A secret report by the Communist-controlled People's Democratic Front (later captured by the Government) estimated that over one-third of the armed forces was already under its control. (One of the issues between the newly-formed government under Vice-President Hatta and the Communists and their followers was the decision to rationalize the unwieldy and swollen Indonesian army and bureaucracy.) The report stated that if the Front's mass campaign to dissolve the government or to reform it with Front members in key posts failed—as it did—then 'we will cut off all relations with the government and continue our struggle under our own leadership either as rebellion or as separate government'.[13]

In August 1948 the veteran Communist revolutionary Musso (who had been more than a decade in Russia) arrived in Jogjakarta, Central Java, the capital of Republican Indonesia (the Dutch were then occupying most of the towns of West and East Java after their 'police action' of July 1947 and they were to attack again in December 1948).* Musso took over the leadership of the Communist Party and expounded his 'Gottwald Plan' to win power (as in the February 1948 Czech *coup*) without the use of armed force if possible, if not, by insurrection. But by mid-September the strengthening and reorganization of the Communist Party had only just begun and Communist leaders did not expect to act with full effectiveness for at least another six weeks. However, on September 19th the matter was taken out of their hands when the local Communist organization and militant youth movement in Madiun, East Java, inspired by dissident military officers, prematurely launched a *coup* (the parallel with the events of September 1965, is remarkable). President Sukarno appealed to the Indonesian people to choose between Musso, founding the Soviet Government in Madiun and attempting to seize the Republic, and the independent Indonesia led by Sukarno and Hatta. Loyal army forces moved in and by the end of October the last rebel unit had been crushed.[14]

Throughout South and South East Asia the purely Communist insurrections failed (the Vietminh, by contrast, was a national movement led by Communists). Firm action by the Indian Government suppressed Communist violence in a number of States and thwarted the proposed nation-wide general strike and railway strike of March 1949, by which the Communist Party, according to Nehru, was 'deliberately seeking to create famine conditions' to 'create a general background of chaos, a breakdown of the administration and mass

* The Dutch at first accused the Indonesian leaders of being 'fascists' because of their wartime collaboration with the Japanese, then of being 'Communists' because some Communists were included in the post-war Republican Government.

uprising'. In Malaya, the Communists who were almost entirely Chinese, never won the backing of the Malay majority, while administrative countermeasures—chiefly resettling and controlling dissident Chinese squatters—isolated the guerrillas from their main source of support. The Burmese Government only gradually brought the various insurrections—of Communists, ethnic minorities, former Kuomintang troops—under control, except in the remote areas. A situation of imminent disaster faced the corrupt and inffective government of the Philippines, but the reforms carried out by Magsaysay (as Secretary of Defence and later President)—land for the landless, free and fair elections, prompt action against abuses—undercut the popular appeal of the rebels and dramatically turned the tide.

In November 1949 Mao's second-in-command, Liu Shao-chi, was still advocating armed struggle in the countryside and 'legal and illegal mass struggles' in the cities. 'Armed struggle,' he told delegates to the Asian-Australasian trade union conference in Peking (another cover for international Communist activities, like the 1948 Calcutta Youth Conference), 'is the main form of struggle for the national liberation struggles of many colonies and semi-colonies'. . . . 'It is necessary to set up wherever and whenever possible a national liberation army which is led by the Communist Party and is powerful and skilful in fighting its enemies.'

But by 1952, with the widespread failure of armed revolt to achieve the overthrow of governments of colonies or independent countries ('semi-colonies'), the emphasis in the Communist world was changing to methods of 'political struggle'—organization, infiltration and subversion. Communist Parties began to seek recognition as mass movements representing workers and peasants and pursuing national aims—not as tightly organized conspiracies bent on the overthrow of bourgeois régimes. Above all, the nationalist parties or leaders were no longer denounced as 'lackeys of the imperialists' but were now considered fellow-members of the 'anti-imperialist, anti-colonialist' camp. As early as December 1950, the Communist Party of India had been criticized by its mentor, Palme Dutt, for waging a 'proletarian revolution'—i.e. against the bourgeois government—instead of a 'national democratic revolution'—against the imperialists. In other words, conditions were not yet suitable—or were no longer suitable—for attempting civil war.

An interesting critique of the post-1948 policy of insurrection is provided by a Filipino Communist, Jorge Maravilla, writing in the November 1965 issue of the Soviet-oriented *World Marxist Review*.[15] The leaders of the Communist Party of the Philippines, he pointed out, were at first divided on whether to pursue all-out armed struggle

—in response to the spontaneous uprising of cadres and peasants—or to fight the 'bourgeois nationalists' through legal channels. Then the party was reorganized in 1948 and became 'more determined' on armed struggle. In January 1950 it decided that a 'revolutionary situation' existed and that the next two years would be the 'preparation for seizure of power': the Huk guerrilla forces would be converted into a regular army and a 'provisional revolutionary government' formed. But an 'obscure and pliable' politician, Ramon Magsaysay, became Secretary of National Defence (and later President): 'Between 1950 and 1956, under the impact of the imperialist counter-offensive, the Huk armed struggle was defeated, the Communist Party cadres were decimated and the movement for national libration received a major setback.'

Why was the Communist struggle defeated? The author gives four main reasons: (1) It was incorrect to estimate that the government's situation in 1950 was 'irrecoverable'; in fact 'the people were susceptible to promises of "reform" '. (2) 'Once a revolutionary situation was declared, the Party put almost all emphasis and cadres into the armed struggle, to the neglect of legal forms of struggle'; the Party failed to form a broad united front and 'antagonized' the national bourgeoisie which allied itself with Magsaysay; and the Huks became isolated. (3) 'Overconfident' of victory, the party was 'careless' of its security. In October 1950 (one of Magsaysay's most daring strokes) the entire Communist Party Secretariat 'and many other top-ranking cadres' were arrested. Complete files of party documents and correspondence were seized. For months, the author states, the remaining cadres were unable to meet and the initiative which had been lost was never regained. Finally (4) the 'national liberation struggle' was 'physically isolated' from its international allies and received virtually no support from abroad.

As a result of the party's 'errors of estimate and tactics' thousands of its cadres and members died fighting—originally there were nine members of the Politburo in 1950 but all were either killed or captured and the same fate befell the entire membership of the party Central Committee: thus the Party was left 'almost without effective cadres'. Only after 1956 did it make a 'tactical shift' to forms of underground and legal struggle.

SINO-SOVIET DISPUTE: (PEOPLE'S) WAR AND PEACE

In the great Communist debate on armed or 'legal' struggle it is significant that the Russians, who chiefly inspired the 1948 revolts (the Chinese Communists being occupied with their own liberation), have come down on the side of 'peaceful' struggle, while the Chinese have identified themselves with the cause of 'national liberation', or as they prefer it, 'people's war'.

Towards the end of 1952 Stalin himself was urging Communist Parties throughout the world to support peace, democracy and national independence (allegedly rejected by the West). But it was his successors who brought about a major shift in Soviet policy. This took two main forms. First, instead of attacking the 'pseudo-independence' attained by bourgeois régimes, the Soviet Union sought to capitalize on feelings of hostility to, or suspicion of, Western policy which influenced men like Nehru, Nasser and Sukarno. Soviet 'friendship'—support for neutrality, offers of trade and aid, promotion of cultural contacts—was intended to point a contrast to the 'militaristic' aims of the West and thus attract the non-aligned countries into the orbit of Soviet foreign policy. The next stage would see the gradual acceptance of the Soviet line in internal affairs—'radical agrarian reforms', abolition of 'feudalism', enlargement of the State sector, expulsion of foreign monopolies, etc.*—and, with this, it was hoped, 'transition to socialism' by peaceful means.

The second feature of Soviet policy was awareness of the disastrous consequences of nuclear warfare in the event of a conflict with the United States. So far from repeating Lenin's famous prediction that 'the existence of the Soviet Republic side by side with imperialist States for a long time is unthinkable . . . a series of frightful collisions between the Soviet Republic and the bourgeois States will be inevitable'—which the Chinese explicitly reaffirmed—Khruschev in his speech at the Soviet Twentieth Party Congress in February 1956, declared that war was 'not fatalistically inevitable' even if imperialism still existed. 'Peaceful coexistence,' he maintained, could avert a nuclear holocaust.

Khruschev's aim was thus to achieve Soviet objectives without risking nuclear war, which he feared might be sparked off by local armed conflicts. † The promotion of 'peaceful transition to socialism' —i.e. to a Communist type of régime without civil war or violent revolution—was a necessary concomitant of the policy of 'peaceful coexistence'. But Khruschev's 'general line' was doubly suspect to the Chinese. Not only in Peking's view was 'US imperialism' the most

* These are the 'national democratic tasks' on which the 'progressive forces of the nation' can unite, according to the Statement of 81 Communist and Workers' Parties, Moscow, December 6, 1960.

† 'The entire experience of the post-war years . . . shows how great in our time is the danger that local wars will grow into a universal war. Also quite real is the danger of thermo-nuclear weapons being used in local wars if countries possessing such weapons—or countries bound by appropriate allied agreements with the nuclear powers—are involved in them. . . .'—Soviet Government Statement, September 20-21, 1963.

ferocious enemy of the people—especially the Chinese people—but America was clearly the major obstacle to the 'liberation' of Taiwan and of near-by countries in South East Asia currently under 'imperialist' control. The militant pursuit of China's national interests was therefore diametrically opposed to Soviet caution in not confronting America, particularly in an area which was not vital to Russia. (Similarly the United States, despite its crusading sentiments, took care not to intervene in the Soviet sphere of influence, both during the 1963 East German revolt and, notoriously, during the 1956 Hungarian uprising.) The basis of coexistence between the two 'super-powers' could not allow for any deviating interests of an ally.

Sino-Soviet differences became apparent in September 1959 when the Russians, instead of supporting China on the Sino-Indian border dispute, adopted an attitude of neutrality. The Chinese not unnaturally complained that Soviet aid should go to Communist countries and not be used to build up bourgeois régimes like India, and that the 'leader' of the Communist camp should support a fellow member. Moreover, as the Chinese were later to argue, a 'socialist country' could not commit 'aggression'—this could only be the act of imperialists or reactionaries. Unmoved by these arguments, the Russians in mid 1960 'perfidiously and unilaterally tore up agreements and contracts they had concluded with a fraternal country'—as the Chinese revealed in February 1963—and withdrew from China all their experts and technicians.

The Chinese had set out their ideological differences with the Russians as early as November 1957—at the Moscow meeting which produced the 'Declaration' of policy of the ruling Communist and Workers' Parties. In a confidential memorandum, the Chinese delegation headed by Mao Tse-tung admitted that Khruschev's advocacy of 'peaceful transition to socialism' was 'advantageous from the point of view of tactics'. But, the Chinese pointed out, 'too much stress' on it, especially on the possibility of a parliamentary majority winning power, was 'liable to weaken the revolutionary will of the proletariat':

'What is most important is to proceed with the hard work of gathering the revolutionary forces. To obtain a majority in parliament is not the same as smashing the old State machinery (chiefly the armed forces). . . . Unless the military bureaucratic State machinery of the bourgeoisie is smashed, a parliamentary majority for the proletariat and their reliable allies will either be impossible . . . or undependable. . . .'

And the memorandum bluntly stated: 'To the best of our knowledge, there is still not a single country where this possibility [of peaceful transition] is of any practical significance.'[16]

As the Chinese leaders were later to argue, violent revolution is a 'universal law of proletarian revolution':

'The key question in the proletarian revolution is that of State power . . . the seizure of State power and the smashing of the bourgeois State machine by violence. . . . [Again] It is absolutely impossible to bring about a fundamental social change by relying on bourgeois parliaments or governments. . . . The active leadership [of the 'proletarian party'] given in day-to-day struggle must have as its central aim the building up of revolutionary strength and the preparations for seizing victory in the revolution when the conditions are ripe. . . . [The struggle is] to prepare for revolution ideologically, politically, organizationally and militarily. . . .'[17]

In theory, this rigorous pursuit of violence was intended to draw a clear line between the true exponents of Marxism-Leninism and its 'betrayers'. In practice, the Soviet Union, having lost the support of most of the South East Asian Communist Parties, legal and illegal, which had gravitated towards Peking, was in any case better prepared for 'governmental' activities unencumbered by revolutionary baggage. The Russians exploited Peking's obsession with violence, claiming that 'the application of the call to armed struggle to countries with national-progressive governments is tantamount to an order for the violent overthrow of those governments which have the respect of the masses and which adhere to an anti-imperialist line'.[18]

This Soviet statement is misleading on two counts. First by declaring that Peking intended the overthrow of 'national-progressive' and not just 'reactionary' régimes; second, by implying that Peking's readiness to use violence was imminent rather than a matter of careful preparation for the time when conditions were ripe. In fact, the Russians, too were opposed to 'reactionary' régimes and what was 'national-progressive' was a matter of interpretation, India qualifying for the Russians but not for the Chinese. . . . Secondly, the Chinese could in practice be just as 'revisionist' as the Russians in their relations with bourgeois governments, for example with Pakistan—a military régime, a member of SEATO and CENTO and an ally of the United States. But the Soviet statement does reveal the *tendency* of the Russians—*faute de mieux*—to deal with governments (rather than Communist Parties) in Asia, and vice versa for the Chinese.

The Russians also believed that their aim of inducing 'national progressive' governments to take the road of 'peaceful transition to socialism' (which, being gradual and non-violent, would avoid armed conflict or outside intervention) was endangered by Peking's campaign for more 'revolutionary' action. Thus, although Moscow was impelled to support 'national liberation movements', if only to prevent them from falling under the influence of the Chinese, it preferred to put stress on their economic rôle once independence had been won. This was in contrast to Peking's view that the 'primary and most urgent task' of the countries of Asia, Africa and Latin America is 'still the further development of the struggle against imperialism, old and new colonialism, and their lackeys. . . . The struggles in all these spheres ['political, economic, military, cultural, ideological'] still find their most concentrated expression in political struggle, which often unavoidably develops into armed struggle. . . .'[19]

Khruschev himself came to recognize that support for 'liberation movements' in South East Asia—an area not of vital importance to the Soviet Union—was not worth the risk of a clash with the Americans. After the Laos settlement of 1962, which had been foreshadowed at his Vienna meeting with President Kennedy in 1961, Khruschev virtually withdrew from any active rôle in South East Asia. But his successors, Brezhnev and Kosygin, anticipating in 1965 an outright military victory by the Vietcong, reversed Khruschev's policy. This was probably to forestall the Chinese, who would otherwise stand to gain too much at the expense of the Russians. But Kosygin's visit to Hanoi to offer military and economic assistance coincided with the start of the US air campaign in February 1965 against targets in North Vietnam. By reasserting their influence in Hanoi the Russians had become inextricably involved in the war in Vietnam.

US REACTION: THE VIETNAM COMMITMENT

By the time John Foster Dulles had been selected as US Secretary of State after November 1952 and was enunciating his policy of 'rolling back Communism' his enemy Stalin had been preparing the shift to a less militant policy, which was taken up more actively by his successors. In a strange reversal of rôles, the new Soviet leaders proceeded to woo the non-aligned nations, while Dulles angrily denounced the 'immorality' of neutralism. Yet another change was to occur under President Kennedy—marked by the *rapprochement* with the Soviet Union (begun under Eisenhower) and the settlement of the Laotian crisis*—while the mantle of Stalinist adventurism,

* Prince Sihanouk aptly retorted to an American correspondent who criticized his 'unpredictability': 'There was a time when your government, which felt great aversion for our neutrality, went so far as to call it immoral. But since then you have gradually learnt to look realities in the face and you finally arrived at desiring for Laos nothing other than this—a neutrality exactly like that of Cambodia, according to your President. Tell me, if you please, if it is you who are changeable or me?' (*Neak Cheat Niyum*, September 3, 1961).

in theory at least, was taken over by the Chinese.[20]

Moreover, though there is a difference in the means employed by 'imperialists' or Communists to attain their ends—corresponding to the different opportunities available to open and closed societies—there is a certain similarity in objectives. Each side, with some justification, sees the other as striving for world domination. Thus Dulles's campaign for the liberation of 'slave States' from Communism was a counterpart of—as well as a reaction to—the Communist drive to liberate colonies and 'semi-colonies' from 'imperialist oppression'. And given an equal assurance of righteousness, each side could feel justified in going to great lengths—'brinkmanship'—because of the vital importance—'inevitability'—of the struggle between them.

In Europe Dulles was unable to take advantage of the opportunities for 'rolling back' Communism afforded by the East German and Hungarian risings (from fear of provoking a nuclear conflict with the Russians), but in South East Asia he had a freer hand. Admittedly his plans for 'united action' in Indo-China to save the French at Dien Bien Phu were turned down by his allies (and his President). But after the 1954 Geneva settlement Dulles worked hard to rebuild a position of strength. This policy had three components: to plug the gap in South Vietnam; to roll back Communism in Laos; and to fortify such 'Free World Bastions' as Taiwan under Chiang Kai-shek, South Korea under Syngman Rhee and Thailand under Marshal Pibun and his police chief Phao. Meanwhile, in neutral countries, the US Central Intelligence Agency was permitted to encourage and support 'anti-Communists', such as the remnants of a Kuomintang army in Burma (even though they were fighting against the Rangoon Government) and the 'separatists' in Indonesia (whose 1958 rebellion against Sukarno was suppressed by the army).

While Dulles's policies remained constant, the Asian situation changed. Four out of the five Right Wing régimes supported by the US in East Asia were overthrown: Rhee in South Korea, Diem in South Vietnam, Pibun in Thailand and Phoumi in Laos. Three times in Laos Prince Souvanna Phouma tried to establish a neutralist régime and three times he was thwarted—twice by the Americans* and once by the North Vietnamese. The Americans put their trust in Colonel (later General) Phoumi Nosavan, ambitious leader of the anti-Communist forces, who helped to dismiss the first neutral-coalition government in 1958 and actually drove Souvanna Phouma out of Vientiane by armed force two years later. It was only under strong pressure by the Kennedy Administration that General Phoumi

* Interview with Prince Souvanna Phouma in Phnom Penh (*New York Times*, January 20, 1961).

reluctantly agreed to the formation of a neutralist-led coalition in 1962, which then foundered on the obstructions of the Pathet Lao and North Vietnamese. Phoumi, after some years of apparent moderation, tried to seize power early in 1965, failed and fled.

In South Korea, fortunately for Washington, the autocratic Syngman Rhee was replaced in 1960 by an equally anti-Communist, but more representative, civilian (and later military) régime; this had also happened in 1957-58, in Thailand. But in South Vietnam the Communist element—legacy of the Vietminh's popular resistance against the French—proved too deeply rooted. Non-Communist adversaries of President Ngo Dinh Diem were unable to overthrow him before his repressive and shortsighted policies had provoked such widespread opposition as to undermine the authority of the State, to the major advantage of the Vietcong. How was it possible for violent change to take place, without leading to Communism, in South Korea, Thailand and Burma (after Ne Win's *coup*), but not in South Vietnam—nor in Nationalist China and French Indo-China? Briefly, in South Korea—the closest 'parallel' to Vietnam—the people had experienced at first hand the brutality of Communist (in Vietnam it was colonial) invasion and military occupation; although they hated Rhee, they hated the Communists still more.*

As for Thailand, no real Communist movement has developed in a relatively prosperous and homogeneous country—although both Pibun and his successors invoked US aid to 'suppress' it. The exception is the poor and (for a long time) neglected north-east provinces bordering Laos where, in addition to subversion in the remote villages encouraged by agents infiltrated from Pathet Lao-held areas in Laos, there are feelings of resentment against (over-privileged) Bangkok.

Compared to the situation in Thailand, Malaysia, Burma or even Laos, the enormous growth of the Communist movement in South Vietnam puts that country in a totally different category. Ironically, it was the very completeness of Diem's initial victories over his opponents in 1954-56—ex-emperor Bao Dai, French supporters, Hoa Hao and Cao Dai religious sects, Binh Xuyen gangsters (con-

* Even the Communists have acknowledged the difference between South Vietnam and South Korea. A North Vietnamese general observed in 1966: 'In the Korean war, what was different from the situation in South Vietnam was that when the Americans introduced (520,000) troops (including satellite troops) in Korea, they sent them all to the front line because their rear base was secure, whereas in South Vietnam, when the Americans introduce 300,000 or 400,000 troops they cannot send them all to the front line. . . .' Confidential address to N.L.F. conference by General Nguyen Van Vinh, recorded in cadre's notebook captured in 1967. 'Viet Cong Documents on the War', *Communist Affairs* (Univ. of Southern California) Nov.-Dec. 1967.

trolling Saigon's police—and brothels), the Vietminh and others—which obscured the underlying reality. South Vietnam was not so much a modern State as a fragmented land, without any real identity, held together by the skill, courage and integrity of Diem at first, but later—and increasingly—by fraud, corruption and repression. Diem imposed the semblance of unity over rival sects, regions and religions, but when he was overthrown the structure fell apart. In a sense, the South still represents 'unfinished business'. The revolution, whether Communist or nationalist, still has to take place. And although the attitudes and methods of the Dulles era have to some extent been disavowed, the US is facing the consequences of these original policies.

In committing the US to Diem, Dulles was building on sand. This commitment was small to start with: Dulles in fact had argued in support of the SEATO treaty in 1954 that the US should deter Communist aggression not by maintaining an army on the Asian mainland (which indeed would not have been acceptable either to Congress, the American public or to military strategists) but by the use of a mobile striking force. But the commitment inexorably increased as the situation deteriorated. For the problem, unlike Korea, was not one of military invasion (though the US was wise to guard against the possibility) but, essentially, of political subversion leading to insurgency.

For many years Communists and Nationalists in Vietnam had struggled against colonial rule, but the Nationalists, less disciplined and organized, had been almost wiped out by ruthless French repression in the thirties. It was the Communists who led the Vietminh's successful resistance to the French—both in North and South. Partition in 1954 along the 17th parallel was an artificial measure, intended as a prelude to reunification. In reality the Vietminh controlled most of the countryside, while the French controlled the towns. Yet by the final stage of the war, even the zones around Hanoi and Saigon had been heavily infiltrated by the Vietminh.

Although some 90,000 Vietminh soldiers were transferred to the North after 1954 (they became the chief source of reinforcement for the Vietcong), many Vietminh military units and Communist cadres in the South simply lay low. Diem's refusal to accept nation-wide elections in 1956, which the Communists had expected to win, was a severe blow.* The Communists in the South then began to reorganize for armed struggle, while Diem, for his part, intensified his campaign

* At the time, the Soviet Union, preoccupied with de-Stalinization and the Polish and later Hungarian revolts, could do little to help, while China was anxious to keep up the 'peaceful' impression made at the Bandung Conference, which had had a favourable effect on Asian opinion.

against 'dissidents', including those who had fought for the Vietminh as well as liberals, socialists or members of sects who disagreed with his policies. When the Communists stepped up their use of terror—chiefly against village headmen, government informers and local officials—as they had done against the French, so Diem, too, ruthlessly sought to suppress all forms of opposition. In March 1959, Diem proclaimed Vietnam as a 'nation at war', while special military tribunals were established for 'repression of acts of sabotage, of infringements of national security and of attacks upon the life or property of citizens'.[21] In November 1959, a year after Diem's Foreign Minister had reported that the threat of internal Communist subversion was under control, the Government of South Vietnam issued a 'White Book' reporting that the Vietcong had murdered nearly 200 people in two years.

In 1960, towards the end of which the National Liberation Front for South Vietnam was formed, the struggle horrifyingly increased. Government forces lost over 6,000 killed, wounded and captured and the Vietcong—the government term for the guerrillas—even more. Guerrilla attacks on small army units and on isolated or poorly defended outposts, ambushes on roads and canals, the destruction of bridges and sabotage of public works became more and more frequent. The aim of the Vietcong was to paralyse the régime by intimidating or destroying the administration at the local level. The Vietcong increased its strength from about 3,000 armed guerrillas in 1955 to 5,000 full-time regular soldiers backed by 30,000 provincial or district troops at the start of 1961—and to 23,000 regulars with 40,000 irregulars a year later.[22] Less than one in seven of Vietcong forces in 1961 had been infiltrated from the North (perhaps one in four of the 'hard core' units).'[23] They were backed locally by 'many thousands of village guards, political cadres, special agents', etc.[24]

At each stage in the grim descent into chaos in Vietnam, the US faced this dilemma: whether to cut its commitments and withdraw from an increasingly difficult, if not irremediable, situation; or to provide more and more support to bolster the régime in the hope of at last turning the corner. The first policy would mean handing over a key area to Communism, which would call in question the entire anti-Communist strategy in South East Asia. The second would tie the US to an arbitrary, unpopular and increasingly incapable régime; for so far from being the 'American puppet' of Communist allegations, Diem both insisted on aid and at the same time spurned the reasonable advice that the US had to offer.

In a two-year cycle, the mounting problems of South Vietnam regularly reached the stage of crisis. First in 1959, when the Vietcong guerrillas stepped up their attacks. Then in 1961 when the US decided that only 'accelerated emergency assistance'—including the formation of a US Military Assistance Command, early in 1962—could save the situation. Once more in 1963, when the US dissociated itself from the Diem-Nhu repression of the Buddhists and allowed the Vietnamese army to overthrow the Diem régime. Again in 1965, when US difficulties came to a head after a disastrous year symbolized by the antics of General Nguyen Khanh who, with American foreknowledge, had ousted the first post-Diem régime. Khanh tried to justify the 'purge' of his former chiefs early in 1964 with the promise of greater zeal, efficiency and personal dynamism. The actual result, however, was further to divide the army, weaken the administration, encourage political intrigues, revive the suspicion of the Buddhists and lose ground before the Vietcong.

The climax of Khanh's dizzy career came in August 1964 when as Prime Minister he proclaimed a State of Emergency, declared the suspension whenever necessary of any law, produced a new Constitution (with American approval) and was duly elected President of South Vietnam. This lasted nine days. Alarmed at the possibility of repression under a new dictatorship, Buddhists, political movements, students and agitators mounted massive demonstrations, which forced Khanh to yield. A month later, some disaffected generals briefly occupied Saigon, but the younger officers rallied to Khanh—still Commander-in-Chief—and the *coup* collapsed. To add to the confusion, a general strike by the trade unions paralysed business in Saigon, and certain mountain tribes, trained by the Americans for 'special operations' against the Vietcong, took up arms against the South Vietnamese authorities instead. By the end of the year, the newest military leaders (Air Vice-Marshal Nguyen Cao Ky and Brigadier General Nguyen Chanh Thi, who were to fall out spectacularly in 1966) deposed the acting legislature, the High National Council, to the chagrin of the Americans. Washington protested bitterly against the removal of this constitutional fig leaf—the irresponsible overthrow of the 'fabric of legal government' as US Ambassador Maxwell Taylor put it. More ominously, the South Vietnamese Army suffered its worst defeat of the war at Binh Gia, a Catholic refugee stronghold only forty miles from Saigon.

Thus 1965 opened for the Americans with the dawning realization that it would not only be impossible to oust the Vietcong as planned,*

* The extraordinary unrealism pervading the US Defence Department—reminiscent of continual French 'victories' over the Vietminh—was reflected in Defence Secretary McNamara's announcement of October 2, 1963, that, assuming the defeat of the Vietcong in 1964, most American forces would be withdrawn by the end of 1965.

but that they would be hard pressed to hold South Vietnam at all. Yet Washington dared not contemplate negotiations to end the conflict—and in fact turned down Ho Chi Minh's proposal, agreed with U Thant in 1964, for a secret meeting with US representatives in Burma*—for fear that the mere suggestion might unbalance the precarious, but anti-Communist, authority of Saigon. However, the existing policy of 'advisory' assistance and the gradual pacification of provinces could no longer be effective, since South Vietnamese government forces had not only lost the initiative (gained with American help after 1961) but faced piecemeal destruction in a protracted war and 'the possibility—indeed . . . the probability—of a Communist military victory'.[25]

The only alternative to the prospect of a humiliating US withdrawal, with all the encouragement this would give to 'national liberation movements' elsewhere, seemed to be US pressure on North Vietnam: that is, military action to compel a political settlement. The American bombing campaign, starting in February 1965, was a bold, even desperate, attempt to offset the disintegration of the South by tackling what was facilely believed to be the nub of the problem —'aggression' by the North. Since Hanoi was responsible for the war, Washington argued,† so the threat of destruction at the hands of the most powerful nation on earth must surely bring it to heel. Failing in this attempt, the US had no alternative but to intervene in strength in the South—where the war all along had to be fought and won— to avert the imminent defeat of the Saigon régime.

INDONESIAN REVERSAL: NEW BALANCE OF POWER?

The situation in Indonesia provides a remarkable contrast to that of Vietnam. The powerful Communist Party of Indonesia (P.K.I.) which had been built up by new leaders after the disaster of 1948—by 1965 it was the third largest in the world—was against all expectations completely routed. While the US was losing out in Vietnam, or barely holding its own—at the cost of millions of dollars in military and economic aid, the despatch of thousands of troops and the employment of massive firepower and the most advanced military techniques—in Indonesia the Communist movement was overthrown, without foreign intervention, almost overnight.

* North Vietnam was ready to discuss the formation of a neutral coalition government in the South, according to United Nations' sources. The first approach was after the fall of Diem in 1963, the second in September 1964, when Burma was willing to act as host. Both were turned down by the United States. [Manchester] *Guardian*, August 9, 1965.

† It was 'a systematic aggression by Hanoi against the people of South Vietnam', according to US Secretary of State Dean Rusk, before the Senate Committee on Foreign Relations, February 18, 1966.

Yet events had seemed to be playing into Communist hands. In the heady atmosphere of confrontation with Malaysia the Indonesian Communists were preparing a 'revolutionary upsurge'. D. N. Aidit, the party's leader, had been touring the villages urging revolt (in the manner of Mao Tse-tung) against landlords and other feudal 'evils'. As early as December 1963, Aidit had called on 'Communists and revolutionaries' to support the peasant struggle against the landlords, adding that the revolution in China, Korea, Vietnam, Algeria, Cuba and other countries had succeeded by relying on the peasantry. The peasants and the villages, according to the P.K.I.'s '45th Anniversary Thesis' of May 1965, were 'a source of foodstuffs, a source of soldiers, a place where the revolution can retreat when beaten in the city, and a base to attack the enemy and wrest back the city'.

In Djakarta, mobs were demonstrating against 'bureaucratic capitalists'—i.e. the party's opponents in the army, administration and state enterprises—on the pretext that they were responsible for food shortages, inflation and the 'sabotage' of the revolution. The press, radio and official news agency had, by early 1965, been taken over by Communist supporters. The P.K.I. was agitating for the arming of workers and peasants—ostensibly against Malaysia:

'The P.K.I. has demanded that the workers and peasants be armed. The P.K.I. is convinced that only the armed people, and especially the armed workers and peasants, can halt the invasion by imperialist troops.'

This was Aidit's 'demand' on May 23, 1965. President Sukarno in his Independence Day speech (August 17, 1965) announced he would 'take a decision' on the proposed 'fifth armed service'.[26]

Meanwhile, according to Army sources, Foreign Minister and First Deputy Prime Minister Subandrio was consorting with the Chinese and retailing—through his own intelligence agency, the B.P.I. which reported directly to the President—Communist-inspired slanders against the military leaders.* President Sukarno himself

* General Nasution, then Armed Forces Chief of Staff, claimed on October 25, 1965—three weeks after the abortive Communist *coup*—that the authors of the plot had prepared for years to infiltrate the armed forces and had 'systematically planted seeds of slander'. He said he had specifically urged President Sukarno to 'establish order within the State's Secret Agencies'—the source of the 'slanderous atmosphere' against the army. Peris Pardede, a captured P.K.I. Central Committee member, testified before the military tribunal in Djakarta on February 15, 1966, that Subandrio had submitted B.P.I. 'Documents' to Sukarno before the *coup*. Subandrio was sentenced to death by the military tribunal on October 25, 1966 for providing the opportunity for the P.K.I. to stage the *coup*.

had 'embraced' the P.K.I., at the huge rally celebrating the P.K.I.'s forty-fifth anniversary in May 1965, as 'thoroughly progressive and revolutionary'. As the party gathered momentum inside Indonesia, so both President and Foreign Minister seemed to become more and more identified with the 'Peking-Djakarta axis', rallying the progressive 'new emerging forces' against the 'imperialists, colonialists and neo-colonialists' ('*nekolim*').

The climax to this feverish political excitement was the attempted *coup* of September 30, 1965, carried out by a dissident officer of the Presidential guard, Lt.-Col. Untung, whose men seized and murdered six senior generals, including the Army Commander-in-Chief, General Yani. Nasution, the foremost military leader (who had been relieved of effective power by Sukarno) escaped only through the courage of his aide, while Suharto, then head of the Army Strategic Reserve, was fortuitously away from home. Had it not been for Suharto's resolution in regaining control of the capital and for the escape of Nasution—the Communists' most determined opponent—Untung's plot might have succeeded—if only for a time, since anti-Communist army units were readily available to put down any uprising. No doubt the 'Revolutionary Council' announced by Untung, including certain leaders of the armed forces, politicians and Communist and other personalities, was intended to serve as a 'front', behind which the P.K.I., having eliminated its chief rivals, could (as in Eastern Europe) gradually but effectively take complete control.

Thus the P.K.I. daily newspaper *Harian Rakjat* came out with an editorial on October 2nd declaring that 'the people will certainly be on the side of the September 30th Movement' formed by Untung. According to the later testimony of captured Communist leaders, the P.K.I. Politburo had discussed the formation of a 'Revolutionary Council' in July 1965. On August 17th, the Politburo was said to have agreed on military operations to frustrate the army's alleged plans to take over power and liquidate the Communists, in the event of the President's death, which the P.K.I. believed to be imminent. A series of meetings between dissident officers and high-level P.K.I. contacts were held in September, according to an Air Force Major implicated in the plot, but only on the morning of September 30th did they decide to take action.*

Yet the P.K.I. irresolution while Suharto rallied his forces, its failure to bring out the party mass organizations in the capital and other cities to retrieve the situation, and its half-hearted attempts at

* Evidence by: Njono, P.K.I. Politburo member responsible for organizing 'combat forces' in the Djakarta area, at his trial by the military tribunal on February 14, 1966; Peris Pardede, February 15, 1966; Major Sujono, February 16, 1966.

guerrilla warfare from its East and Central Javanese strongholds, all these indicate either that the P.K.I. really was ignorant of Untung's activities (despite later confessions) or, if it was involved at least to some extent (which seems more likely) that it was caught off balance, first, by the premature nature of the *coup* and, second, by the speed of the army's retaliation.

In reality, the P.K.I. was not in nearly so strong a position as its 'revolutionary' propaganda had been making out. It was not so much Sukarno who was the 'prisoner' of the P.K.I.—the fear of many Western observers—as the reverse. For the actual power of the P.K.I. was 'severely restricted'; it was the Army which was becoming 'a State within the State' (not the Communists); the P.K.I.—unlike the Army—had no ministerial functions in the Cabinet; yet as the 'weaker partner' in Sukarno's *Nasakom* (nationalists, religious, Communists) concept, it had to share governmental responsibility without having a major influence on policy.[27]

Aidit, it seems, was deluded by the sheer weight of numbers—the millions of party members and of the party-controlled trade union, peasant, women and youth organizations—into exaggerating his and his party's own importance and the effectiveness of the 'mass organizations'; and this perhaps led him into adventurous courses. Almost a year after the attempted *coup*, a statement by the P.K.I. Politburo (published another year later by Peking), roundly criticized Aidit's belief in 'numerical strength' and his 'unprincipled' reliance on Sukarno and warned: 'The armed struggle to defeat armed counter-revolution, as a revolution, must not be waged in the form of military adventurism, in the form of a putsch, which is detached from the awakening of the armed masses.'[28]

It seems clear that the P.K.I. had it been able to choose its moment, would not have resorted to violence at that time. Only after many more months of preparations could it have consolidated its position under Sukarno, perhaps persuaded him to sanction an armed force of workers and peasants and have stepped up its infiltration of the lower ranks of the army to a crippling extent. But time (as at Madiun in 1948) was not its to choose. For Sukarno, according to the Chinese doctors treating him in August 1965, was believed to be mortally ill; with the President removed from the scene, nothing would prevent the army leaders from ending the Communist threat while it still had the capacity to do so.

No doubt the army, aware of Sukarno's illness, had prepared contingency plans to deal with the Communists. But the ease with which Untung was able to kidnap its leaders does not indicate that the army—contrary to later Communist propaganda and to Subandrio's intelligence—was at any active stage of preparations. All the signs are that Untung (possibly in the belief that the President was on the point of death) acted impulsively, without effective co-ordination with the P.K.I.

Sukarno's motives remain ambiguous. There seems little doubt (despite his later denials) that he accepted Subandrio's reports of a *coup* being planned by a 'Council of Generals' on Army Day (October 5th) and was privy to what he understood to be a move to discipline them—or even to 'eliminate' the leading Right Wing generals—because of their opposition to his policy of bringing the Communists more effectively into power.

It seems unlikely that Sukarno would have supported an all-out Communist *coup,* since by removing the army leaders this would have undermined the basis of his support, established by balancing between the army and the P.K.I. However, Sukarno was present at the Halim Air Base (where the six generals were killed by Communist fanatics) a few hours after Untung's *coup.* He is reported to have approved the activities of the dissident army officers, and to have met the Communist and Air Force leaders in the plot.* Only when he heard of Nasution's escape and Suharto's recovery did he apparently abandon his intention to fly with Aidit to Central Java and there to proclaim his support for the 'Revolutionary Council'.[29]

While Sukarno indecisively awaited the outcome of the struggle, the army leaders rapidly crushed the revolt in Central and East Java and incited the P.K.I.'s opponents to take their revenge. In a matter of weeks, thousands of Communists were rounded up and massacred and the party organization virtually destroyed. Aidit himself was captured, interrogated by the army, and shot.

These shattering events transformed the situation both in Indonesia and abroad. At one blow the Chinese had lost a major ally against the Russians—the P.K.I. had come out in violent opposition to the 'revisionists'—an important source of international support—through the formation of the 'Peking-Djakarta axis'—and, most important of all, the confident expectation of a Communist Indonesia.†

Instead of mainland South East Asia being squeezed between China and a Communist Indonesia, the situation has been reversed.

* Air Vice-Marshal Dani, the former Air Force Commander-in-Chief implicated in the plot, testified at his trial in Djakarta on December 6, 1966, that Sukarno had arrived at Halim Air Base on October 1st and had received a report from the senior dissident officer, Brigadier General Supardjo, on the *coup.*

† In McNamara's words: '. . . to the south is what the Chinese Communists may consider the greatest prize of all—Indonesia's resources, territory, and the world's fifth largest population, whose strategic location straddles and dominates the gateway to the Indian ocean.' From his report on 'US Policy in Vietnam' of March 26, 1964.

If General Suharto's régime can restore order out of chaos, then the foundations may be laid for a regional association of Indonesia, Malaysia, Thailand and the Philippines, all with a common interest in opposing Peking.

Although there is no evidence that the Chinese leaders were involved in the attempted *coup* in Indonesia, their repeated insistence on violence and armed struggle could not fail to be linked in people's minds with the P.K.I.'s attack on the generals and its bloody aftermath. The Chinese found themselves doubly discredited; first among their opponents for having openly encouraged revolutionary violence while the P.K.I. was on the 'upsurge' in Indonesia; but above all among their friends for having done nothing to help the P.K.I. in its hour of trial.

DOMINO-LAND*

If Indonesia has turned out, perhaps temporarily, to be a failure for the Chinese, Vietnam remains 'the most convincing current example of a victim of aggression defeating US Imperialism by a people's war'.[30] As seen from the other side:

'It is my unshakeable conviction that, should South Vietnam fall into the hands of the Communists, the floodgates would be open for Communism to sweep across the peninsula to Malaysia, the Philippines and the rest of South Asia to the South, and through Cambodia, Thailand, Burma and other newly-independent countries to the West.'[31]

This is a full-blooded expression of the 'domino theory' that if South Vietnam falls—before that it was Laos—the rest of South East Asia will follow. And not just South East Asia. According to the US Defence Secretary in 1965, the 'outcome of this struggle' in South Vietnam 'could have grave consequences not only for the nations of South East Asia but for future of the weaker and less stable nations everywhere in the world.'[32]

Now, although United States' spokesmen no longer accept the 'pat simplicities' of the domino theory—that the fall of one country automatically means the collapse of others—'What happens in South Vietnam will determine,' according to President Johnson, 'Yes, it will determine, whether ambitious and aggressive nations can use guerrilla warfare to conquer their weaker neighbours.'[33] As if by way of confirming this, US Secretary of State Dean Rusk pointed out

* Much of this section has appeared under the title 'Vietnam and the Domino Theory' (*Australian Outlook*, April 1967).

that the Communists themselves do not see the problem in isolation: 'They see the struggle in South Vietnam as part of a larger design for the steady extension of Communist power through force and threat.'[34]

China and the US are at least agreed on this. 'The US aggressors,' Lin Piao argues, '. . . are deeply worried that their defeat in Vietnam will lead to a chain reaction. . . . The people in other parts of the world will see still more clearly that US imperialism can be defeated and that what the Vietnamese people can do, they can do too. . . .'

This is, of course, precisely the reasoning behind the 'domino theory'. Just as Washington has a 'crucial stake' in defeating 'Communist aggression' ('people's war') in Vietnam to prevent the habit spreading to other countries—'the loss of Indo-China will cause the fall of South East Asia like a set of dominoes', in President Eisenhower's famous phrase—so China insists that the 'Vietnamese people's heroic struggle . . . goes far beyond the borders of Vietnam. This contributes enormously to the anti-US struggle of the people in Indo-China and South East Asia, to the national liberation movement in Asia, Africa and Latin America, to the revolutionary movement of the people of the whole world. . . .'[35]

And the reverse applies. America's 'stake' in holding on to South Vietnam is also China's 'domino' fear of the result of North Vietnamese and Vietcong defeat. The following passage from the *People's Daily*, with appropriate substitutions, will qualify for either side:

'If the US [Communist] aggressors, instead of being driven out, are allowed to hang on in South Vietnam, then US imperialism [Chinese Communism] will still more unscrupulously push forward its plot to subjugate its victims one by one, more furiously suppress the national-liberation [free world] movement in Asia, Africa and Latin America, launch "special [guerrilla] wars" everywhere and more truculently commit aggression and intervention in the new-emerging independent countries in Asia and Africa. . . . This will greatly help US imperialism [Chinese Communism] in its war [insurgent] adventures. It will launch a war [revolution] in one region today and in another tomorrow. It will undermine peace at will in Asia today and in Africa, Latin America and Europe the next. . . .'[36]

Such a belief inspired the conclusion of the US State Department's 1961 'White Paper' on Vietnam: 'For Vietnam's neighbours the consequences of a Communist victory in all Vietnam would be far-reaching. . . . The present balance of forces between independent and Communist States in Asia would be tipped perilously if Vietnam,

Cambodia and Laos, fell under Communist domination. What then would be the prospects for Thailand and Burma, for Pakistan and India, for Malaya and Indonesia?'

Even Defence Secretary McNamara, who observed in May 1966 that the 'US has no mandate from on high to police the world' and that 'we have no charter to rescue floundering régimes who have brought violence on themselves by deliberately refusing to meet the legitimate expectations of their citizenry'[37] (which would seem to apply to South Vietnam), is no less affected by domino considerations. In his important policy statement of February 18, 1965, McNamara asserted:

'South East Asia remains for us and for the entire Free World the area in which the struggle against Communist expansion is most acute, and, in that area, South Vietnam is the keystone. Here, the North Vietnamese and the Chinese are putting into practice their theory that any non-Communist government of an emerging nation can be overthrown by externally supported, covert armed aggression, even when that government is backed by US economic and military assistance. Indeed, the Chinese Communists have made South Vietnam the decisive test of that theory. . . . Thus, the stakes in South Vietnam are far greater than the loss of one small country to Communism. It would be a serious setback to the cause of freedom throughout the world.'

The remarkable feature of the domino theory is the way both China and the United States universalize a specific situation—Vietnam. This is unduly favourable to the Chinese point of view and unfavourable to the American. Vietnam encourages the Chinese to paint a rosy picture of revolutions breaking out elsewhere, while it leads the Americans to view the Asian scene in unnecessarily gloomy tones.

Mao Tse-tung in the past had to criticize a similar tendency among his followers to 'unwittingly generalize and exaggerate their momentary, specific and limited situation'.[38] What is important or decisive, he noted, should be determined 'not by general or abstract considerations, but according to the concrete circumstances'.[39] It is just these 'concrete circumstances' which are neglected by the domino theorists in Washington and by the present doctrinaire exponents of worldwide revolution in Peking.

Although certain broad tendencies may be common to a number of countries, each country has its unique features. South Vietnam, it is true, would probably have succumbed to Communism without massive American intervention, but there is no reason to suppose that Thailand or Malaysia would automatically follow. Even if it is assumed that Communism pursues the same destructive course in every country—a large assumption even for diabolists—the obvious differences in its effectiveness throughout the world indicate that the *conditions* in which it works do vary, region by region and country by country.

Psychologically, of course, the fall of South Vietnam (that is, the collapse of the South Vietnamese army and administration) would clearly encourage revolutionary movements elsewhere and correspondingly depress the existing régimes. The latter might then believe that Communism was 'inevitable' and make the necessary accommodation to it. But they might just as well be alerted to a danger greater than they had anticipated and thus be galvanized into taking more effective action.

What, after all, is the danger they face? Is it Communist armed aggression, in the style of North Korea's invasion of the South? Outright invasion would quite probably bring in American, not to speak of United Nations', armed forces. The danger is much more likely to be one of 'indirect aggression' or 'creeping subversion', encouraged and perhaps aided and directed, from outside. But it is this that has all along had to be faced in South East Asia: the only difference would be the psychological impetus provided by its successful employment elsewhere.

Thus the internal situation determines the action to be taken in response to an external threat—and not, like the domino theory, the other way round. If a government judges that it cannot overcome insurgency backed from outside—presumably because it lacks enough support within the country to deal with the revolt—it may well decide to come to terms with the 'enemy'. But it is unlikely to do this merely because the psychological pressure has increased. After all, the leading personnel of the régime—the suppressors of the revolution—could hardly expect to retain for long the favour of their opponents' backers, even after most humble confessions. (This is what keeps the South Vietnamese army in the war.)

The belief that when one country falls the rest will fall is sheer defeatism (nor does it show much confidence in the staying-power of the 'free world'). For it implies that the state of disintegration of Laos or South Vietnam is *typical* of the situation of other countries.* Only such an assumption could justify McNamara's plea—in his prepared statement before the US House of Representatives—that the 'choice is not simply whether to continue our efforts to keep

* Though it seems incredible now, Laos once took the place of South Vietnam in domino calculations. 'If Laos is lost to the Communists,' as the *New York Times* expressed it on October 9, 1960, 'the entire balance of power in South East Asia will be changed.'

South Vietnam free and independent but, rather whether to continue our struggle to halt Communist expansion in Asia. If the choice is the latter, as I believe it should be, we will be far better facing the issue in South Vietnam.' Only a strategist who was not aware that better defensive positions were available would choose to fight on the least favourable ground.

If the domino theory is correct, why did the Communist takeover in Czechoslovakia in 1948 not result in the collapse of Western Europe? And why was Castro's revolution in Cuba not followed by a wave of successful revolts throughout Latin America? If the answer is that the situation in Europe, and in Latin America, is different to that in South East Asia that makes a point. But if a regional difference is conceded, why not differences within that region?

Domino theorists, however, have another argument to fall back on—the supposed analogy with Europe at the time of Munich. There was 'no reaction' by the democracies to Hitler's aggression. Therefore the lesson of appeasement in the 1930s, in the colourful if confusing imagery of a US Government spokesman, is that 'successful aggression feeds on itself and begets further aggression. . . . If aggression is permitted to occur unchecked it snowballs and soon there is a world in flames.'[40] The Munich analogy is also cited from time to time by Dean Rusk to justify American 'firmness' in resisting North Vietnamese 'aggression'.* The same idea underlies President Johnson's assurance to US troops on his visit to South Vietnam of December 23, 1967: 'Because of what you men are doing here today, you may very well prevent a wider war, a greater war, a World War III.'

It was expressed in the President's State of the Union message of January 10, 1967: 'We have chosen to fight a limited war in Vietnam in order to prevent a larger war—a war almost certain to follow if the Communists succeed in taking over South Vietnam by force.' He had previously implied in his Baltimore speech on April 7, 1965, that if the US were not fighting in Vietnam, the 'battle would be renewed in one country and then another'. For the 'central lesson of our time is that the appetite of aggression is never satisfied'.

But *how* would the 'battle be renewed'? An outright invasion—in the Hitler manner—has not taken place in South Vietnam,† so how

* e.g. 'The clearest lesson of the 1930s and '40s is that aggression feeds on aggression.' US policy is to 'demonstrate that aggression must be stopped at its earliest stages'. Before the US Council on Foreign Relations, May 24, 1966. See also his statement of October 30, 1967, that the US was resolved 'not to repeat the blunders' which led to the Second World War.

† There was infiltration rather than invasion by North Vietnamese regular units, after 1965.

could it be 'renewed' in Thailand, Laos or Cambodia, Vietnam's neighbours? And if the North Vietnamese have aided and directed an indigenous subversive movement in South Vietnam—and Washington does not deny that most Vietcong guerrillas are local South Vietnamese*—then for the 'snowball' technique to succeed elsewhere the North Vietnamese must have an equally effective indigenous movement of Thais, Malays or others to work on (if they can).

If this is 'aggression' then it is not Hitler's form of aggression. Therefore the methods which should have been used against Hitler are not applicable to Vietnam. Invasion is a case in which military methods obviously apply; and since it is a breach of national frontiers it is by definition an international problem. Subversion, on the other hand, is essentially a political matter; and since it occurs within the boundaries of a State, it is a national problem. ('Incitement' from outside can only stimulate what is already there.)

To sum up: aggression is a clear-cut military problem of a 'universal' nature, to which other countries can and should respond. Subversion, which may or may not lead to insurgency, is a complex 'local' political problem; it is directly related to the conditions of the country; and it can basically be met only by the government concerned. Subversion which cannot achieve its aims by political means (or where it finds a suitable terrain) may turn to insurgency—the use of armed force. Once insurgency is under way it then becomes a security, and perhaps a military, problem as well. But the tendency, and not only in the United States, is to consider both Laos and South Vietnam, for example, as 'victims' of aggression rather than subversion, as military rather than as political problems, and as models of what must apply elsewhere—the domino theory—rather than as specific cases, to be treated on their own terms.

It is natural to confuse these issues. Most governments prefer to blame outside intervention rather than face the fact that subversion springs from (usually bad) local conditions. But this confusion is compounded in the US State Department brief, as expressed, for example, by the Assistant Secretary for Far Eastern Affairs, William Bundy. In Bundy's words, the US has a 'deep stake in preventing the

* According to US official estimates, there were at the start of 1966 between 215,000 and 245,000 Vietcong regulars, irregulars and cadres in South Vietnam; the *total* amount of these infiltrated from the North—disregarding casualties—from 1959 to 1965 inclusive was 56,100: see Roger Hilsman, *To Move a Nation* (Doubleday, 1967) table on p. 529. McNamara himself pointed out on March 26, 1964: 'Clearly, the disciplined leadership, direction and support from North Vietnam is a critical factor in the strength of the Vietcong movement. But the large indigenous support that the Vietcong receives means that solutions must be as political and economic as military. . . .'

success of what in this instance [South Vietnam] is a North Vietnamese effort fully supported by Communist China, which would advance the Communist Chinese view of the need for violence and which, if successful, would not only impel the Chinese Communists towards new aggression but might conceivably induce the Russians to resume a more violent general posture'.[41]

Considering that it is the US—rightly or wrongly—and not China that is fighting in South Vietnam, what is this 'aggression' that Bundy is referring to? It is little wonder that Dean Rusk should have declared, though he intended it against his critics, that 'much of the confusion about the struggle in South Vietnam has arisen over a failure to understand the nature of the conflict'. In his view, as he told the Senate Foreign Relations Committee in February 1966, it was 'a systematic aggression by Hanoi against the people of South Vietnam'.

Such is the official US line *after* the start of the bombing campaign against North Vietnam, in February 1965. Before 1965 the emphasis was on the Vietcong insurgency (even if 'directed' by the North) in South Vietnam. As late as July 1964 the Prime Minister of that period, General Khanh, was reminded that his demand for an advance to the North was contrary to his agreement in March 1964 with the US to concentrate on the war against the Vietcong, fully mobilize domestic resources and try to win over the peasantry. . . .[42]

The conflict in Vietnam is thus a war on two levels. The first is a civil war between the Vietcong and the Saigon régime, the second, overlapping it, is a war between North and South (the South, too, has sent guerrillas and saboteurs against the North, but without success). The first has its origins in the Vietminh 'liberated areas' set up during the struggle against the French. The second is the continuation of that struggle, with the resumption of Ho Chi Minh's drive, thwarted in 1954 (the Geneva ceasefire) and in 1956 (Diem's refusal, for obvious reasons, to accept nation-wide elections), to found a unified, independent Vietnam under Communist control. Neither of these wars is aggression in the Hitler manner, as implied by Rusk.* And it is misleading to characterize either of them as 'aggression . . . against the people of South Vietnam'. If the 'people' had supported Saigon in the first place there would have been no war.

For Washington, the notion of a 'victim of aggression' is needed to evoke a clear and sympathetic response, both from the US public

* Of course, North Vietnam might use the same argument Taiwan does to justify forcible unification. 'When we do use force,' according to the Nationalist Chinese Ambassador to Australia, 'it is certainly not a case of invasion because it will be a case of our own forces returning to our own territory.' (*Canberra Times*, January 10, 1967).

and from America's allies. Even the term 'indirect aggression', which was once in vogue, blurs the distinction between aggression and subversion, since it introduces the complexity of local factors—how else could aggression be 'indirect'? But in presenting the situation in black-and-white, both in order to justify American intervention and to explain away the successive internal crises in South Vietnam, Washington even in its peace proposals has become the prisoner of its own unreality.*

Tactics and strategy are inextricably confused. Are US troops in South Vietnam—and US planes bombarding the North—to fulfil the pledge, as President Johnson says, made by three Presidents to defend the 'people' of Vietnam? Or are they there, as President Johnson pointed out in the same policy statement of April 7, 1965, because 'there are great stakes in the balance', that is, the need to end the 'deepening shadow' in Asia of Communist China? If US policy is usually announced in terms of the first reason—'defence of the people' evading the problem of the legitimacy of South Vietnamese governments after Diem—the motives for that policy are largely the second. As liberal Americans have pointed out, America's aim to support national independence in South East Asia has for years been overlaid by the primary objective of the containment of China.[43]

This is where the domino theory fits in. It is not so much the belief that conditions in South Vietnam and the rest of South East Asia are so similar that the fall of one must lead to the fall of others, but the fear that China will benefit so greatly from North Vietnam's conquest of South Vietnam as to appear irresistible to other Asian States. This is not so much the fear of Communism (Russia, after all, can be accommodated) but the fear of *Chinese* Communist expansion—a national as well as an ideological contest.† As the

* Although written more than two years ago, Max Frankel's observation (from Saigon) is very much to the point. He noted the complaints of US troops in the field about Washington's 'repeated and confusing offers of peace'. The troops 'believe there is now no easy way out of the morass. . . . They simply cannot imagine any peace until the village-by-village organization of the Vietcong—the infrastructure of political agents and paddy fighters—is first uprooted and eventually replaced. . . .' (*New York Times*, internat. ed., November 26-27, 1965).

† This was clearly brought out by Dean Rusk at his news conference of October 12, 1967, when he raised the spectre of a 'billion Chinese on the mainland, armed with nuclear weapons' within a decade or two. The 'free nations' of Asia, he added, 'don't want China to overrun them on the basis of a doctrine of world revolution'. The US, he inferred, had a 'tremendous stake' in fighting in Vietnam to prevent the world being 'cut in two by Asian Communism reaching out through South East Asia and Indonesia, which we know has been their objective . . .'. (*Department of State Bulletin*, October 30, 1967.)

State Department puts it, 'We are Peking's great enemy because our power is a crucial element in the total balance of power and in the resistance by Asian States to Chinese Communist expansionist designs in Asia.'[44] And in McNamara's words, 'South East Asia remains for us . . . the area in which the struggle . . . is most acute, and, in that area, South Vietnam is the keystone.' Therefore, as an American military commentator frankly described the issue, the 'reasons we must fight for Vietnam have little to do with making Saigon safe for "democracy" or "freedom" ', but with the 'defeat of Communist attempts to extend their control deep into South East Asia'.[45]

However, there are three points to consider.

First, in making Vietnam the 'test case' for the defeat of China's alleged designs, the Americans are facing an uphill struggle in the very area where conditions most favour Communist subversion and people's war.

Second, there seemed little doubt that the might and mobility of US power in Vietnam would eventually prevail—until the Vietcong offensive in the cities from January 1968 demolished over-optimistic expectations.* But whether winning or losing the Americans will ultimately withdraw—either after the cessation of serious fighting (assuming the success of General Westmoreland's 'four phases') or as a result of a political settlement. Then it may still be the Communists, if they can rally the forces of change or discontent, who will win in the end.

Finally, for America, the war in Vietnam may not just be a tactical error but a strategic illusion. For the national interests of China and Vietnam are not identical—far from it, in the past. A unified Vietnam, under any system of government, is likely to be an obstacle to Chinese expansionism.† (It might be a threat to its neighbours as well, but is this, for America, a matter of vital concern?) It is a supreme irony, and a tragic one, that in pursuing the lesser objective of blocking—at such heavy cost—the ambitions of the North Vietnamese, the US is thereby thwarting its major role of halting the Chinese.

* 'I can bring you the assurance of what you have fought to achieve: The enemy cannot win, now, in Vietnam. He can harass, he can terrorize, he can inflict casualties—while taking far greater losses himself. But he just cannot win. . . .' President Johnson to US forces at Korat Air Base, Thailand, December 23, 1967.

† Consider—in contrast to the US view of China's role—Air Vice-Marshal Ky's assurance that there is 'no possibility' of North Vietnam asking for Chinese troops as military aid, 'because if the Hanoi leaders do so then I am sure that all the Vietnamese from the North and South will unite in one group and stand up and destroy the régime and defend our land'. At a Press Conference in Canberra on January 19, 1967.

REFERENCE NOTES TO CHAPTER I

1. Karl Marx, 'The Eighteenth Brumaire of Louis Bonaparte', *Selected Works* (Lawrence and Wishart, 1942), p. 315.
2. See Philippe Devillers, *Histoire du Viet-Nam: de 1940 à 1952* (Editions du Seuil, 1952), pp. 299-301, 318.
3. Ellen J. Hammer, *The Struggle for Indo-China 1940-1955* (Stanford Univ. Press, new ed. 1966). p. 313.
4. *Ibid.*, p. 117.
5. *Ibid.*, p. 200.
6. Hugh Tinker, *The Union of Burma* (Oxford Univ. Press, 3rd ed. 1961), pp. 32, 34-5.
7. J. H. Brimmell, *Communism in South East Asia: A Political Analysis* (Oxford Univ. Press, 1959), pp. 258-9.
8. M. R. Masani, *The Communist Party of India* (Macmillan, 1954), pp. 89-90, 281-2.
9. Ruth T. McVey, *The Calcutta Conference and the Southeast Asian Uprisings* (Cornell Univ., Interim Reports series, 1958), p. 19.
10. *Ibid.*, pp. 21-2.
11. *The Danger and Where it Lies* (Information Services, Federation of Malaya, Kuala Lumpur, 1957), p. 14.
12. Brimmell, *op. cit.*, p. 320. And see Charles B. McLane, *Soviet Strategies in Southeast Asia: An exploration of Eastern Policy under Lenin and Stalin* (Princeton Univ. Press, 1966), pp. 385-90.
13. George McT. Kahin, *Nationalism and Revolution in Indonesia* (Cornell Univ. Press, 1952), pp. 269-71.
14. *Ibid.*, pp. 272, 275, 284, 292-3.
15. 'Upsurge of the Anti-Imperialist Movement in the Philippines' (*World Marxist Review*, Prague, Nov. 1965), pp. 40-4.
16. 'The Origin and Development of the Differences between the Leadership of the Communist Party of the Soviet Union and Ourselves . . .' (joint article by Editorial Departments of *People's Daily* and *Red Flag*, Peking, September 6, 1963).
17. 'The Proletarian Revolution and Khruschev's Revisionism' (*People's Daily* and *Red Flag*, March 31, 1964).
18. *Pravda*, September 16, 1963: Governments of Algeria, Burma, India, UAR were considered to be taking the 'non-capitalist path of development'.
19. 'Apologists of Neo-Colonialism' [the Soviet leaders] (*People's Daily* and *Red Flag*, October 21, 1963).
20. 'Stalin's Life was that of a great Marxist-Leninist, a great proletarian revolutionary'—*People's Daily* and *Red Flag*, 'On the Question of Stalin', September 12, 1963.
21. Philippe Devillers, 'The Struggle for the Unification of Vietnam' (*China Quarterly*, special issue on North Vietnam, January-March, 1962).
22. Roger Hilsman, *To Move a Nation: The Politics of Foreign Policy in the Administration of John F. Kennedy* (Doubleday, 1967), table on p. 529, using US official estimate revised in 1966.
23. *Loc. cit.*
24. US State Department, *A Threat to the Peace: North Vietnam's Effort to Conquer South Vietnam* (Washington, December 1961), pp. 9-10.
25. William P. Bundy, US Assistant Secretary for Far Eastern Affairs, in a speech of May 23, 1966, referring to events 'a year ago' (*Department of State Bulletin* [henceforth D.S.B.] June 20, 1966).

26. Arthur J. Dommen, 'The Attempted Coup in Indonesia' (*China Quarterly,* January-March, 1966).
27. W. F. Wertheim, 'Indonesia before and after the Untung Coup' (*Pacific Affairs,* Spring-Summer, 1966). The author disbelieves in P.K.I. responsibility for Untung's actions.
28. 'Statement by the Political Bureau of the Central Committee of the Indonesian Communist Party' (August 1966) in *Peking Review* No. 29, July 14, 1967. In the same issue, *Red Flag* editorial commenting on the P.K.I. 'Statement' and its 'Self-Criticism'; excerpts from the latter are given in *Peking Review* No. 30, July 21, 1967.
29. Seymour Topping, *New York Times* (internat. ed.) August 23, 1966, reporting army sources. Dommen, *op. cit.*
30. Lin Piao, 'Long Live the Victory of People's War' (*Peking Review,* September 3, 1965, and reprinted August 4, 1967).
31. Opening speech at the SEATO Council meeting in Canberra, June 27, 1966 (*Current Notes on International Affairs,* Department of External Affairs, Canberra, June 1966).
32. Robert S. McNamara, US Secretary of Defence, before the Armed Services Committee of the US House of Representatives (*New York Times,* February 19, 1965).
33. Speech at Omaha, June 30, 1966 (D.S.B., July 25, 1966).
34. Before the US Senate Foreign Relations Committee, February 18, 1966 (D.S.B., March 7, 1966).
35. *People's Daily* Editorial, April 16, 1965 (*Peking Review,* April 23, 1965).
36. *Ibid.*
37. Speech at Montreal, May 18, 1966 (D.S.B., June 6, 1966).
38. *Selected Works of Mao Tse-tung* (Peking, Foreign Languages Press, 1965), Vol. I, p. 120.
39. *Ibid.,* p. 185.
40. Douglas MacArthur II, Assistant Secretary for Congressional Relations in Brussels, October 12, 1966 (D.S.B., November 14, 1966).
41. 'Vietnam and US Objectives in the Far East' (D.S.B., June 20, 1966).
42. *New York Times,* March 14 and July 24, 1964.
43. See Max Frankel, *New York Times,* February 12, 1965. And George McT. Kahin, at a National Teach-in on Vietnam (Marcus G. Raskin and Bernard B. Fall, eds., *The Viet-Nam Reader: Articles and Documents on American Foreign Policy and the Viet-Nam Crisis,* Random House, 1965), pp. 289-96.
44. William Bundy, speaking on the United States and Communist China, February 12, 1966.
45. Hansom Baldwin, 'US Choices in Vietnam', *New York Times,* Internat. ed., March 2, 1965.

II THE MODEL

China: Conditions for Success

'To rely on the peasants, build rural base areas and use the countryside to encircle and finally capture the cities—such was the way to victory in the Chinese revolution. . . .

In these base areas, we built the [Communist] Party, ran the organs of State power, built the people's armed forces and set up mass organizations. . . . Our base areas were in fact a State in miniature. . . .

Guerrilla warfare is the only way to mobilize and apply the whole strength of the people against the enemy, the only way to expand our forces in the course of the war, deplete and weaken the enemy, gradually change the balance of forces between the enemy and ourselves, switch from guerrilla to mobile warfare, and finally defeat the enemy. . . .

The history of people's war in China and other countries provides conclusive evidence that the growth of the people's revolutionary forces from weak and small beginnings into strong and large forces is a universal law of development. . . .

Comrade Mao Tse-tung's theory of the establishment of rural revolutionary base areas and the encirclement of cities from the countryside is of outstanding and universal practical importance for the present revolutionary struggles of all the oppressed nations and peoples, and particularly for the revolutionary struggles of the oppressed nations and peoples in Asia, Africa and Latin America against imperialism and its lackeys. . . .

In the final analysis the whole course of world revolution hinges on the revolutionary struggles of the Asian, African and Latin American peoples. . . .'[1]

These passages from Lin Piao's article on people's war admirably summarize the experience of the Communist movement in China and, based on it, Peking's expectation of world-wide revolution.

People's war was the way to power in China. And the Communist takeover in China, drastically transforming the balance of power, is of incalculable consequence in Asia. Moreover, the Chinese revolution is seen as a model for the developing countries of the world. There are 'many similarities', Lin Piao claims, between the 'basic political and economic conditions' of 'old China' and the Afro-Asian and Latin American nations today. Not only are the peasants the main force in the 'national-democratic' revolution; but 'the countryside, and the countryside alone, can provide the revolutionary bases from which the revolutionaries can go forward to final victory'. Finally, the encirclement of the cities from the countryside—the key to Chinese Communist success—is projected on a world-wide scale: 'If North America and Western Europe can be called "the cities of the world" then Asia, Africa and Latin America constitute "the rural areas of the world".'

So far these bold generalizations have hardly been vindicated, either as the way to victory in the developing countries or even as a means of weakening the 'imperialists'. Yet conditions in Latin America would seem remarkably suited—in view of the oppressive contrast between selfish landowners and a poor, exploited peasantry—to an upsurge of people's war. But apart from sporadic guerrilla fighting in Bolivia—where Che Guevara was killed in October 1967—Venezuela and Colombia, neither feudal nor democratic régimes have been shaken by peasant revolt. Even in Africa, the disintegration of the Congo rebellion has largely extinguished the 'flames of people's war'. In Asia, the success of people's war in South Vietnam is more than counter-balanced by its failure to develop in Indonesia—a country of far greater importance than Vietnam.

It is ironical that Aidit himself should have originated the theme of Asia, Africa and Latin America being the 'village of the world, while Europe and North America are the town of the world'—an expression quoted with approval by Peng Chen (another ill-fated personality) at the P.K.I.'s 45th anniversary celebrations in May 1965. Mao Tse-tung sent a personal message to the 'great and heroic Communist Party of Indonesia' on this anniversary—'no force on earth can destroy', he said, the revolutionary unity of the Chinese Communist Party with its 'close and staunch comrade in arms'. But Peking's inability to prevent the subsequent destruction of its ally may well have impaired the confidence of the 'world's revolutionary people' in such judgements. For the Chinese leaders' doctrinaire application of their revolutionary past to the present situation is in marked contrast to the practical—and flexible—way in which they themselves gained power.

The successful outcome of people's war, judging from the Chinese experience, depends on six conditions: peasant support, protracted war, national appeal, leadership, organization and the breakdown of the opposing régime. (A seventh factor is useful, but not essential: external aid and the existence of a 'privileged sanctuary'.)

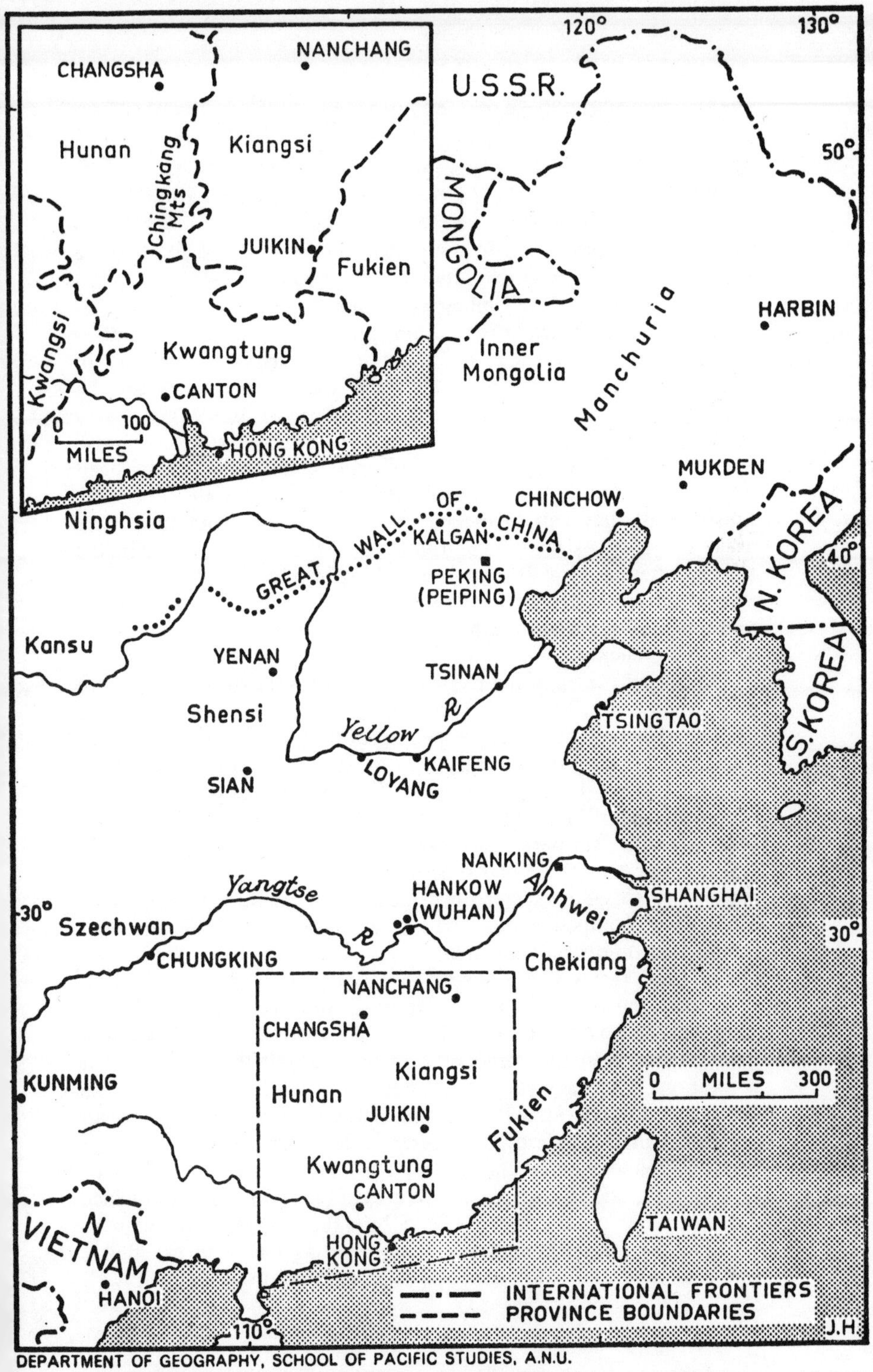

China Proper and Manchuria. Inset, 'revolutionary area' 1924-34

Mao Tse-tung recognized that the peasantry—rather than the proletariat—was the main force of revolution in China. 'The Chinese revolution is essentially a peasant revolution,' Mao wrote in 1940, 'and the resistance to Japan now going on is essentially peasant resistance. . . . As every schoolboy knows, eighty per cent of China's population are peasants. So the peasant problem becomes the basic problem of the Chinese revolution and the strength of the peasants is the main strength of the Chinese revolution.'[2]

Second, Mao realized the need for 'protracted war' in the countryside—rather than instant revolution in the cities—as the way in which a weak movement could face the strong. 'Because the reactionary forces are very strong, revolutionary forces grow only gradually, and this fact determines the protracted nature of our war,' Mao wrote in 1936.[3] In the period of protracted war Mao envisaged guerrilla fighting from secure revolutionary bases; 'the guerrillas must do all they can to extend guerrilla warfare from their base areas as widely as possible and hem in all the enemy's strongholds, thus threatening his existence and shaking his morale'.[4] The strategic role of guerrilla warfare was twofold: to 'support regular warfare and to transform itself into regular warfare' for the counter-offensive against the enemy.[5]

The aim of the opposing régime was to crush the insurgents before they could consolidate their position in the remote areas, prepare impregnable bases and secure widespread support. The aim of the revolutionaries, on the contrary, was to stave off the enemy and thus gain time to survive and to expand. The enemy was powerful in its use of modern means of warfare but the régime was not united and the basis of its support was uncertain. These 'contradictions' made possible the emergence and growth of Communist power in certain regions. A Communist base became a 'state in miniature', as Lin Piao puts it, competing with and eventually supplanting government administration over a wide area.

The third factor is the appeal to nationalism—before 'socialism'—to form the broadest 'united front' against the common enemy. The Chinese revolution, Mao declared in 1940, embraced two distinct stages: 'first the democratic revolution and then the socialist revolution'. And these stages must not be confused. This was because the major struggle at that time was between Japanese imperialism and the Chinese nation; only after it came the conflict between 'feudalism' and the peasant masses. This was a complete reversal of Communist policy during the early years of the revolution. But in face of the grave external threat to China, 'was the Party to continue with the civil war and the agrarian revolution,' as Lin Piao asked, 'or was it to hold aloft the banner of national liberation, unite with all the forces that could be united to form a broad national united front. . . . ?' And he answered: 'If we abandon the national banner . . . and thus isolate ourselves [from the masses] it is out of the question to exercise leadership.' It was as the advocate of national unity—instead of 'worker-peasant' dictatorship—that the Communist Party developed from a struggling revolutionary movement, as in the first fifteen years of its existence, into a powerful countrywide force. With the reversal of policies came the reversal of the balance of forces inside China. By the end of the war against Japan (but not before) it was the Communists who professed and more truly represented national interests, and the Kuomintang which had degenerated into an oppressive, sectarian minority.

The fourth factor is leadership: success clearly testifies to leadership, but leadership is more than 'success'. Leadership is the imposition of will on (often recalcitrant) men and conditions. Certainly, Mao Tse-tung's finest period of leadership was in the most desperate of circumstances. Both Mao and Chiang Kai-shek were indisputably leaders, each at the expense of the other. Chiang's rise to power over the Kuomintang was marked by the virtual destruction of the early Communist movement: with Mao as a hunted outlaw, discredited even in his own party, Chiang became President of the Republic of China. Although the Generalissimo appeared at the height of his power and prestige at the end of the war against Japan—acknowledged leader of one of the 'Big Five'—it was a hollow triumph. The foundations of Kuomintang rule had been undermined; in less than five years Mao was Chairman of the Chinese People's Republic and Chiang was a refugee on Taiwan.

Perception of the underlying 'trend' of events and the ability to change course accordingly: perhaps this is the key to leadership. As Mao observed, 'preliminary investigation and study' can pose a problem but cannot solve it. For this analyisis is needed: otherwise, faced with a chaotic and bewildering mass of phenomena, you will not be able to discern where the problem or contradiction lies'.[6] And when conditions change, tactics must change accordingly. 'The making and changing of tactical, campaign and strategic plans in accordance with scope and circumstances is a key factor in directing a war; it is the concrete expression of flexibility in war.' The 'ancients' said: 'Ingenuity in varying tactics depends on mother wit.' 'This "ingenuity",' Mao commented, 'which is what we mean by flexibility, is the contribution of the intelligent commander. . . .'[7]

The factor of leadership—the importance of personality—inevitably raises problems for Marxists. It is a supreme irony that such personalities as Lenin, Stalin, Trotsky, Tito, Mao Tse-tung, Ho Chi Minh and others should have played such a dominant role in the rise to power of Communist movements. Whether success would have been achieved without these leaders is, of course, impossible to say. But there seems to be little doubt that it was their ability to discern and act upon the vital issue at the decisive moment—usually after years of 'protracted' struggle—which led to victory. 'Conditions' might, in time, have produced the same result; by this argument, the leader is merely the catalyst who activates the latent process. But 'in the long run' could prove so lengthy as to alter the entire situation; some form of revolution might still take place, but it would not necessarily be a Communist one. If leadership is the inspiration, hardly less important is organization—the fifth condition of success. The organization of the party, the army and the administration in a territorial base was an enormous achievement in China. The Red Army was not—like its enemies—a conventional army of professional soldiers or mercenaries, but of men imbued with a sense of mission. Like the party cadres of that era they were dedicated to the task of revolution: not to study the world, or administer it, but to change it.

Mao stressed the political role of the army: 'The Red Army should certainly not confine itself to fighting . . . it should shoulder such important tasks as doing propaganda among the masses, organizing the masses, arming them, helping to establish revolutionary political power and setting up Party organizations. . . . Without these objectives, fighting loses its meaning and the Red Army loses the reason for its existence.'[8] To carry out these objectives required a major effort to counter the 'purely military viewpoint' which was at first 'very highly developed' among a number of party members: 'They do not understand that the Chinese Red Army is an armed body for carrying out the political tasks of the revolution.'

Mao himself faced an open revolt by part of the Red Army against his political and personal leadership in 1930, an 'incident' so grave, he told Edgar Snow, that 'to many it must have seemed that the fate of the revolution depended on the outcome of this struggle'.[9] The revolt was finally suppressed and between 2,000 to 3,000 officers and men were 'liquidated' in the bloodiest purge in pre-1949 Chinese Communist Party history.[10] Mao concluded from this bitter experience that 'Communists do not fight for personal military power (they must in no circumstances do that . . .) but they must fight for military power for the Party. . . . Every Communist must grasp the truth, "Political power grows out of the barrel of a gun."* Our principle

* This famous phrase has been much misunderstood—a symptom of wider misunderstanding. It is *not* an expression of militarism or militant expansionism, as is often claimed, but rather the opposite: it is a plea for civilian, i.e. Party, control of the military.

is that the Party commands the gun, and the gun must never be allowed to command the Party.'[11]

Organization is the infusion of leadership in mass activities. The Party's task is to mobilize the 'common people throughout the country' to 'create a vast sea in which to drown the enemy'. Political mobilization 'means telling the army and the people about the political aim of the war. It is necessary for every soldier and civilian to see why the war must be fought and how it concerns him. . . . Without a clear-cut concrete political programme it is impossible to mobilize all the armed forces and the whole people to carry the war . . . through to the end.'[12]

Leadership without the masses is 'fruitless effort', but mass activity alone—in Mao's rather sinister phrase, 'without a strong leading group to organize their activity properly'—prevents popular action being 'sustained for long, or carried forward in the right direction, or raised to a high level'. Mao recognized that 'the masses in any given place are generally composed of three parts, the relatively active, the intermediate and the relatively backward'. The task of leadership—and this is no less valid for 'counter-insurgency' operations—is to 'unite the small number of active elements around the leadership', rely on them to 'raise the level' of the majority in the intermediate range and 'win over' the backward elements. Mao is perhaps rather more optimistic about popular participation than most counter-insurgency specialists would allow. In Sir Robert Thompson's experience of Malaya and Vietnam, the activists among the insurgents usually amount to 1 per cent or less of the total population, while the government's hard core supporters are also small, maybe 10 per cent, but no more than 20 per cent. 'The remaining 80 or 90 per cent of the population is neutral or near neutral as between the government and the insurgents.' If the government strength were over 20 per cent and the rest were not neutral but supporters there would be no insurgency.[13] As the French writer, David Galula, puts it: which side gives best protection, which one threatens the most, which one is likely to win—these are the criteria governing the people's stand.[14]

A conventional war, Galula points out, is for the conquest of territory and the destruction of forces. But in a revolutionary war, the insurgent holds little or no territory and refuses to fight for it. If the situation is untenable for the guerrillas they will simply transfer their activity to another region. It becomes a vicious circle: intelligence is the chief source of information needed in locating and fighting the guerrillas and it must come from the people: 'But the people will not talk unless it feels safe, and it does not feel safe until the insurgents' power has been broken.'[15]

If, however, counter-insurgency forces are so strong that they can saturate the country with garrisons, conventional military operations will, of course, work. But saturation, Galula adds, can seldom be afforded.[16] Saturation 'worked' in Chiang Kai-shek's block-house strategy against the limited Communist areas of 1933-34. It is also 'working' with the US armies in South Vietnam(?). But it did not work with the Japanese, who were unable to garrison effectively the large areas of China they had overrun, nor with the Kuomintang against vastly more numerous and effective post-war Communist forces, nor with the French in Indo-China.

Thus the final condition is the breakdown or severe incapacity of the existing régime. It was the Japanese occupation of large parts of China and South East Asia which proved the turning point both for the Kuomintang and for the colonial régimes, even though they seemed to have emerged victorious from the war. The apparent power and prestige of these régimes rendered all the more cataclysmic the completeness of their downfall. In South East Asia, the French administration in Indo-China never really recovered from the humiliating concessions it had to make to the Japanese. who finally overthrew it, creating a vacuum into which the Vietminh could move. (The Dutch likewise never regained their authority over the Indonesian people; and the British had to concede independence to India, Burma and eventually Malaya.) Similarly the Kuomintang, apparently at the zenith of its fortunes in 1945, had been fatally weakened by the loss of territory, the isolation of the years in Chungking and the failure to compete with the Communists either in intellectual appeal or in mobilizing the masses.

Did the Kuomintang fall more as a result of its own weaknesses—popular revulsion against the incompetence, corruption and repressiveness of its leaders; overstretched resources; the uncontrolled inflation which ruined the bourgeoisie; the rabid persecution of its critics? Or was it rather a result of the superior skill, foresight and determination of the Communists? Kuomintang weaknesses had been evident before the Japanese period; the exhausting years of war aggravated them. Yet the Communists, no less than the Kuomintang, had been targets for Japanese attacks. In the grim test of war one survived and grew; and the other stagnated and fell. Without external pressure (by the Japanese) the internal 'contradictions' of the Kuomintang régime might not have proved so calamitous. Yet it is true to say that all the other factors—peasant revolt, protracted guerrilla warfare, growing national appeal of the Communists, their leadership and organizational abilities—were moving in the same direction to undermine the basis of Kuomintang support. These 'conditions' for the success of people's war have been analysed separately; but they operated more or less simultaneously. To put it in a sentence: *leadership* of the *peasant* struggle provides the *organized* means for the *eventual* ('protracted') *nation-wide* victory over a *disintegrating* enemy régime.

The inter-relationship of these elements is significant. It takes extremely harsh conditions before the peasants—known for the fatalism with which they normally endure natural calamities and social oppression—are driven to take up arms in revolt. In other words the existence of peasant revolt posits a breakdown or at least severe mal-functioning of the established system of rule. 'Intolerable social and economic conditions had created the conditions for revolution,' Peng Teh-huai told Snow; 'it was only necessary to give leadership, form and objectives to this rural mass movement.'[17]

It was the organization and discipline of the Chinese Communist Party which transformed the 'roving guerrilla bands' of Chinese history into a systematic and enduring force capable of establishing its own authority and of overthrowing the existing government. Communism—'Marxism-Leninism'—provided an explanation of events, which fitted Chinese conditions—both the predatory role of imperialism and the oppressive and backward state of landlord-dominated society; which imbued the masses with faith in the justice of their cause; and which convinced them of ultimate success. 'Communism,' as Mao extolled it in *New Democracy*, 'is at once a complete system of proletarian ideology and a new social system. It is different from any other ideology or social system, and it is the most complete, progressive, revolutionary and rational system in human history. . . . The Communist ideological and social system alone is full of youth and vitality, sweeping the world with the momentum of an avalanche and the force of a thunderbolt. . . .'[18]

Yet, to repeat: the Communists had achieved only a limited success, on social and economic grounds, in their early years in south east China. Resistance to Japan reversed the situation. Northern China, hitherto largely immune to Communism, became its major stronghold, while the old guerrilla bases in the south only slowly revived. Foreign destruction of the established order and the peasants' need for protection were the chief reasons for this momentous change in Communist support. This tends to confirm the view that the mass of the 'people' at any given time are politically 'neutral' between the government and the 'opposition'; security to till the land in peace is their aim; whoever provides it, on whatever grounds, gets their support.

Finally, the question of foreign aid for the revolutionaries and the availablity of a 'sanctuary'. Soviet assistance played little part in the success of Chinese Communism; Chinese support was not essential for the victories of the Vietminh; and even North Vietnamese intervention was not a decisive factor in the crumbling of Saigon's resistance. Stalin's attitude towards the Chinese Communists was ambiguous to say the least. If the Russians handed over captured Japanese weapons to the Communists in Manchuria in 1945, they also handed over the cities to the Kuomintang. According to Vladimir Dedijer, Stalin early in 1945 spoke of his advice to Chinese Communist delegates shortly after the end of the Japanese war: 'We told them bluntly that we considered the development of the uprising in China had no prospect, and that the Chinese comrades should seek a *modus vivendi* with Chiang Kai-shek, that they should join the Chiang Kai-shek Government and dissolve their army. The Chinese comrades agreed here with the view of the Soviet comrades, but went back to China and acted otherwise. . . . Now, in the case of China, we admit we were wrong.'[19]

To sum up: these 'conditions for success'—outlined above—are abstractions from the specific, and changing, circumstances of China over a period of many years. The factors operate simultaneously—but in a geographical, economic and historical context. They cannot be properly understood apart from it. Indeed Mao's theories of 'people's war' did not and could not spring fully armed from his or anyone else's head. They are the product of thought on circumstance. Moreover, he had to start from scratch. When the conventional doctrines proved worse than useless in an unexpected situation (the problem that the Americans also face in Vietnam) Mao was forced to think and act for himself. It is important to reveal this process at work, particularly in a revolutionary war, where there can be no simple 'mechanical' copying of other people's experiences. This calls for a historical approach, though it may be slow and cumbersome, to show the development of the theory corresponding to the development of the situation: imperfect, faltering, ebbing and flowing, vague, uncertain. It may seem unsatisfactory compared to clear-cut definitions and abstract conclusions, but it is the way it happened. 'In real life,' as Mao says, 'we cannot ask for "ever-victorious" generals. . . .'

PEASANT REVOLT: MAO'S SEPARATE COURSE

In stressing three main themes—peasant revolt, protracted war and finally 'national-democratic' appeal—Mao was either ahead of or against the conventional line of the Communist movement; and in the first two he was opposed to the Chinese Communist Party leadership as well. As Mao summed up his views in the early years of the Japanese war: the main 'contradiction' was between Japanese imperialism and the Chinese nation; then came the conflict between feudalism and the (peasant) masses. Because the 'enemies of the Chinese revolution' were extremely powerful, the revolution cannot be other than protracted and ruthless . . .'. Since the enemy controlled the large cities, 'it is imperative for the revolutionary ranks to form the backward villagers into advanced consolidated base areas, into great military, political, economic and cultural bastions'. The Chinese revolution, Mao argued, 'can be won first in the rural areas' in the form of 'peasant guerrilla warfare led by the Chinese Communist Party'. But the final objective remained the 'capture of cities'.[20]

By that time Mao had been five years the acknowledged leader of the Chinese Communist Party. But before 1935 it was a different story. For more than a decade Mao had been in a minority and almost continually at odds with the party Central Committee. In 1930 Mao's 'idea that for a long time we should employ our main strength to create rural base areas and use the rural areas to encircle the cities' was rejected by the party leadership as 'utterly erroneous . . . localism and conservatism characteristic of peasant mentality'.[21]

In 1928, when Mao was political commissar of the newly formed 4th Red Army—defending the first Communist 'base area' in the Chingkang Mountains, far from the Central Committee in Shanghai —Mao was among 'strongly dissenting comrades' who criticized the 'mechanical enforcement' of orders by the Province Party Committee, which he said, had 'failed to grasp the actual situation'. Mao complained that the Province Committee had advocated three different plans within a few weeks, each of which was stated to be 'absolutely correct' and to be carried out 'without the least hesitation'. These 'rigid directives', Mao wrote, 'put us in a real dilemma, because failure to comply would be tantamount to disobedience, while compliance would mean certain defeat'.[22] So Mao's attitude was one of 'outward obedience—inner disobedience'.[23]

The main clash between Mao as the exponent of 'protracted war' and the 'Left adventurist' line then dominating the party leadership came in the early 1930s. By the end of 1931 Mao was Chairman of the 'Central Soviet Government' formed in the southern Kiangsi 'base area' and was devoting himself almost exclusively to the work of organizing the Soviet régime. But the Central Committee in Shanghai, divorced from practical considerations, continued to advocate an extremist line of 'down with everything'—including the seizure of the big cities and the declaration of a general strike—in the belief that the 'situation for an immediate revolution now exists'.[24] In 1931 the 'central leadership', according to the later party resolution 'rectifying' these errors, 'made an entirely wrong appraisal' of Mao's work in the base area. The 'most disastrous consequence' of the Left line was the failure to defeat Chiang Kai-shek's fifth 'encirclement and suppression' campaign, which drove the Communists out of the area with heavy losses. Only in January 1935, during the Long March, was a new Central leadership established, headed by Mao Tse-tung.

Indeed, few could have foretold the eventual success of Communism in China from the experience of the early years of the party. At one stage (1923-26) junior partner in coalition with the Kuomintang; at the next, virtually shattered by Chiang Kai-shek's bloody *coup*. The organizer of frantic uprisings (1927-30) which were rapidly crushed; driven out by overwhelming force from its last rural stronghold; finally, after losing thousands in its epic Long March (1934-35) occupying an obscure, sparsely-populated province remote from the centres of power. It was Mao Tse-tung who jettisoned Communist dependence on the proletariat and actively espoused the revolt of the peasantry—the inexhaustible source of revolutionary strength in China—which finally brought the Communists within sight of their goal.

What were the conditions in China at the time of Mao's emergence to leadership? After the downfall of the Manchu Dynasty in 1912, China was in a state of virtual anarchy with changing coalitions of warlords fighting each other for control. 'The civil wars and the reign of the generals,' according to an American historian of the period, 'deepened the misery in the countryside. Exactions increased. Land was laid waste. Agricultural production declined. . . . Famines and unchecked floods took heavy tolls in human life. Millions of peasants, driven off the land, swelled the hordes of the militarist armies or took to banditry, often much the same thing. . . .'[25]

The situation in the 1920s—the first phase of the Communist movement in China—demonstrated the turbulence and ferment in the country: the Kuomintang's challenge to warlord rule; labour upsurges in Shanghai, Canton and other cities, with strikes and wage demands; student anger against 'imperialist' intervention, intensified by the shooting of demonstrators in the foreign concessions; and finally, peasant risings in south and central China.[26]

As another historian describes it, 'the flight of the rich from the countryside, the prevalence of banditry hardly differing from the exactions of the military destroyed the balanced economy of the countryside, drove the peasants down further into misery, drained money away to the coast, and left the great irrigation and drainage works uncared for and in decay . . . all contributed to the ruin of the older order of society. . . .'[27]

Over-population, natural disasters, and an unjust social order; such were the causes of peasant revolt. A vast increase in population had taken place in China during the ninteenth and early twentieth centuries. While the population—more than eighty per cent peasants—increased, the small cultivable area remained much the same. As Mao himself pointed out in 1955: 'The situation in China is like this. Its population is enormous, there is a shortage of cultivated land (only three *mou* [half an acre] of land per head taking the country as a whole; in many parts of the southern provinces the average is only one *mou* or less; natural calamities take place from time to time—every year large numbers of farmers suffer more or less from flood, drought, gales, frost, hail or insect pests—and methods of farming are backward.'[28] Mao Tse-tung's father, who owned two and a half acres in Hunan Province, south of the Yangtse river, was considered a 'middle peasant'. When he bought just over one acre more he became 'rich'.[29]

The crushing poverty of most of the people of China was made worse, and even unbearable, by landlord oppression, heavy rents and taxes, drought, floods and famine. Landlords kept about half the crop of tenant farmers, who were particularly numerous in the south—some two-thirds of all peasants in Fukien and Kwangtung Provinces, and even more in Hunan, a birthplace of peasant revolt. Throughout the centuries, Chinese peasants, driven to despair, had broken out in violent revolt. A century ago the famous Taiping rebellion, partly inspired by Christianity, had come near to destroying the decaying Manchu Empire. But it was left to Mao Tse-tung to grasp the prize which had evaded the Christian revolutionary and thus to emulate the peasant founders of the great Han and Ming Dynasties.

Mao has described the 'deep impression' made on him by a peasant uprising in Hunan Province in 1906, when he was thirteen years old. 'There had been a severe famine that year,' he told Edgar Snow, 'and in Changsha [the provincial capital] thousands were without food.' When the civil governor turned down their pleas for relief 'the people . . . became very angry. They held mass meetings and organized a demonstration . . . and drove out the governor. . . . A new governor arrived, and at once ordered the arrest of the leaders of the uprising. Many of them were beheaded and their heads displayed on poles as a warning to future "rebels".'[30]

Mao became a teacher in Hunan; he attended the first Congress of the Chinese Communist Party in 1921 and in the following year was made Secretary of the Hunan party branch. In 1923, at Soviet prompting, came the Communist alliance with the Kuomintang (then in precarious control only of the Canton region), whereby Communists would join the Kuomintang as 'individuals' but continue to maintain a separate party organization. To win power against the warlords, the Kuomintang had been reorganized along 'democratic centralist' lines, following the agreement between Sun Yat-sen and the Soviet envoy Joffe: China was to be united under the 'tutelage' of the Kuomintang, in coalition with the Communists and with the support of the Russians. This was the first attempt at a 'united front' in China; but the Kuomintang at that time was a 'revolutionary' organization—even Chiang Kai-shek, who was sent for military training to Russia, was denounced as a 'Bolshevik' by the West.

Mao was given responsibility by the Communist Party for work among the peasants. Ironically he was considered unsuitable for the 'more important' task of organizing the proletariat because of his inexperience of urban life; moreover with his country upbringing, he could not command the respect of intellectuals needed for 'united front' work.[31] Sent back to Hunan in 1925, Mao formed more than twenty peasant unions, for the peasantry had become 'very militant'.[32]

'The present upsurge of the peasant movement,' Mao declared in his report on conditions in Hunan, 'is a colossal event':

'In a very short time, in China's central, southern and northern provinces, several hundred million peasants will rise like a mighty storm . . . so swift and violent that no power, however great, will be able to hold it back. . . .They will sweep all the imperialists, warlords, corrupt officials, local tyrants and evil gentry into their graves. Every revolutionary party and every revolutionary comrade will be put to the test. . . . There are three alternatives. To march at their head and lead them? To trail behind them, gesticulating and criticizing? Or to stand in their way and oppose them? Every Chinese is free to choose, but events will force you to make the choice quickly.'[33]

The basis of China's autocratic government, Mao pointed out, was the 'patriarchal-feudal class' of local tryrants, evil gentry and lawless landlords: therefore 'to overthrow these feudal forces is the real objective of the national revolution'. And he caustically added: 'In a few months the peasants have accomplished what Dr Sun Yat-sen wanted, but failed, to accomplish in the forty years he devoted to the national revolution. . . .'[34]

To Mao the spontaneous revolt of the peasantry opened the way for an attack on the whole 'feudal-patriarchal system and ideology . . . binding the Chinese people'. But to the leaders of the Chinese Communist Party the turbulence in the countryside was at best irrelevant, at worst a source of anxiety. Doctrinally, they considered the growth of the peasant movement distracted from the tasks of urban revolution. In practice they also feared that their policy of alliance with the 'national bourgeoisie'—the Kuomintang—would be endangered by peasant 'excesses'.

In Moscow's view, the way to seize power in China was through the Kuomintang army (with its landowning officers). Therefore agrarian revolution must be avoided. Moreover the Russians believed that they could 'use' the Kuomintang to defeat the warlords and then simply cast it aside. In Stalin's own words in April 1927, only a week before Chiang Kai-shek's successful *coup* against the Communists in Shanghai, 'Chiang Kai-shek is submitting to discipline. . . . At present we need the Right. It has capable people, who still direct the army and lead it against the imperialists. . . . So they have to be utilised to the end, squeezed out like a lemon, and then flung away.'[35] In a situation of treachery and intrigue, in which the Communists are usually considered past masters, they were the ones to be 'squeezed'.

The doctrinaire attitude, both of Moscow and of the Chinese Communist Party, proved disastrous. Stalin, engrossed in Moscow in his struggle for power with Trotsky, veered from one extreme to the other. And the academic leaders of the Chinese Communist Party continued to believe, in the face of the evidence, that the Communist movement in China depended on the minute 'vanguard' of urban workers and not on the vast masses of the peasantry. As Chen Tu-hsiu, the party's first Secretary-General, asserted in 1923, three factors prevented the peasants from taking part in the revolution. First, they were widely scattered, and so were difficult to organize. Second, their low cultural standards gave them a 'conservative' outlook. And finally, because of the ease of movement inside China, they tended to evade difficulties and become 'complacent'.[36] Even after Mao had successfully organized a territorial base among the peasantry, following the debacle of the alliance with the Kuomintang, the Comintern in Moscow still condescendingly considered that Mao's 'peasant activities have become an important side current'.[37]

Chen Tu-hsiu had been purged for 'Right opportunism', that is for (reluctantly) carrying out Stalin's policy of alliance with the Kuomintang. Li Li-san, the next main leader, was dismissed for 'Left adventurism', that is for failing to succeed in Moscow's new policy of 'armed uprising' against the Kuomintang. Both, however, continued to believe that the urban proletariat formed the basis of the revolution. Unfortunately, Li Li-san admitted in November 1928, 'our union organizations have been reduced to a minimum, our party units in the cities have been pulverized and isolated. Nowhere in China can we find one solid, industrial cell.'[38] As a result of Kuomintang repression, Communist Party membership which amounted to nearly 60,000 at its height in early 1927, had been reduced by four-fifths in one year. M. N. Roy, the Comintern emissary, estimated that 25,000 Communists had been killed in the 1927 'white terror'. Hundreds of members of peasant associations had also been slaughtered.[39] But according to Li Li-san's assessment of the situation, with the collapse of the proletariat, 'peasant mentality is now reflected in our party . . . (but) the peasantry is petty-bourgeois and cannot have correct ideas regarding socialism'. Indeed he reasserted the orthodox Communist view that, 'unless we proceed to correct the dangers involved in this peasant mentality, it may lead to a complete destruction of the revolution and of the party'.[40]

It was Mao, unlike the city intellectuals of the Communist Party, who saw clearly the revolutionary ferment working over much of the Chinese countryside. Even in the period of collaboration with the Kuomintang, the main objective, in his view, must be to overthrow feudal rule, not to compromise with it, to organize peasant associations, not to hinder them. Mao also noted, and this was to prove of great importance, that during a revolutionary upsurge many joined the struggle—including middle and 'rich' peasants—who at other times would vacillate or 'wait and see'. But Mao's views were rejected by the party Central Committee; the peasants were held back; and their organizations—after Chiang Kai-shek gained control of the Kuomintang—were destroyed.

PROTRACTED WAR

(1) *Contradictions*

Between the fiasco of the Communist armed uprisings and the pitiless repression of the Kuomintang, urban membership of the Communist Party was almost wiped out. Scattered Communists, like Mao Tse-tung, painfully resumed the struggle at the head of small peasant and guerrilla bands. Meanwhile the party Central Committee, from its underground headquarters in Shanghai, continued a parallel but largely powerless existence.

Mao had been dismissed from the party Politburo after the failure of his 1927 'autumn crop uprising'.[41] With about a thousand men he sought refuge in the mountain stronghold of Chingkang, on the border of Hunan and Kiangsi Provinces. The population there was less than two thousand and the yield of rice was low. 'We are keenly aware that the revolutionary tide is on the ebb in the country as a whole . . . ,' Mao wrote a year later. 'Wherever the Red Army goes, the masses are cold and aloof. . . . Whatever enemy units we face, there are hardly any cases of mutiny or desertion to our side. . . . We have an acute sense of isolation which we keep hoping will end.'[42]

It was during these bleak years that Mao Tse-tung developed the strategy and tactics of 'protracted war'—the way in which the weak can defeat the strong. It was a matter of necessity to rely on the peasantry, rather than the proletariat, to set up liberated areas in the remote countryside, rather than incite urban insurrection, and to wear out the enemy by guerrilla warfare, rather than risk defeat in a head-on clash. But it was also the way to build up strength, to be ready to strike when the opportunity came.

Mao was concerned, not so much with the (by now) abstract theory of proletarian revolution in China, but with the practical question of the 'survival and growth' of an 'armed independent régime of workers and peasants' (in fact, chiefly peasants). This, he noted, required the following conditions:

1. a sound mass base,
2. a sound Party organization,
3. a fairly strong Red army,
4. terrain favourable to military operations, and
5. economic resources sufficient for sustenance.[43]

But it also depended on 'splits and wars' within the 'enemy' régime. When provincial warlords were fighting each other—for Chiang Kai-shek's formation of a Nationalist Government at Nanking did not put an end to warlord rivalry or even rebellion—Mao considered that 'our strategy can be comparatively adventurous and the area carved out by military operations can be comparatively large'. But when the ruling classes had achieved a certain stability, only a gradual advance was possible. Then the 'worst thing is to divide our forces for an adventurous advance . . . to scatter our personnel and neglect to lay a solid foundation'.[44]

Mao's call to 'vary party strategy', depending on whether the 'ruling class régime' was stable or divided, foreshadows his later elaborate analyses of the 'contradictions' within the enemy, which he was brilliantly to exploit. Mao's objective was the painstaking accumulation of revolutionary strength in the face of a powerful enemy, to be ready to 'turn to good account all such fights, rifts and contradictions in the enemy camp. . . .'[45]

The same need for 'protracted war' was recognized by the Viet-minh against the French twenty years later. In General Vo Nguyen Giap's words:

'The balance of forces decidely showed up our weaknesses against the enemy's power. . . . All the conceptions born of impatience and aimed at obtaining speedy victory could only be gross errors. It was necessary to firmly grasp the strategy of a long-term resistance . . . to maintain and gradually augment our forces, while nibbling at and progressively destroying those of the enemy; it was necessary to accumulate thousands of small victories to turn them into a great success, thus gradually altering the balance of forces, in transforming our weakness into power and carrying off final victory.'[46]

Mao himself had to educate the party to take the long-term view. Writing in January 1930, he opposed both the facile optimism of the Central Committee in Shanghai—which sought to launch a 'nation-wide armed insurrection'—as well as the gloomy opinions of the 'pessimists' who, after being 'defeated in battle or encircled or pursued by strong enemy forces', felt that the 'prospects of victory for the revolution were remote'. The issue, in Mao's view, could only be decided by 'making a detailed examination to ascertain whether the contradictions leading to a revolutionary high tide are really developing'.[47]

Above all, Mao rejected the prevalent theory (held by the Central Committee) of the need to win over the masses 'on a country-wide scale and in all regions' before any form of political power could be established. The actual state of the Chinese revolution, Mao argued, was different. Because of the lack of unity in the ruling régime, on the one hand, and the 'gravity of the peasant problem', on the other, the situation in China was *not uniform*: on the contrary, it revealed the 'unusual phenomenon' of the 'existence and development of small Red areas encircled by the White régime'.[48] The power of the enemy permitted it to contain and even defeat the small Communist forces; but the 'contradictions' within the existing régime, added to peasant support for the revolutionaries, gave the latter the opportunity to grow and to advance.

The Central Committee was still wedded to the concept of armed uprisings in the cities. Li Li-san insisted in April 1930 that 'all talk of "encircling the city with the country" or of relying on the Red Army to take the cities is sheer nonsense'.[49] For Mao Tse-tung, however, the 'establishment and expansion of the Red Army, the guerrilla forces and the Red areas' was not only the 'highest form of peasant struggle' but also the 'most important factor' in accelerating the revolution. Mao in 1930 was already advocating the 'correct' policy—

'of establishing base areas: of systemically setting up political power: of deepening the agrarian revolution: of expanding the people's armed forces by a comprehensive process of building up first the township Red Guards, then the county Red Guards, then the local Red Army troops, all the way up to the regular Red Army troops: of spreading political power by advancing in a series of waves . . .'[50]

It was this 'systematic' and 'comprehensive' process of organization and expansion which enabled the Communist movement, starting from secure bases—the 'liberated areas'—to fan out over the country and, profiting from the mistakes and weaknesses of the 'enemy' finally to seize power. The Vietminh movement followed a similar course in Indo-China. In Giap's words, 'the strategy of long-term resistance required . . . a gigantic effort of organization in both military and economic fields'. 'Once the political bases were consolidated and developed, we proceeded one step further to the consolidation and development of the semi-armed and armed forces. . . .'[51]

Mao's policy was to ascertain and take full advantage of the favourable factors—the revolutionary situation in the countryside—and ruthlessly to exploit all that was unfavourable to the enemy. Despite the appearance of strength, he contended, the political organs and armed forces of the 'reactionary ruling classes' were weak, 'resting as they do on the backward and fragile social and economic structure of China'. The result he argued in 1930, was that:

'In the wake of the contradictions among the reactionary ruling cliques—the tangled warfare among the warlords—comes heavier taxation. . . . In the wake of . . . heavier government taxation, etc., comes the deepening of the contradiction between the landlord class and the peasantry, that is, exploitation through rent and usury is aggravated. . . .

Because the reactionary government, though short of provisions and funds, endlessly expands its armies and thus constantly extends the warfare. . . . Because of the . . . rise in rent and interests demanded by the landlords and the daily spread of the disasters of war, there are famine and banditry everywhere. . . .

Once we understand all these contradictions, we shall see in what a desperate situation, in what a chaotic state, China finds herself. . . .'[52]

China's entire development, Mao wrote six years later, was uneven:

'a weak capitalist economy coexists with a preponderant semi-feudal economy; a few modern industrial and commercial cities coexist with a vast stagnant countryside; several million industrial workers coexist with several hundred million of peasants and handicraftsmen labouring under the old system; big warlords controlling the central government coexist with small warlords controlling the provinces; two kinds of reactionary armies, the so-called Central Army under Chiang Kai-shek and "miscellaneous troops" under the warlords in the provinces, exist side by side; a few railways, steamship lines and motor roads exist side by side with a vast number of wheelbarrow paths and footpaths. . . .'

This was the 'first characteristic' of the 'revolutionary' situation in China. The second was the size and power of the 'enemy':

'The Kuomintang is a party that has seized power and has more or less stabilized its power. It has gained the support of the world's principal counter-revolutionary states. It has remodelled its army . . . this army is much better supplied with weapons and material than the Red Army. . . . The Kuomintang controls the key positions or life-lines in the politics, economy, communications and culture of China; its political power is nation-wide. . . .'

The third characteristic was the small size and weakness of the Red Army:

'Our political power exists in scattered and isolated mountainous or remote regions and receives no outside help whatsoever. . . . The revolutionary base areas embrace only rural districts and small towns. These areas were extremely small in the beginning and have not grown much larger since. . . . The Red Army is numerically small, its arms are poor, and it has great difficulty in obtaining supplies. . . .'

The fourth characteristic was Communist Party leadership and the agrarian revolution:

'Victory is possible because it is under the leadership of the Communist Party and has the support of the peasantry. Thanks to this support, our base areas, small as they are, are politically very powerful. . . . Small, as it is, the Red Army has great fighting capacity, because its members, led by the Communist Party, are born of the agrarian revolution and are fighting for their own interests. . . .'[53]

These 'characteristics' are the key to the success or failure of 'people's war'. They exist simultaneously, Mao observed, 'that is, there are favourable factors and there are difficulties. . . . He who has eyes but fails to see this fundamental law cannot direct China's revolutionary war':

'The four principal characteristics of China's revolutionary war are: a vast semi-colonial country which is unevenly developed politically and economically and which has gone through a great revolution; a big and powerful enemy; a small and weak Red Army; and the agrarian revolution.'

It followed from the first and fourth characteristics 'that it is possible for the Chinese Red Army to grow and defeat its enemy'. But it also followed from the second and third 'that it is impossible for the Chinese Red Army to grow very rapidly or defeat its enemy quickly'. Thus, Mao concluded, 'the war will be protracted and may even be lost if it is mishandled'.[54]

The uneven development of the country did provide the long-term opportunity of revolutionary success. But in the short term it was the Communists themselves who faced disaster. True, Mao hoped in 1930 to seize most of Kiangsi and parts of Fukien and Chekiang Provinces—where there were few provincial troops—and indeed easily repulsed Chiang Kai-shek's first two 'extermination' campaigns. But even at the height of their power in south-east China in the early 1930s the Communists were never strong enough to hold more than a few big towns and their scattered rural areas were divided by roads and rivers controlled by the Kuomintang. The 'Central Soviet Government' established at Juichin, in southern Kiangsi, ruled a population of only three million. The Red Army led by Chu Teh, numbered only 40,000 men at first and was to face, in successive campaigns, 100,000 men, 200,000, 300,000 and finally a million men advancing irresistibly from concrete blockhouses and with artillery and airplane support. The Communists were driven out of their stronghold in 1934 and barely survived the year-long 6,000 mile 'Long March' to the far north-west.

(2) *Mass Support*

'It is absolutely necessary,' Peng Teh-huai,* commander of the Communist First Front Army, told Edgar Snow in 1936, 'for the partisans to win the support and participation of the peasant masses. If there is no movement of the armed peasantry in fact, there is no partisan base and the army cannot exist.'[55] Mao, too, underlined the need for 'active support of the population' as the 'most important' condition in preparing for the counter-offensive. With active popular

* There is some evidence of early rivalry between Peng, one of the Communists' leading military commanders and Mao. Both came of 'rich' peasant families in the same county in Hunan Province. Peng was later Deputy Commander-in-Chief (to Chu Teh) of the People's Liberation Army, commander of the Chinese 'volunteers' in Korea and Minister of Defence. He was dismissed in 1959 partly because of his opposition to the Mao-inspired Great Leap Forward campaign, which Peng considered was having a bad effect on the morale of the (peasant) soldiers.

support—which 'means having a base area'—Mao claimed it was then easy to achieve three other conditions: discovery of the enemy's weak spots, reducing him to a 'tired and demoralized state' and inducing him to make mistakes.[56]

However, popular support (in a small area) had not saved the Communists two years earlier from the determined assault of an overwhelmingly more powerful enemy (Soviet suppression of the Hungarian national revolt in 1956 is a similar case). In this respect, popular support is clearly subordinate to 'contradictions' in the enemy régime as a factor in Communist success. Where Chiang Kai-shek had been able, free from other distractions, to *concentrate* his forces against the Communists—as in the 1933-34 year-long blockade of Juichin which finally wore down and starved out the defenders—the more powerful force had won. The Communists had also made the mistake of fighting a positional war—a war to defend territory—and not a war of movement as in previous campaigns, which would deploy the Red Army to its best advantage; thus the Communists contrary to Mao's principles, had engaged the enemy on ground of the latter's choosing.

In the third 'suppression' campaign of 1931, Chiang had had to call off the attack—at a point where it had penetrated far into the Communist base area—because of the threat from the Japanese occupation of Manchuria. The Communists were once more saved in Yenan in 1936, when Chiang Kai-shek was (forcibly) prevented from mounting a further campaign against the 'Communist bandits' by the insistence of his own troops on uniting instead against the Japanese invader. Resistance against Japan provided the Communists with the broad national support they had hitherto lacked. Yet it was not merely their strong resistance and their militant patriotism—in contrast to the more defensive or even passive behaviour of the Kuomintang—which won them support; or if this secured it initially, allowed them to maintain it. What did so was undoubtedly the belief that the Communists represented the interests of the mass of the people—certainly to a much greater extent than did the Kuomintang—and would actively defend them.

To win popular support for the revolutionaries, Mao had long pointed out, meant assuring the 'well-being of the masses'. 'Our comrades,' Mao observed in 1934, 'should in no way neglect or underestimate the question of the immediate interests, the well-being of the broad masses. For the revolutionary war is a war of the masses; it can be waged only by mobilizing the masses and relying on them.'[57] As Peng Teh-huai put it, 'because the masses are interested only in the practical solution of their livelihood, it is possible to develop partisan warfare only by the immediate satisfaction of their most urgent demands'.[58] Such a 'reformist' approach might not produce good Communists but it turned out good supporters of the Communists.

The peasants wanted land, but they also needed assistance in 'all the practical problems' of their everyday life. Mao was one of the first to recognize the importance of agrarian reform and what is now known as 'community development' to win the 'hearts and minds' of the people:

'We must lead the peasants' struggle for land and distribute the land to them . . . safeguard the interests of the workers, establish co-operatives, develop trade with outside areas, and solve the problems facing the masses—food, shelter and clothing, fuel, rice, cooking oil and salt, sickness and hygiene and marriage. . . . The women want to learn ploughing and harrowing. Whom can we get to teach them? The children want to go to school. Have we set up primary schools? The wooden bridge over there is too narrow and people may fall off. Should we not repair it? . . .

We should convince the masses that we represent their interests, that our lives are intimately bound up with theirs. We should help them to proceed from these things to an understanding of the higher tasks we have put forward . . . so that they will support the revolution and spread it throughout the country, respond to our political appeals and fight to the end. . . .'[59]

Land to the tiller—Sun Yat-sen's slogan which the Kuomintang failed to carry out—this was the 'link' between the peasant masses and the revolution. The way to obtain the land for the peasants was by overthrowing the 'local tyrants, evil gentry and lawless landlords' —the basis of autocratic government; and this 'is the real objective of the national revolution', as Mao perceived in his early report from Hunan. 'Every revolutionary comrade should know that the national revolution required a great change in the countryside.' If the rich peasants were not 'enthusiastic' and the middle peasants vacillated— 'they have rice cooking in their pots and no creditors knocking on their doors'—the poor peasants, the great majority of the population, were the 'main force in the bitter fight in the countryside . . . leadership by the poor peasants is absolutely necessary. Without the poor peasants,' Mao proclaimed, 'there would be no revolution.'[60]

In 1927 when the Kuomintang broke with the Communists, Mao was already calling for a 'peasant-worker revolutionary army' and the confiscation of landlord property. In the Chingkang mountain base, a year later, Mao regarded the two main tasks as to 'divide the land and to establish Soviets'.[61] This programme was adopted in

1930 at a party conference in South Kiangsi, where the first 'Soviet government' was later set up, with Mao as chairman. Mao told Snow that the 'peasants responded with a warm, enthusiastic support which helped, in the months ahead, to defeat the extermination campaigns of the Kuomintang armies'.[62]

In this poor and backward region of China where peasants lived in squalid mud hovels with few possessions, paying rents of up to 70 per cent of their crop, indebted to moneylenders and suffering from the exactions of provincial and local armies, the Communists appeared as deliverers. 'We never had to lay seige to any village,' said Chu Teh, the Red Army's commander. 'Whole villages poured out and often walked for miles to wait for us, but the strongholds of the landlords had to be taken by storm.'[63]

The 'hundred-headed' landlords, as the peasants called them, lived in large towns and cities, safe behind their walls.[64] Here they acted—as Mao had reported from his investigations in Hunan—as officials, judges, juries and executioners. The pessimism of the peasant, his indifference to fate, only began to crumble when he heard of the 'poor man's army' led by 'Chu Mao against the nobles'. The peasants fought, Chu Teh recalled, with their own primitive weapons until they were crushed by the landlords' militia from the cities. Then the heads of captured rebels were mounted on poles as a warning to offending villagers.[65]

'With enemies who so ruthlessly suppress the Chinese revolution . . . ,' Mao later observed, 'the principal means or form of the Chinese revolution must be armed struggle, not peaceful struggle. For our enemies have made peaceful activity impossible for the Chinese people. . . .'[66] As it was, Mao claimed, the peasants had been driven to take up arms because of the tyranny of their oppressors. His early report from Hunan noted that the 'most violent revolts and the most disorders have invariably occurred in places where the local tyrants, evil gentry and lawless landlords perpetrated the worst outrages'.[67] When the landlords had been in power, Mao argued, they slaughtered peasants wholesale. 'A revolution is not a dinner party, or writing an essay, or painting a picture, or doing embroidery,' Mao sarcastically reminded the intellectuals then leading the Communist Party. 'It cannot be so refined, so leisurely and gentle, so temperate, kind, courteous, restrained and magnanimous'—the traditional Confucian 'virtues'. 'A revolution is an insurrection, an act of violence by which one class overthrows another.'[68]

Certainly the Communists were to have their fill of violence. Mao's first wife and his younger sister were executed by the Kuomintang.[69] Chu Teh's third wife was tortured and beheaded, and her head mounted on a pole in one of the main streets of Changsha, where she had been born.[70] The peasant and labour unions of Hunan, 'probably the most effectively organized in the whole country', were 'completely smashed'.[71] Twenty thousand people were reported to have been executed in Hunan province in 1927. And the Kuomintang itself admitted that about a million people had been killed or starved to death during the successful blockade of the Communist base area in 1933-34.[72]

It is not surprising that in the violence of their reaction the Communists should have behaved ruthlessly against their oppressors. Yet, as Mao recognized, the Communists were in a dilemma. For although forcible measures against the landlords might win the support of the poor peasants, they also had the effect of alienating the middle and rich peasants (whose lands were often confiscated) as well as the 'middle class' merchants, on whom the Communist areas depended for trade and thus, in effect, for survival. As Mao observed in 1928, when party policy was one of 'complete confiscation and thorough distribution' of landlord property (including that of the 'intermediate class' of small landlords and rich peasants), 'having been under attack during the revolutionary upsurge, the intermediate class deserted to the enemy . . . it was precisely the small landlords and rich peasants who led the reactionary troops'. This was because they had 'received too heavy a blow from the revolution'.[73]

Similarly, as a result of the party's insistence on expropriating 'middle' merchants in the towns, the 'ultra-left policy of attacking the petty-bourgeoisie drove most of them to the side of the landlords'.[74] As a result of the anti-Communist blockade and of 'our mishandling of the petty bourgeoisie', trade almost ceased, necessities such as salt, cloth and medicines were scarce and costly, and agricultural products could not be disposed of, 'so that the peasants' cash income is cut off'. The poor peasants were more disposed to endure these hardships but the 'intermediate class', Mao believed, would go over to the landlords 'when it can bear them no longer'. Under such conditions Mao doubted if the 'small independent Red régimes' could survive; 'for not only is such economic strain intolerable to the intermediate class, but some day it will prove too much even for the workers, poor peasants and Red Army men'.[75]

By force of necessity Mao adapted his policy to circumstance. In 1934 he was speaking of mobilizing the peasants 'within the framework of small-scale peasant economy'; 'of course, we cannot as yet bring up the question of state or collective farming'. And he went on to propose, not hampering, but promoting and encouraging the private sector of the economy. 'For the development of private enterprise is essential to the interests of the State and the people at the present stage.'[76]

The later broadening of Communist political support—through united front policies with the 'petty' and 'national' bourgeoisie against Japan—entailed still greater 'concessions' to capitalists and even landlords (the 'enlightened gentry'). Yet Mao did not neglect the peasant masses, on which the Communists based their support. 'Party and government personnel at the county and district levels,' he declared in 1943, following the worst period of the Japanese war, 'should devote nine-tenths of their energy to helping the peasants increase production, and only one-tenth to collecting taxes from them. . . . It is wrong simply to demand grain and money from the masses (as does the Kuomintang) without making every effort to help them to increase production . . . for all such activity is in the interests of the revolutionary cause.'[77]

The Communists were not, of course, 'agrarian reformers'—they had different ends in view. But the important point, in the 'national-democratic' stage, was that (unlike their rivals) they behaved as such.

(3) *Base Area*

Mao's contribution to Marxism-Leninism, affirms an American historian, was not in the realm of theory, but of practice. It was the 'creation of a State within a State—a party, an army and mass support in a territorial base'.[78] As Lin Piao recalled in his 1965 report on people's war, 'in these base areas, we built the Party, ran the organs of State power, built the people's armed forces and set up mass organizations. . . . Our base areas were in fact a State in miniature . . . [and] became the springboard for the people's war of liberation.'

Yet a revolutionary base area, initially established in a remote or 'inaccessible' region, was not so much a condition of victory—as of survival. How 'one or more small areas under Red political power' could survive when 'completely encircled by the White régime' was Mao's first consideration. He believed that this 'phenomenon' could occur only in backward 'semi-colonial' China—not in an industrialized country or a colony, where the imperialists were in full control (Mao was later to change his mind about colonies). This was similar to Lenin's view that revolution could break out, not so much in the highly organized industrial countries (as Marx predicted) but at the 'weakest link' in the imperialist chain. Mao realized that the régime in China exerted only a precarious control over large areas of the country and was subject to 'prolonged splits and wars'; thus the revolutionaries, weak as they were, could escape the full brunt of the enemy's attack. Mao also recognized that 'Red power' could survive at this time, not in China's northern and western provinces, which were 'unaffected by the democratic revolution', but in the centre and south, where the 'masses of workers, peasants and soldiers' had arisen and waged 'many economic and political struggles'.[79]

The area suitable for a revolutionary base was narrowed down still further. It must be neither 'too close to the enemy's big political centres', which would leave it dangerously exposed, nor yet too far away, since it would then be unable to exert any political influence on the population. Mao and his followers, after the initial rout of the Communists in 1927, 'traversed the whole range of mountains' extending across the four most turbulent provinces of south-east China. It was in the central range that Mao established an 'excellent military base, the Chingkang Mountains'. This had a further advantage in that it was sited on the border of two provinces (Hunan and Kiangsi) and thus could influence the lower valleys and the rivers—the natural means of transport and the chief areas of settlement in a mountainous region—'an influence endowing it with much more political importance'. But the disadvantage, which was to prove insuperable, was that it had long been blockaded by the enemy and 'its economic problems, especially the shortage of cash, are extremely difficult'.[80]

As a result of the enemy blockade, Mao noted in October 1928, 'necessities such as salt, cloth and medicines have been very scarce and dear . . . which has upset, sometimes to an acute degree, the lives of the masses . . . the soldiers are under-nourished, many are ill, and the wounded in the hospitals are worse off'. Trade with 'white' areas had almost ceased (thanks in part to to 'mishandling of the petty bourgeoisie'). Though 20 per cent of the crop in the central base area had been collected by the Communists as tax, other parts of the 'independent régime' were hilly areas 'where the peasants are so poverty-striken that any taxation is inadvisable'.[81] As the blockade tightened, so Communist troops faced starvation. Peng Teh-huai, the deputy commander, was left on Chingkang with 1,500 soldiers, while Mao Tse-tung and Chu Teh led a force of 4,000 through the driving snow to break the blockade. Soon after, the stronghold was taken by storm and the sick and wounded were hunted down and slain. Peng with 700 survivors fled by the same escape route Mao and Chu had taken.[82] They finally joined forces at Juichin in southern Kiangsi, which in November 1931 became capital of the 'Chinese Soviet Republic'.

It was from Juichin that Mao advocated to a sceptical Central Committee his 'policy of establishing base areas; of systematically setting up political power, of deepening the agrarian revolution; of expanding the people's armed forces. . . .' This, to repeat his views, was the 'highest form of peasant struggle' and the most important factor in accelerating the revolution. Particularly significant were the 'three objective conditions' stated by Mao for the establishment of the new base:

> *First, the economy of Kiangsi is mainly feudal,* the merchant-capitalist class is relatively weak, and the armed forces of the landlords are weaker than in any other southern province.
>
> *Secondly,* Kiangsi has no provincial troops of its own and has always been garrisoned by troops from other provinces. Sent there for the 'suppression of Communists' or 'suppression of bandits', *these troops are unfamiliar with local conditions,* their interests are much less directly involved than if they were local troops, and they usually lack enthusiasm.
>
> *And thirdly,* unlike Kwangtung which is close to Hongkong and under British control in almost every respect, *Kiangsi is comparatively remote* from imperialist influence.
>
> Once we have grasped these three points, we can understand why rural uprisings are more widespread and the Red Army and guerrilla units more numerous in Kiangsi than in any other province.[84]

What is also significant about these conditions is that they are contrary to the orthodox 'centralized' Communist Party doctrine. It was from an entirely practical point of view that Mao decided on a backward, remote agrarian province, far from the (suppressed) proletariat in the coastal cities of Canton and Shanghai. It was not from within the stronghold of capitalism—such as it was in China—that revolution was most likely to break out, but at the 'weakest link in the chain', where 'enemy' control was least effective. Not seeking a head-on clash, but taking advantage of the enemy's weak points: this is the most striking feature of what was later to be known as 'people's war'. Thus, a Mao-ist revolutionary movement could survive and grow as a purely 'local' phenomenon, not dependent on the existence of a nation-wide upsurge, as in the French or Russian Revolutions.

Depending on the terrain—and the mountainous or jungle regions of much of South East Asia proved to be as suitable for insurgent bases as the vast expanses of China—local armed strongholds could be established, screened from the 'enemy' by a sympathetic population and replenishing their strength from the same source. The authorities, equipped with modern means of State power, could without difficulty suppress organized opposition in the areas under their control (particularly any 'subversive' concentrations in the towns and cities); but modern techniques could no longer be used to advantage when dispersed over a large and hostile countryside or when dealing with jungle or mountain conditions.

This made possible the 'co-existence' in one country of 'pockets' of rebellion encircled by government-controlled territory. It was the 'uneven development' of countries like China—the relatively small impact of modernization in certain areas compared to widespread 'stagnation' under the traditional system—which enabled the revolutionaries to exploit these 'contradictions' and survive; though these factors could not altogether protect them, while still weak, from the possibility of defeat at the hands of a more powerful enemy.

(4) *Guerrilla Warfare*

'Guerrilla warfare,' as Lin Piao pointed out in his report on people's war, 'is the only way to mobilize and apply the whole strength of the people against the enemy, the only way to expand our forces in the course of the war . . . gradually change the balance of forces between the enemy and ourselves, switch from guerrilla to mobile warfare and finally defeat the enemy.'

And as General Giap expressed it:

'Guerrilla warfare is the form of fighting of the masses of the people, of the people of a weak and badly equipped country who stand up against an aggressive army which possesses better equipment and technique. This is the way of fighting the revolutionary war . . . avoiding the enemy when he is the stronger and attacking him when he is the weaker, now scattering, now regrouping one's forces, now wearing out, now exterminating the enemy, determined to fight him everywhere, so that wherever the enemy goes he would be submerged in a sea of armed people. . . .'[85]

And in a famous passage: 'There was no clearly defined front in this war. It was there where the enemy was. The front was nowhere, it was everywhere.'[86]

As Mao Tse-tung had explained years before, the absence of fixed battle lines was one of the 'outstanding characteristics' of Red Army operations. 'In a revolutionary civil war,' he wrote in December 1936, there cannot be fixed battle lines. . . . Our base areas are constantly expanding and contracting, and often as one base area falls, another rises. This fluidity of territory is entirely a result of the fluidity of the war.' The party exponents of regular warfare, whom Mao blamed for the disastrous outcome of Chiang Kai-shek's fifth encirclement campaign in 1934, denied this fluidity and opposed 'guerrillaism'. The result, Mao pointed out, was an 'immense fluidity'—the Long March.[87]

'We must adapt our thinking and our work to the circumstances,' Mao declared. 'We should honestly admit the guerrilla character of the Red Army. It is no use being ashamed of this. On the contrary, this guerrilla character is precisely our distinguishing feature, our strong point, and our means of defeating the enemy.' 'Fight when you can win, move away when you can't win'; this, Mao said, was the way to describe their methods.[88]

Mao's tactics were two-fold. To disperse Communist forces to 'arouse the masses'—a rôle which Giap was to call 'armed propaganda'; and to concentrate these forces when attacking the enemy. 'These tactics are just like casting a net; at any moment we should be able to cast it or draw it in. We cast it wide to win over the masses and draw it in to deal with the enemy.'

'The enemy advances, we retreat;
The enemy camps, we harass;
The enemy tires, we attack;
The enemy retreats, we pursue.'[89]

Concentration of troops, Mao reiterated, was the 'first and most essential condition' in battle. In this way the revolutionaries could make up for their overall lack of numbers by bringing a tactical local superiority to bear. 'Our strategy is "pit one against ten" and our tactics are "pit ten against one".'[90] But Mao advised, 'we should strike only when positively certain that the enemy's situation, the terrain and popular support are all in our favour and not in his. Otherwise we should rather fall back and carefully abide our time. There will always be opportunities; we should not rashly accept battle.'[91]

There is nothing original in these tactics. 'Avoid the enemy when he is full of vigour, strike when he is fatigued and withdraws,' recommended Sun Tzu, the celebrated Chinese strategist of the fifth century BC, whom Mao regularly quoted with approval. It is standard military practice to achieve local superiority before attacking. But the Communists were able to strike from a position of their own choosing more often than their opponents; this was not only because they knew the terrain and were usually well-informed about the movements of the 'enemy'—whether Kuomintang or Japanese—but because the latter was of necessity largely tied down in the static rôle of defence of towns and communications; and given the need to defend an extensive area, enemy forces were likely to be overstretched.

This situation is brought out with admirable clarity by General Giap:

'[The French] colonial war had no other aim than to occupy and dominate our country. . . . [The] object of the war forced the enemy to scatter his forces to occupy the invaded localities . . . a continuous process of dispersal of forces. The enemy divisions were split into regiments, then into battalions, companies and platoons, to be stationed at thousands of points and posts. . . .The enemy found himself face to face with a contradiction: without scattering his forces it was impossible for him to occupy the invaded territory; in scattering his forces, he put himself in difficulties. His scattered units would fall easy prey to our troops. . . . [For] we chose the positions where the enemy was relatively weak to concentrate our forces there and annihilate his manpower. As a result, the more we fought, the stronger we became. . . .'[92]

Indeed, the Indo-China war disproves Mao's original thesis that only in a 'semi-colonial' country and one as vast as China could such a revolutionary war develop. Actually Ho Chi Minh and Giap were more successful in protracted war than the Chinese Communist leaders, who on several occasions faced disaster. It was only after the peasant war became a national war (against the Japanese) that the Chinese Communists really made headway. Despite the relatively greater strength and efficiency of the French colonial régime, compared to wardlord or even Kuomintang rule, the Vietminh from the beginning possessed the inestimable advantage of being a nationwide resistance movement; it was sheltered by the people, lived among the people and derived its strength from them. The difficulty of the terrain, particularly the jungles and mountains of north and central Vietnam, made up for the country's lack of size. (Even in Malaya, where British and local forces both in operational skill and in numbers were superior to the Communist guerrillas, it took twelve years to weed the latter out from the jungles; and a remnant is still holding out along the Thai frontier.)

The basic issue facing insurgent movements is this: starting with a small and weak force they must keep up the initiative against a more powerful enemy in order, eventually, to change the balance of power. But if they are initially successful in winning control over certain areas, where conditions are particularly favourable, they then face the problem of defence of these areas: in other words they are in the *same* situation as the enemy. If the guerrillas simply disperse before the onslaught of a more powerful enemy, the guerillas themselves may be saved, but the bases will be lost. But if they stand and fight—as the Chinese Communists tried to do in 1934—they will be annihilated. Mao's solution was therefore neither to flee nor to attempt to hold 'every inch of territory', but to 'lure the enemy in deep'; a favourite military device to deceive the enemy into thinking he has defeated the retreating forces and then to counter-attack when he is off-guard.

Mao argued that 'luring the enemy in deep'—even at the temporary sacrifice of territory*—is the policy a weak army fighting a strong force must adopt in the initial stages of a war.[93] (It was precisely the strategy of 'trading space for time' adopted by the Kuomintang against the Japanese.) As Mao put it, 'if the attacking enemy is far more numerous and much stronger than we are, we can accomplish a change in the balance of forces only when the enemy has penetrated deeply into our base area and tested all the bitterness it holds for him'.[94]

Since they lived in the countryside, the retreating guerrillas could choose the most suitable terrain for fighting: 'But this condition alone is not enough and must be accompanied by others. The first of these is popular support. The next is a vulnerable enemy, for instance, an enemy who is tired or has made mistakes, or an advancing enemy column that is comparatively poor in fighting capacity.... In the absence of these conditions, even if we have found excellent terrain, we have to disregard it and continue to retreat in order to secure them'. Thus in the enemy-held areas, Mao admitted in 1936, 'there is no lack of good terrain, but we do not have the favourable condition of active popular support'. Therefore there was usually no alternative but to retreat towards the base area, because that is where the population is most active in supporting the Red Army'.[95]

Chu Teh, the Red Army commander, confirmed the vital importance of the peasantry providing information about the enemy. The Red Army had early established an intelligence network in the Communist areas and far 'underground' into enemy-held territory. It was manned entirely by peasants, some of whom could cover thirty miles a day without much effort. 'There came a time,' Chu told Agnes Smedley, 'when enemy armies were afraid to advance after they had sighted even one barefoot peasant watching them from a distance.' The villagers 'spied on the Kuomintang, waylaid and destroyed small units and captured their transport columns'. In one campaign the Red Army knew everything about the enemy defences. The peasants, who were forced to build them, had told the Communists their location and explained how deep the trenches were, how many loopholes each fort had and even drew rough sketches in the dust to show each path leading up to them.[96]

Certain 'rules' of guerrilla warfare were evolved by the Red Army: 'Partisans must never remain stationary,' Chu's deputy, Peng Teh-huai, told Snow, 'to do so is to invite destruction. They must constantly expand, building around themselves ever new peripheral and

* 'If what we lose is territory and what we gain is victory over the enemy, plus recovery and also expansion of our territory, then it is a paying proposition. . . .' (*Problems of Strategy in China's Revolutionary War*).

protective groups.' Again, 'partisans must not fight any losing battles. Unless there are strong indications of success, they should refuse any engagement. . . . Static warfare must be avoided. The partisan brigade has no auxiliary force, no rear, no line of supplies and communications except that of the enemy. In a lengthy positional war the enemy has every advantage, and in general the chances of partisan success diminish in proportion to the duration of the battle. . . .'[97]

Mao himself pointed out that though the war would be long, battles must be quickly decided; 'if we fail to gain a quick decision in attacking one of the enemy detachments, all the others will converge upon us'. The Red Army at that time usually finished a battle within a few hours, or sometimes a day. In the first 'encirclement' campaign of 1930, it fought two battles in five days. In the second, it marched over 200 miles, fought five battles and captured 20,000 rifles in fifteen days. The third campaign in 1931 dragged on for three months, while the fourth in early 1933 was over in three weeks and 10,000 rifles were captured in two battles—the Red Army, Mao observed, 'gets almost all its supplies from the enemy'.[98] But for the fifth campaign of 1933-34, Chiang Kai-shek mobilized nearly a million men. On the advice of German experts, the troops advanced over a period of months from concrete blockhouses with tank, artillery and airplane support. The Red Army, fighting to defend its major base, suffered heavy casualties and was compelled to retreat.

Most guerrilla units, as Mao admitted during the war against Japan, 'operate in very difficult circumstances, fighting without a rear, with their own weak forces facing the enemy's strong forces, lacking experience (when the units are newly organized), being separated, etc.'.[99] But he added: 'The Chinese peasants have very great latent power; properly organized and directed, they can keep the Japanese Army busy twenty-four hours a day and worry it to death.'[100]

To Mao, guerrilla warfare behind the enemy lines 'cripples the enemy, pins him down, disrupts his supply lines and inspires the regular forces . . .'.[101] The aim is the 'accumulation of many minor victories to make a major victory'.[102] Although guerrilla war was supplementary to regular war, which could alone decide the outcome, this did not mean it was unimportant. 'Its rôle in the strategy of the war as a whole,' Mao said, 'is second only to that of mobile warfare, for without its support we cannot defeat the enemy.'[103]

Mao discerned three 'strategic stages' of the war. In the first, where the enemy was penetrating deeply into the country, 'the form of fighting we should adopt is primarily mobile war [to check the enemy advance] supplemented by guerrilla and positional warfare', and there should be no attempt to fight entirely from fixed positions. The second stage was one of 'strategic stalemate', because of the invader's shortage of troops amidst increasing national resistance; the 'enemy will attempt to safeguard the occupied areas'. But 'taking advantage of the fact that the enemy's rear is unguarded, our guerrilla warfare will develop extensively . . . and many base areas will be established, seriously threatening the enemy's consolidation of the occupied areas'.[104]

This was the most ruthless stage of the war, Mao declared, 'and the country will suffer serious devastation'. If successful, the guerrilla forces might regain up to two-thirds of the occupied territories. Yet this 'very painful period', Mao warned, could last a long time: 'The two big problems will be economic difficulties and the disruptive activities of the traitors', especially the 'puppet government' set up by the enemy. Moreover because of the 'loss of big cities and the hardships of war, vacillating elements within our ranks will clamour for compromise [with the enemy] and pessimism will grow to a serious extent'. It was the most difficult stage, but a 'pivotal' one: 'If we can persevere . . . China . . . will gain the power to change from weakness to strength' ready for a 'brilliant last act': the recovery of the lost territorities.[105]

In the West, in recent years, there has been something of a fetish made of Mao's three stages. Thus political and military commentators have vied with each other in 'forecasting' when the Vietcong would enter, or asserting that they already had entered, the famous 'third stage'. But, as Mao makes clear, it is the period of *protracted* war—when the enemy is seeking to consolidate his initial gains and the resistance movement is painstakingly preparing for the counter-offensive—which is the really decisive stage. All the Vietminh successes were in this stage: even the victory at Dien Bien Phu, however effective psychologically, only eliminated a small proportion of total French armed strength. (International politics dictated the Geneva ceasefire, though there is little doubt that the Vietminh, if the war had gone on, would sooner or later have overrun the entire country.) In China, the surrender of the Japanese put an end to the struggle while it was still in the stage of protracted war. Mao actually acknowledged that, even in the third stage, 'China's strength alone will not be sufficient' to drive out the Japanese: 'We shall also have to rely on the support of international forces and on the [revolutionary] changes that will take place inside Japan, or otherwise we shall not be able to win.'[106]

However, protracted war, although not put to the final test against Japan, proved remarkably effective when the 'process' was applied to the Kuomintang:

'The process of war will present to China the possibility of capturing many Japanese prisoners, arms, ammunition, war-machines and so forth. A point will be reached when it will become more and more possible to engage Japan's armies on a basis of positional warfare.... Japan's economy will crack under the strain of a long, expensive occupation of China and the morale of her forces will break under the trial of a war of innumerable but indecisive battles. . . .'[107]

NATIONAL APPEAL

(1) *Resistance to the Enemy*

The Japanese invasion marked the turning point in Communist fortunes in China. Before 1937 the Communists had achieved a limited success on economic grounds; but only after the invasion did they come to be a major popular force because of their resistance to the enemy. 'Logically,' as Mao pointed out, 'a national war should win broader mass support than an agrarian revolutionary war.'[108] After the initial upsurge of the 1926-27 revolutionary movement in south and central China had subsided it was only with difficulty that the Communists—suppressed in the towns—were able to form small rural bases in remote areas of south-east China. Their ranks, gradually increasing in the years of rural struggle, were decimated in the disastrous campaign of 1933-34 and in the heroic Long March that followed.* At the end of 1935 they found shelter in the sparsely populated north-west province of Shensi where, as Mao admitted, they could pose little threat to the government in Nanking. But they were in a position to threaten the flanks of the Japanese army poised to advance in north China.

The Communists had for some years vigorously opposed Japanese expansionism, without being able to do much about it. In fact their anti-Japanese appeals in the early 1930s were designed more to distract the Kuomintang from pursuing its anti-Communist campaigns than in the expectation of creating a real united front against the common enemy. Thus the object of the party's 'tactical line', decided by the Political Bureau in December 1935, was to 'arouse, unite and organize' all the revolutionary forces throughout China 'to oppose the chief enemy confronting them, namely Japanese imperialism and the arch-traitor Chiang Kai-shek'.[109]

A year later occurred the famous incident at Sian, which led to

* 'All the revolutionary bases except the Shensi-Kansu border area were lost, the Red Army was reduced from 300,000 to a few tens of thousands, the membership of the Chinese Communist Party fell from 300,000 to a few tens of thousands and Party organizations in the Kuomintang areas were almost all destroyed.' (*Selected Works*, Vol. I, p. 195.)

a complete reversal of policy by both the Communists and the Kuomintang. Sian, capital of Shensi Province, was the headquarters of Chang Hsueh-liang, the 'Young Marshal' of Manchuria, whose forces had been driven out by the Japanese when they occupied the region in 1931. The Manchurian troops, not surprisingly, were increasingly reluctant to attack the Communists—as Chiang Kai-shek had ordered—to the profit of their common enemy. When Chiang arrived in Sian in December 1936, to direct the 'extermination' campaign against the 'Red bandits', he was kidnapped by the Young Marshal and saved from death only by Communist intercession. The latter needed the Nationalist leader to rally the people of China—which they alone could not do—against Japan.

Chiang Kai-shek was released, the civil war was called off and a united front was formed against Japan. Under the terms of this extraordinary bargain:

(1) the Communist-led government in the Shensi-Kansu-Ninghsia revolutionary base area will be renamed the Government of the Special Region of the Republic of China and the Red Army will be redesignated as part of the National Revolutionary Army, and they will come under the direction of the [Chiang Kai-shek] Central Government in Nanking and its Military Council respectively;

(2) a thoroughly democratic system will be applied in the areas under the Government of the Special Region;

(3) the policy of overthrowing the Kuomintang by armed force will be discontinued; and

(4) the confiscation of the land of the landlords will be discontinued.

In return for these concessions, 'the Kuomintang abandons the policy of civil war, dictatorship and non-resistance to the common foe', as Mao put it. Moreover he insisted that 'the preservation of the Communist Party's leadership over the Special Region and in the Red Army, and the preservation of the Communist Party's independence and freedom of criticism in its relation with the Kuomintang—these are limits beyond which it is impermissible to go'.[110]

To carry out the bargain, the more anti-Japanese elements of the Kuomintang had to put pressure on the anti-Communist 'die-hards' to reverse their policy; and Mao also had to convince his own doctrinaire followers that 'a great change' had taken place: 'When the revolutionary situation changes, revolutionary tactics and methods of leadership must change accordingly.' Because of the enormity of the Japanese threat and the weaknesses of the revolutionaries, Mao argued, it was only by organizing and rallying millions of people, through a united front with the 'national bourgeoisie', that

China could be saved.[111] The 'Party's new tactics' stemmed from the 'two fundamental facts that Japanese imperialism is bent on reducing all China to a colony and that China's revolutionary forces still have serious weaknesses'. What was needed was to 'organize millions upon millions of the masses' and move a mighty army into action. 'The plain truth,' Mao declared, 'is that only a force of such magnitude can crush the Japanese imperialists and the traitors and collaborators.'[112]

In these circumstances, Mao pointed out, it was wrong to advocate 'closed-door tactics' in the fixed belief that the 'forces of the revolution must be pure, absolutely pure', that the national bourgeoisie was 'entirely and eternally counter-revolutionary', that 'not an inch must be conceded to the rich peasants' and the 'yellow trade unions must be fought tooth and nail'. On the contrary, Mao observed, like every activity in the world 'revolution always follows a tortuous road and never a straight one . . .'.[113]

As Lin Pio confirms, if the party abandons a nationalist appeal—and thus isolates itself from the masses—'it is out of the question to exercise leadership and develop the people's revolutionary cause'. So successful was the Chinese Communist Party's united front policy in the war against Japan—and later against the Kuomintang—that it became a key feature (sometimes more in appearance than in reality) of post-war 'national liberation movements'. The Vietminh was just such a consciously 'national' grouping led by dedicated Communists in the struggle for independence. In Giap's words:

'The [Communist] Party devoted itself entirely to this work, to the regrouping of all the national forces, and to the broadening and strengthening of a national united front, the Vietminh . . . which was a magnificent model of the unity of the various strata of the people. . . . In fact, this front united the patriotic forces of all classes and social strata, even progressive landlords; all nationalities in the country—majority as well as minority; patriotic believers of each and every religion . . . we waged a people's war. . . . The national factor was of first importance.'[114]

Mao's dramatic switch in the tasks of revolution—from fighting for the confiscation of landlord property and for the establishment of Soviets to the formation of a national alliance (and the postponement of social changes)—necessitated a new attitude on the part of the Communists. This Mao rationalized in his 'two-stage' theory of revolution: 'The present task of the [national-democratic] revolution is to fight imperialism and feudalism, and socialism [the second stage] is out of the question until this task is completed.' But the two stages were 'two parts of an organic whole, guided by one and the same Communist ideology'.[115]

The Communists both stimulated, and made use of, the strong patriotic feelings in China inflamed by the Japanese invasion. As a Japanese political report noted in January 1940, there was 'intense' Chinese Communist consciousness of opposition to the enemy, owing to a 'certain clumsiness' of the Japanese forces and to a 'comparative decline in the consciousness of the Kuomintang. . . . At present, the fact of an intense anti-Japanese attitude on the part of the Chinese armies and masses is beyond dispute.'[116]

The very word 'Communism', Johnson states in his analysis of Japanese wartime reports, hardly appeared in a Communist political worker's training manual captured by the Japanese from the [Communist] New Fourth Army. Patriotic resistance came before support for popular interests.[117] According to another Japanese report: 'When the New Fourth Army first reaches a certain village, the political workers distribute anti-Japanese and anti-Wang [Wang Ching-wei, a former Kuomintang leader, who headed the pro-Japanese 'puppet' government at Nanking] leaflets. Then they reduce taxes by 20 to 30 per cent and distribute food and other necessities to refugees and the poor.' [118]

Japanese brutality above all forced the Chinese peasants to take up arms in self-defence. As Johnson broadly states, 'prior to 1937, the population of north China was more willing than the Chinese of other areas to countenance Japanese-sponsored government. . . . In actual fact, the devastation and exploitation that accompanied the Japanese invasion produced a radical change in the political attitudes of the northern Chinese.* The peasants of north China gave very strong support to the Communist organizational initiatives during the war and the largest number of Communist guerrilla bases was located in the rural areas of the north.'[119]

The policy of the Japanese commander of the North China Area Army—'kill all, burn all, destroy all',[120] reminiscent of Nazi German behaviour in Russia and other parts of occupied Europe—drastically reduced the Communist-held areas, but it also cemented the alliance of the Communists and the peasantry; this was not only from a common hatred of the invader but as a means of survival. The threat of terror and destruction created by the Japanese 'pacification' campaigns, Johnson points out, was a constant ingredient in Chinese

* The Chinese Communists did, however, have popular support, because of their radical social and economic programme, in Shansi Province; this was before the war against Japan enabled them to utilize patriotic feelings. (Donald G. Gillin, reviewing Johnson's 'Peasant Nationalism and Communist Power', in *Journal of Asian Studies,* February 1964.)

rural life throughout the eight years of war. The Communist Party 'met this challenge with an effective policy and the organizational ability to make this policy work won the support of the peasant population as no other political group has done in recent times'.[121] The Japanese themselves reported after the first 'mopping up' operation early in 1938: 'Although the enemy suffered heavy losses during these operations the desired result was not achieved. Communist troops . . . were not completely wiped out and powerful forces continued to roam the countryside harassing the Japanese rear.'[122]

Particularly instructive is a Japanese document comparing Chiang Kai-shek's successful campaign against the Communists in 1934 with current Japanese operations against the Communists in late 1941. Firstly, there was the matter of popular support. Chiang, according to the Japanese, was able to mobilize the country against the Communists in 1934; but the Japanese Army and (puppet) Nanking Government in 1941 'certainly do not possess the confidence of the broad masses'. Secondly, Chiang was dealing with a limited area (part of Kiangsi province); but Japanese troops were fighting Communist forces in some eight provinces throughout north and central China. Thirdly, the Red Army in 1934 numbered only 75,000 regular soldiers; in 1941 it amounted to 350,000 with another 100,000 in village self-defence corps. Fourthly, Chiang was able to concentrate his forces against the Communists, while the Japanese had also to fight the Kuomintang and to provide against the international threat. Finally, the Red Army in 1934 was 'not necessarily indigenous', but 'today it champions Army-civilian integration and is continuously organizing local armies. As a consequence it is extraordinarily difficult to separate bandit from citizen in Communist destruction work'.[123] The peasant farmer, in other words, had also become a patriotic guerrilla fighter.

The practical consequences of the Japanese invasion of China were of enormous significance for the Communists. In the first place, the rapid Japanese advance in 1937 and 1938 forced the Kuomintang armies to give ground; as they retreated, officials and the landed gentry fled with them, abandoning the peasantry.[124] The result was the disruption of the traditional social order and the creation of a vacuum into which the Communists, sometimes evading, sometimes attacking the Japanese, were able to move. Secondly, the brutality of the Japanese occupation compelled popular resistance; again the Communists were the most active in mobilizing and organizing the villagers for self-defence. Finally, and perhaps most important of all, the Nationalists [Kuomintang] were unable to compete effectively with the Communists in mobilizing mass support. This was because of the fear that stimulating popular resistance to the Japanese would also undermine the social base of the Kuomintang régime.

As the American historian, J. K. Fairbank, points out, there was a shift in the nature of the Kuomintang's support when it abandoned Nanking to the Japanese and withdrew to Chungking, in distant Szechwan Province, for the duration of the war: 'The Szechwan landlords and militarists took the place of the Shanghai bankers. Although the financial and mercantile class of the treaty ports had maintained close ties with landlordism, it had been in the forefront of modernization and of the Nationalist movement and had supported reform, though not revolution, in the countryside. The landed magnates of the interior, on the other hand, were conservatives of an earlier generation. . . . The Kuomintang faced the alternative of competing directly with the Communists by encouraging mass resistance through social revolution, or fighting on two fronts against foreign invasion and domestic revolt at the same time. About 1938 they chose the latter course. This obviously sprang from a deep bureaucratic distrust of mass movements and popular initiative, and an easily rationalized determination to retain power at any price. . . .'[125]

As Mao Tse-tung not unfairly described the issue in August 1937: 'The step forward taken by the Kuomintang on the question of resistance [to Japan] is to be commended; it is what the Chinese Communist Party and the people of the whole country have for years been hoping for. . . . But the Kuomintang has not changed its policies on such matters as the mobilization of the masses and the introduction of political reforms. . . . Some Kuomintang members say, "Let political reforms be instituted after victory." They think the Japanese aggressors can be defeated by the government's efforts alone, but they are wrong. A few battles may be won in a war of resistance fought by the Government alone, but it will be impossible to defeat the Japanese aggressors thoroughly. This can be done only by a war of total resistance by the whole nation.'[126]

Chiang Kai-shek at that time had welcomed the Communists, fighting 'shoulder to shoulder with the rest of the nation', but mutual suspicion of each other's ulterior motives remained strong. After a series of 'demarcation disputes' in central China, there occurred the January 1941 Anhwei 'incident' when part of the Communist New Fourth Army was wiped out by the Kuomintang. The united front was irreparably damaged. For the remainder of the war the Communists and Kuomintang spent more time preparing to fight each other than in resisting the Japanese.[127] The Communists, however, continued to expand their control in alliance with local guerrillas left behind after the retreat of the Kuomintang. As Mao observed while the united front was still in being, 'the enemy, employing his small forces against a vast country, can only occupy some big cities and main lines of communication and part of the plains. Thus there are extensive areas in the territory under his occupation which he has had to leave ungarrisoned, and which provide a vast arena for our guerrilla warfare.'[128]

This aspect of the Japanese occupation is particularly relevant to later attempts to deal with people's war: the problem of rural 'pacification'. The Japanese for the most part relied on ferocious reprisals and brutality to cow popular resistance; but they also attempted a more subtle and 'enlightened' political approach, chiefly in central China, where the resistance struggle was less acute. Ironically before 1937, it was in northern China that the Japanese had had most success in controlling large areas by 'political' pressure and influence on local Chinese warlords. However, the development of this policy was threatened by the revival and growth of popular anti-Japanese feelings, culminating in the 1937 agreement between Communists and Kuomintang. The Japanese Army therefore decided on a full-scale armed invasion which they confidently expected (like the Germans invading Russia in 1941) would force the enemy to sue for peace. In fact the Kuomintang was driven out of vast areas, but not destroyed; and so far from being compelled to surrender, was strengthened in its determination to resist.

The Japanese were not only faced with the prospects of a long war, but found it difficult to govern the large territory that had proved so easy to invade.[129] Their reaction took two forms: the 'mopping up' of Communists who had moved to fill the 'vacuum' resulting from the Japanese advance; and the establishment, in 1940, of a Japanese-controlled central government in Nanking—under the collaborator Wang Ching-wei—intended to rival both the Nationalists at Chunking and the Communists in their guerrilla bases. But like the Emperor Bao Dai (set up as a rival to Ho Chi Minh in French-controlled Vietnam) Wang was unable to demonstrate his independence of the foreign power which established him. The Japanese, moreover, did not really trust Wang, who had been leader of the Left-Kuomintang in its early alliance with the Communists. (They would have preferred one of the old warlords.)[130] By the time they had been persuaded to concede more powers to the Wang régime, so that he could compete more effectively in national appeal with the Communists, it was too late: the latter had already won the allegiance of a large part of the rural population. Above all, Wang faced an insuperable obstacle—his identification with the hated invader.

Where Japanese repression was less severe—in central China—a more effective policy of 'constant positive action' to eliminate resistance was undertaken. The aim was to work through local authorities subordinate to the Wang 'government', and particularly by 'encouraging the Chinese authorities to popularize the Mutual Guarantee System'—the Japanese Central China Army command decided in 1939.[131] This was the traditional system known as *Pao-Chia* and dating back to the Sung Dynasty, which placed on village households collective responsibility to report 'disturbances', keep order, collect information, supervise schools, repair roads, take a census of the population, and control movements between villages. It had already been found useful by the Japanese in maintaining order in Taiwan.[132]

A further development was the 'Rural Pacification Movement' launched in 1941 by Japanese and 'puppet' forces in strategic areas of the Yangtse valley. Its objective—similar to that of the Americans at present in South Vietnam—was to establish 'Model Peace Zones'. In these the guerrillas would be exterminated and the zones would then be rehabilitated, policed and systematically controlled by the Nanking (Wang) Government. 'In these zones Japanese forces were used only in the anti-guerrilla phase; all political and social affairs were handled by the Nanking Government.'[133]

The Model Peace Zones set up near large urban areas in Central China were generally immune to Communist penetration until 1944, when it became clear that Japan was losing the war.[134] By then the population of the zone had little to gain from collaboration with Nanking officials. The North China 'puppet' government sent a mission to inspect the peace zones in July 1943. But the military situation in the north had already deteriorated to too great an extent for 'pacification' to be effective.[135]

(2) *United Front Tactics*

In contrast to the limited success of Japan's model peace zones in central China was the enormous increase in Communist popular support in both north and central China. This was achieved by guerrilla warfare, by defence of the peasantry and by the united front. 'To subordinate the class struggle to the present national struggle against Japan,' Mao declared, 'such is the fundamental principle of the united front.'[136] In doing so Mao had to restrain the 'ultra left tendency' ('still the main danger in the Party'[137]) which wished to attack capitalists, petty-bourgeoisie and rich peasants in the belief that the Communist revolution was at hand. But when the greatest danger came from Japan, Mao had to keep up a united front with these bourgeois allies—at the same time without yielding to the 'anti-Communist diehards' forming the Right-Wing of the Kuomintang.

Mao's tactics are of great interest and subtlety. His declared aim was to 'isolate' the diehards, win over or at least neutralize the moderates and expand the 'progressive' forces. The moderates included such varied elements as the 'national bourgeoisie', which sought power by constitutional methods (but feared the working class), the 'enlightened gentry' who were anxious to resist Japan (but feared agrarian reform) and finally 'regional power groups' of big landlords, certain troop commanders and wealthy merchants and financiers (who feared revolution of any kind but were also opposed to the Kuomintang Central Government). These could, and must, be won over, Mao recommended, 'given certain conditions. These are (1) that we have ample strength; (2) that we respect their interests; and (3) that we are resolute in our struggle against the diehards. . . . The middle forces carry considerable weight in China and may often be the decisive factor in our struggle against the diehards; we must therefore be prudent in dealing with them.'[138]

Part of the anti-Communist forces, like Wang Ching-wei, had 'capitulated to Japan', but another part—the leadership of the Kuomintang—favoured resistance. Towards the latter, Mao advocated co-operation in resistance to Japan, and at the same time, 'struggle tactics' to combat its 'reactionary policy'. In this dual struggle with and against the 'diehards'—to parry their attacks and to prolong their wartime resistance—Mao insisted on three principles. First, self-defence: 'We must never attack others without provocation, but once attacked we must never fail to return the blow'. Second, assurance of victory: 'We must never fight without a plan, without preparation, and without certainty of success'. Third, restraint: 'After repulsing one diehard attack, we should know when to stop . . . we should then take the initiative in seeking unity'.[139]

By 'isolating' the diehards ('we . . . must not take on too many of them at a single time, but must direct our blows at the most reactionary of them first') and winning over or neutralizing the middle groups, the Communists were free to 'develop the progressive forces' through the united front movement. Besides expanding the Communist armies, this meant 'establishing anti-Japanese democratic base areas on an extensive scale, building up Communist organizations throughout the country, developing national mass movements of the workers, peasants, youth, women and children, winning over the intellectuals in all parts of the country, and spreading the movement for constitutional government among the masses as a struggle for democracy'.[140] This painstaking and thorough work of organization in the Communist-held areas laid the foundations, if not for the defeat of Japan, for victory in the civil war that followed.

The 'base areas' were the hub of Communist power. As a means of developing mass support through the united front the Communists in 1940 established the 'three-thirds' system of political power. One-third of seats in the 'organs of political power' went to the Communists; one-third to the 'left-progressives' among the petty-bourgeoisie; 'and the remaining one-third to the middle and other elements, representing the middle bourgeoisie and the enlightened gentry'. At the lowest level, Mao advised, the 'ratio may have to be somewhat modified to prevent domination by the landlords and evil gentry, but the fundamental spirit of this policy must not be violated'. All political parties, whether Kuomintang or any other, Mao went on, must be granted legal status 'so long as they co-operate with and do not oppose the Communist Party'. Every Chinese of eighteen years and over who favoured 'resistance and democracy' had the right to elect and be elected, 'irrespective of class, nationality, party affiliation, sex, creed or educational level'.[141]

The 'common programme' of the united front was said to be based on Sun Yat-sen's Three Principles; Nationalism—'by firmly resisting Japanese imperialism'; Democracy—by establishing the 'revolutionary democratic political power of the anti-Japanese National United Front'; and People's Livelihood—'by abolishing exorbitant taxes and miscellaneous levies, reducing land rent and interest, enforcing the eight-hour working day, developing agriculture, industry and commerce'. All these points, Mao observed, were also in the Kuomintang's published programme, but it had failed to carry out any of them except resistance to Japan. 'It is a simple enough programme', Mao pointed out, 'yet many Communists fail to use it as a weapon for mobilizing the masses and isolating the diehards'.[142] From now on 'we should keep attention focused' on it and popularize it continually. Testimony to the effectiveness of this policy is provided by the US War Department's 1945 study of the Chinese Communist Movement:

'[The three-thirds] system supports the claims of the Communists that they are maintaining a democratic, united front government. But no real opposition towards the Communists could, it appears, develop from any other party or class or group, since the electoral vote is controlled by the masses and the masses are controlled by the Communists. Anyone is free to stand as a candidate, but in practice nearly all the candidates are proposed by the mass movement associations and the choice offered the electors is usually limited . . . The Communists' control of (or loyalty from) the masses, combined with universal suffrage, is the chief cause of Communist power and political and military control.'[143]

As Mao saw it, establishment of 'united front political power' in

Communist areas would serve as a model for extension on a national scale. It was a 'new type of revolution' led by the proletariat with the aim, in the first place, of establishing a 'new-democratic society under the joint dictatorship of all the revolutionary classes';[144] that is, all those taking part in the united front against Japan. While the 'old democratic form' of bourgeois republic was 'out of date', Mao declared, the Soviet system was also not suitable for colonial and semi-colonial countries, at least 'for a certain historical period'.[145] Instead, Mao's 'third form' of State structure provided a semblance of national as well as class support; and this inevitably became a model for Communists in the developing countries of the post-war world, whose proletarian foundations in any case were none too strong.

Excerpts from Mao's reports during the Japanese war reveal the skill, determination and foresight needed to carry out and perfect the united front policy, *in all its facets,* in contrast to the negative attitude of the Kuomintang:

Tactics:

'Our tactics [in the united front] are guided by the same principle: to make use of contradictions, win over the many, oppose the few and crush our enemies one by one.'[146]

Patriotism:

'Can a Communist, who is an internationalist, at the same time be a patriot? We hold that he not only can be but must be. . . . Only by fighting in defence of the motherland can we defeat the aggressors and achieve national liberation.'[147]

Communism:

'Communists must consciously shoulder the great responsibility of uniting the entire nation. . . . Every Communist engaged in government work should set an example of absolute integrity, of freedom from favouritism in making appointments and of hard work for little remuneration. . . . It must be realized that Communists form only a small section of the nation, and that there are large numbers of progressives and activists outside the Party with whom we must work.[148]

Underground Work:

'In the Kuomintang areas our policy is to have well-selected cadres working underground for a long period, to accumulate strength and bide our time. . . . Our members should penetrate the *pao chia* [local security] and the educational, economic and military organizations everywhere; they should develop extensive united front work, i.e. make friends, in the Central Army and among the [provincial] troops. . . . Our Party organizations in the Kuomintang areas must be kept strictly secret . . . no one open to the slightest suspicion should be allowed to remain in any of these leading bodies.'[149]

Labour Policy:

'We must strictly guard against being ultra-leftist; there must not be excessive increases in wages or excessive reductions in working hours. . . . Once a contract between labour and capital is concluded, the workers must observe labour discipline and the capitalists must be allowed to make some profit. Otherwise factories will close down.'[150]

Land:

'It must be explained to Party members and to the peasants that this is not the time for a thorough agrarian revolution . . . the landlords shall reduce rent and interest, for this serves to arouse the enthusiasm of the basic peasant masses for resistance to Japan, but the reductions should not be too great.'[151]

Intellectuals:

'Many of the army cadres are not yet alive to the importance of the intellectuals . . . and are even inclined to discriminate against them. . . . All this is due to failure to understand the importance of the intellectuals for the revolutionary cause.'[152]

Traitors, Prisoners:

'We must firmly suppress the confirmed traitors and anti-Communists . . . but there must not be too much killing, and no innocent person should be incriminated . . . the stress must be on the weight of evidence and confessions should not be taken on trust. Our policy towards prisoners captured from the Japanese, puppet or anti-Communist troops is to set them all free, except for those who have incurred the bitter hatred of the masses and must receive capital punishment. . . . Among the prisoners, those who were coerced into joining the reactionary forces but who are more or less inclined towards the revolution should be won over in large numbers to work for our army.'[153]

Red Army:

'So long as the leadership of the army is left in the hands of the Party (this is an absolute and inviolable necessity), we need not be afraid of drawing large numbers of sympathizers into the work of building up the military and technical departments of our army . . . otherwise it will be impossible to win the sympathy of the whole country and expand our revolutionary forces.'[154]

New Democracy:

'United front political power under Communist leadership is the chief mark of a new-democratic society. . . . When the example of the anti-Japanese base area is extended throughout the country, then the whole of China will become a new-democratic republic.'[155]

China's Destiny:

'What the Kuomintang has gained from looking on with folded arms for five and a half years is the loss of its fighting capacity. What the Communist Party has gained from fighting and struggling hard for five and a half years is the strengthening of its fighting capacity. This is what will decide China's destiny. . . . For more than ten years we have been in the countryside and have had to encourage people to know the countryside well and to build the rural base areas. During these ten years and more the task of preparing insurrections in the cities . . . was not and could not have been carried out. But now it is different. . . . While we are in the base areas, we must learn how to administer the industry, commerce and communications of big cities, or otherwise we shall not know what to do when the time comes.'[156]

DOWNFALL OF THE REGIME

(1) *America's Dilemma*

One-fifth of China's population was under Communist control by the end of the war against Japan. But it had taken fifteen years for Mao's prediction to come true: 'It is certain that the masses will soon shed their illusions about the Kuomintang. In the emerging situation no other party will be able to compete with the Communist Party in winning over the masses.'[157]

As US Secretary of State Dean Acheson pointed out in 1949 in his foreword to the official record *United States Relations with China*:

'The reasons for the failures of the Chinese Nationalist Government . . . do not stem from any inadequacy of American aid. Our military observers on the spot have reported that the Nationalist armies did not lose a single battle during the crucial year of 1948 through lack of arms or ammunition. The fact was that the decay which our observers had detected in Chungking early in the war had fatally sapped the powers of resistance of the Kuomintang. Its leaders had proved incapable of meeting the crisis confronting them, its troops had lost the will to fight, and its government had lost popular support. The Communists, on the other hand, through a ruthless discipline and fanatical zeal, attempted to sell themselves as guardians and liberators of the people. The Nationalist Armies did not have to be defeated; they disintegrated. History has proved again and again that a régime without faith in itself and an army without morale cannot survive the test of battle. . . .'[158]

It was not by advocating Communism that the Communist Party came to power: but as promoters of clean government, political reforms and land for the peasant. 'The Communists are not in fact Communists,' announced US Ambassador Hurley in February 1945, 'they are striving for democratic principles.' (But he also believed that the 'one man personal Government of the Kuomintang is not in fact fascist, it is striving for democratic principles'.[159]) American policy at that time was to bring the two sides together; this was dictated by the imperative needs of the war against Japan. With the collapse of Japan a few months later the Americans tried the same policy of settlement to achieve a stable, united China. The Chiang Kai-shek Government, according to US Secretary of State Byrnes in December 1945, 'affords the most satisfactory base for developing democracy', but it must be broadened to include hitherto unrepresented 'large and well organized groups' (including the Communist Party).[160]

However, reports from US Foreign Service Officers, who 'had a unique opportunity through travel and contacts with American and Chinese military authorities, to observe conditions', presented instead a 'depressing picture of a deteriorating situation, characterized by internal squabbles and apathy'.[161] Even before the end of the war with Japan, their reports quoted in the official record, showed the 'development of the following themes':

'1. Russian intentions with respect to the Far East, including China, are aggressive.
2. The Chinese Communists have a background of subservience to the USSR, but new influences—principally nationalism—have come into play which are modifying their outlook.
3. The Chinese Communists have become the most dynamic force in China and are challenging the Kuomintang for control of the country.
4. The Kuomintang and Nationalist Government are disintegrating.
5. The rivalry between these two forces threatens to culminate in a civil war which (a) would hamper the conduct of the war against

Japan, (b) would press the Communists back into the arms of the USSR and (c) might well lead eventually to American Soviet involvement and conflict.
6. The Communists would inevitably win such a war because the foreign Powers, including the United States, which would support the [Nationalist] Government, could not feasibly supply enough aid to compensate for the organic weaknesses of the Government.
7. In this unhappy dilemma the United States should attempt to prevent the disaster of a civil war through adjustment of the new alignment of power in China by peaceful processes. The desirable means to this end is to encourage the reform and revitalization of the Kuomintang so that it may survive as a significant force in a coalition government. If this fails, we must limit our involvement with the Kuomintang and must commence some co-operation with the Communists, the force destined to control China, in an effort to influence them further into an independent position friendly to the United States. We are working against time because, if the USSR enters the war against Japan and invades China before either of these alternatives succeeds, the Communists will be captured by the USSR and become Soviet satellites.
8. A [US] policy of this description would also—and this is a decisive consideration in the war against Japan—measurably aid our war effort.'[162]

These proposals were recommendations from the field, *not* official US policy. But after the downfall of the Kuomintang in 1949 they inevitably gave rise in Right-Wing circles of America to accusations of defeatism and even treachery. Yet the experience of US relations with China entirely confirms Acheson's view that the 'ominous result of the civil war in China was beyond the control of the Government of the United States . . . it was the product of internal forces, forces which this country tried to influence but could not'. Now, it may have been naïve of the US Foreign Service officers—later to be made scapegoats for the 'loss' of China—to have expected that a sympathetic policy towards the Chinese Communists would influence them into adopting an 'independent position friendly to the United States'. But it was no less naïve of their opponents to have believed that US intervention in China—for which American opinion was utterly unprepared—could have succeeded in propping up the faltering Kuomintang régime.*

* Even such vehement critics of the United States' China policy as Senator Knowland and General Chennault were opposed to direct American intervention and the use of American ground forces for combat duties in China. Thus any positive action was ruled out: either (a) *to increase aid,* because

The magnitude of the disaster to US foreign policy—the change-over from a friendly if incompetent ally to a ruthlessly hostile régime controlling the most populous country in the world—was obvious. But it was also unavoidable, given the inability of the Kuomintang to reform itself. The US could put pressure on Chiang Kai-shek, but it could not compel him to make those drastic changes which alone might have kept him in power. In the ensuing emotional wave of feeling which swept America and which was exploited by the political opponents of the Administration— a situation also the 'product of internal forces'—these lessons were lost. The United States, under a different Administration, was again to face the problem of a disintegrating 'friendly' régime—in Indo-China—which US aid and advice alone could not save. Washington then recoiled from the 'brink' of armed intervention; it did so again in Laos; and even in South Vietnam after the downfall of Diem. However, massive intervention, which had been rejected in the case of the largest country in the world was finally (in 1965) felt necessary to 'save' one of the smallest.

The 'American dilemma' in China, which was also to be that in Indo-China, Laos and South Vietnam, was summed up by Dr Leighton Stuart, the last US Ambassador in Nanking: 'We are opposed to the spread of Communism all over the world and anxious to assist in preventing this in China, but, on the other hand, we cannot do this through a Government that has lost the support of its own peoples; to do so would be contrary to those democratic principles, the violation of which is the principal reason for our objection to Communism.'[163] And in a further despatch to Washington, also in December 1948: 'It is distressing to observe how completely he [Chiang Kai-shek] has lost public confidence. . . . [The] view is not infrequently expressed that he is best asset Communists have.'[164]

The tragedy of China was the lack of a middle way. The 'greatest obstacle to peace', reported the US 'Special Representative in China', General George C. Marshall, to President Truman in January 1947, 'has been the complete, almost overwhelming suspicion with which the Chinese Communist Party and the Kuomintang regard each other. . . .' He went on:

the Kuomintang was too incompetent and corrupt to use it properly; or (b) *to commit troops,* because of Congressional opposition and the rapid demobilization of US forces after the surrender of Japan (an Army of over eight million was cut down to less than one million by mid 1947, including only 140,000 in the whole of the Far East). 'Civil Strife and Armed Intervention: Marshall's China Policy', Tang Tsou, *Orbis,* Spring, 1962. See also Tang Tsou, *America's Failure in China 1941-50* (Univ. of Chicago Press, 1963), p. 363.

'On the side of the National Government, which is in effect the Kuomintang, there is a dominant group of reactionaries who have been opposed, in my opinion, to almost every effort I have made to influence the formation of a genuine coalition government. This has usually been under the cover of political or party action, but since the Party was the Government, this action, though subtle or indirect, has been devastating in its effect. . . . On the side of the Chinese Communist Party there are, I believe, liberals as well as radicals, though this view is vigorously opposed by many. . . . Nevertheless, it has appeared to me that there is a definite liberal group among the Communists, especially of young men who have turned to the Communists in disgust at the corruption evident in the local governments. . . . [But] the dyed-in-the-wool Communists do not hesitate at the most drastic measures to gain their end as, for instance, the destruction of communications in order to wreck the economy of China and produce a situation that would facilitate the overthrow or collapse of the Government. . . .

Sincere efforts to achieve settlement have been frustrated time and again by extremist elements of both sides. The agreements reached by the Political Consultative Conference a year ago* were a liberal and forward looking charter which then offered China a basis for peace and reconstruction. However, irreconcilable groups within the Kuomintang, interested in the preservation of their own feudal control of China, evidently had no real intention of implementing them. Though I speak as a soldier, I must here also deplore the dominating influence of the military. Their dominance accentuates the weakness of civil government in China. . . .

Between this dominant reactionary group in the Government and the irreconcilable Communists . . . lies the problem of how peace and well-being are to be brought to the long-suffering and presently inarticulate mass of the people of China. The reactionaries in the Government have evidently counted on substantial American support regardless of their actions. The Communists by their unwillingness to compromise in the national interest are evidently counting on an economic collapse to bring about the fall of the Government, accelerated by extensive guerrilla action against the long lines of rail

* In January 1946, representatives of the Kuomintang, Communist Party, Democratic League and others, agreed to: the convention of a National Assembly to draw up a Constitution; pending the meeting of the Assembly, the formation of a State Council as supreme organ of government, composed half of Kuomintang, half of non-Kuomintang members, with President Chiang Kai-shek's power of veto being overridden only by a three-fifths majority; legalization of political parties; and finally military reorganization, envisaging the reduction in eighteen months of Government divisions to fifty and Communists to ten, later to be integrated.

communications—regardless of the cost in suffering to the Chinese people. . . .'[165]

All efforts to achieve a settlement foundered on insuperable distrust. The Kuomintang would not accept the Communists in a coalition government unless they gave up their armed forces. But to do so without a guarantee of legal political status, the Communists argued, would mean their destruction: in Mao's well-known phrase, 'political power grows out of the barrel of a gun'. In other countries, Mao admitted, there might be no need for political parties to have an armed force under their direct command. 'But things are different in China, where, because of the feudal division of the country, those landlord or bourgeois groupings or parties which have guns have power, and those which have more guns have more power.'[166]

In such a situation, the 'liberal' solution advocated by General Marshall was doomed to failure. The 'salvation' of the country, he reported, 'would be the assumption of leadership by the liberals in the Government and in the minority parties, a splendid group of men', but who, he conceded, 'as yet lack the political power to exercise a controlling influence'.[167] Mao himself denied any possibility of a third choice. The aim of his most influential publication *On New Democracy*, written in 1940, was precisely to show that 'either you co-operate with the Communist Party or you oppose it'. Since opposition to Communism was the policy of the Japanese imperialists, 'the moment you oppose the Communist Party you become a traitor, because you can no longer resist Japan'. There was also no alternative, in Mao's view, to an alliance with the Soviet Union. 'Unless there is the policy of alliance with Russia, with the land of socialism, there will inevitably be a policy of alliance with imperialism':

'Once the conflict between the Socialist Soviet Union and the imperialist powers grows sharper, China will have to take her stand on one side or the other. This is an inevitable trend. Is it possible to avoid leaning to either side? No that is an illusion. The whole world will be swept into one or the other of these two fronts and "neutrality" will then be merely a deceptive term.'[168]

'There is no third choice.' In reality there was little enough choice in China, but Mao was determined to exlude even that. Wholehearted co-operation with the Communists, or be treated as an enemy: these were Mao's terms. In this summary fashion he brushed aside Sun Yat-sen's famous 'Three People's Principles'—Nationalism, Democracy and People's Welfare—which were intended to represent a genuine alternative both to Communism and to Warlord rule, and which might have done so had the Kuomintang lived up to them.* Instead the choice evidently lay between a military dictatorship, which became increasingly oppressive, and a Communist dictatorship which professed, and appeared then to be acting by, democratic principles. Virtually the only 'third force' in China was a group of intellectuals, notably in the Democratic League—at times supported by certain Kuomintang generals at odds with Chiang—which had little influence and less power. This third force distrusted, with good reason, both the Communists and the militarists. The former in effect ignored it; the latter repeatedly harassed and finally suppressed it altogether.

This was the state of China even before the end of the Japanese war, according to US Foreign Service reports: 'The Chinese Communists are so strong between the Great Wall and the Yangtze that they can now look forward to the post-war control of at least North China. . . . The reason is . . . positive and widespread popular support.'[169] On the Nationalist side:

'Morale is low and discouragement widespread. There is a general feeling of hopelessness. . . . The governmental and military structure is being permeated and demoralized from top to bottom by corruption, unprecedented in scale and openness. . . . The intellectual and salaried classes, who have suffered the most heavily from inflation, are in danger of liquidation. . . . Peasant resentment of the abuses of conscription, tax collection and other arbitrary impositions has been widespread. . . . The Kuomintang shows no intention of relaxing the authoritarian controls on which its present power depends. . . . The Kuomintang is unwillingly to take any effective steps to check inflation which would injure the landlord-capitalist class. . . . It does nothing to stop large-scale profiteering, hoarding and speculation—all of which are carried on by people either powerful in the Party or with intimate political connections.'[170]

By the time of the surrender of Japan, China's economy was in a precarious state and transport was almost totally disrupted; but militarily at least the Nationalist government enjoyed a superiority of five to one over the Communists in troops and rifles, a practical monopoly of heavy equipment and transport, and an unopposed air force. The United States, which had been supplying arms and assistance to the Government (but not, despite their pleas, to the Communists), air-lifted almost half a million Nationalist troops to

* 'The spread of Communism today is a result of our failure to put into effect the principles we believe in. . . .' Sun Fo, President of the Executive Yuan (Prime Minister), on February 5, 1949.

re-occupy east and north China, against bitter local resistance by Communist forces.[171]

General Wedemeyer, Commander of US Forces in China, had advised the Nationalists to consolidate south of the Great Wall before entering Manchuria. He considered Chiang Kai-shek could 'stabilize' the situation in south China if he accepted the assistance of foreign administrators and technicians and engaged in 'political, economic and social reforms through honest, competent civilian officials'. But, he reported to Washington in November 1945, it would take months or even years to occupy and administer north China, unless a satisfactory settlement could be reached with the Communists. Such a settlement, the General added, 'appears remote'.[172]

This estimate was correct. Mao in his report *On Coalition Government,* written not long before the defeat of Japan, effectively contrasted the Kuomintang's 'policy of active repression of the people' resulting in 'military setbacks, enormous territorial losses, financial and economic crises', with the doubling of the Communist army (to nearly one million men) and the development of nineteen 'liberated areas' throughout north and central China.[173] These areas had a total population of 95 million, and 'local coalition governments'—of Communists, progressives and patriots—were already in existence. The Kuomintang 'ruling clique' on the other hand (Mao argued), represented only the interests of China's 'big landlords, big bankers and big compradors; who monopolized all the important military, political, economic and cultural organizations under the government.[174] It was inconceivable, Mao argued, for the Communists to hand over their liberated areas, their local governments and armed forces in exchange, not for participation in a genuine coalition government (as the Communists insisted), but for only a 'few posts' in the 'defeatist, fascist and dictatorial' Kuomintang Government.[175]

Mao reaffirmed his belief in New Democracy 'at the present stage', including 'land to the tiller' and the growth of private capitalist economy.[176] But perhaps his most telling stroke was to put forward a whole series of popular demands. Among them: 'Punish the reactionaries . . . traitors . . . agents of the Japanese; liquidate the reactionary secret service and all its repressive activities. . . . Recognize the legal status of all democratic parties and groups. . . . Allow the Chinese people to arm themselves and defend their homes and country. . . . Punish corrupt officials and institute clean government. . . . Abolish exorbitant taxes. . . . Introduce rural reforms. . . . Check the unbridled inflation and rocketing prices. . . . Improve the livelihood of the workers. . . . Protect the interests of the youth, women and children . . .', etc.[177] In fact, something for (almost) everyone.

The country, Mao declared, was faced with two prospects. Either the continuance of the 'fascist dictatorship' of the Kuomintang and the possibility of civil war 'dragging China back into her old miserable state'. Or else 'abolishing the Kuomintang's fascist dictatorship, carrying out democratic reforms . . . and building an independent, free, democratic, united prosperous and powerful new China'.[178] Put in this way, which made more sense to more people than the propaganda—and still more, the activities of the Kuomintang—there was really no choice. But it was through war and not through peace that it came about; for as Mao had stated years before in his *Problems of War and Strategy*: 'Whoever has an army has power and . . . war decides everything.' Chiang Kai-shek had understood this vital point and 'in this respect we ought to learn from him'.[179]

The basis of Mao Tse-tung's policy—during the uncertain peace and the civil war that soon followed—continued to be peasant support: 'The main body of the masses,' he noted, 'consists of the workers, peasants (soldiers being chiefly peasants in uniform) and other working people.'[180] But whereas the need to maintain a united front against Japan had compelled the Communists to restrain peasant demands for land (rent and interest reductions only being permitted), there was no such need for restraint—on the contrary—during the struggle against the Kuomintang: a struggle against 'imperialism, feudalism and bureaucrat-capitalism', as Mao called it.

In May 1946 the Communists therefore reversed their policy. They insisted, as in the days before the United Front, on confiscation of the land of landlords and its distribution among the peasants. The 'Outline Land Law' approved by the Party's National Land Conference in September 1947 declared: 'The peasant associations of the villages shall take over the draught animals, farm tools, houses, grain and other properties of the landlords, requisition the surplus of such property of the rich peasants, distribute all this property among the peasants and other poor people who are in need of it and allot the same share to the landlords.'[181] Mao noted three months later the 'two fundamental principles' that the 'demands of the poor peasants and farm labourers must be satisfied' and that there must be 'firm unity' with the middle peasants, whose 'interests must not be damaged'.[182]

'The whole Party must understand,' Mao declared in the same report, 'that thoroughgoing reform of the land system is a basic task of the Chinese revolution in its present stage.' Because the party had stood 'resolutely on the side of the peasants' so the Army's rear areas were much more consolidated than they were a year and a half ago. The effect of peasant support for the Communists is confirmed by a Japanese adviser to the Kuomintang forces who was captured by the Communists in July 1948. The People's Liberation Army, he pointed out, readily split up larger enemy forces and destroyed them piecemeal. They were able to do so under conditions of local superiority because of popular support. The peasants, given the ownership of land by the Communists, gladly supplied 10 per cent of their grain to the Liberation Army (in contrast to the 70 per cent they had often had to provide to the landlords). The villagers would carry supplies and ammunition to Communist troops, while the local militia guarded the supply lines. Sons and brothers of 'liberated' former poor hired peasants volunteered to join the Communist forces to protect their land.[183]

Indeed from the military point of view, as General Marshall told the US Congress in February 1948:

'It was clear from V-J Day in 1945 that the Chinese Government was confronted by a military situation which made it, in the opinion of virtually every American authority, impossible to conquer the Communist armies by force. Geographically, the odds were too heavy against the government—thousands of miles of communications bordered by mountains affording easy retreats for guerrilla forces, numerous vulnerable river crossings and tunnels easily subject to destruction; the strategical and tactical characteristics of guerrilla warfare, permitting a concentration of guerrilla forces at a desired point where the government was weakest; and the governmental military necessity of covering all points, therefore weakly and thus vulnerable to surprise attack. . . . The odds were too heavy against them.'[184]

General Barr, Commander of the US Advisory Group in China, put it more bluntly in November 1948: 'Their [Kuomintang] military débâcles in my opinion can all be attributed to the world's worst leadership and many other morale destroying factors.'[185]

(2) *The Débâcle*

The final struggle between the Communists and the Kuomintang after the defeat of Japan followed three distinct phases: (1) The race to occupy Manchuria, the cease-fire and US efforts at mediation (the Marshall Mission 1945-46). (2) Renewed outbreak of civil war in 1947, with the initiative passing to the Communists. (3) Kuomintang troops on the defensive, mass defections and surrenders, the loss of Manchuria (1948), north China (March 1949), the crossing of the Yangtse, and the proclamation of the Chinese People's Republic (October 1949).

As the Americans had foreseen the crisis came to a head over

Manchuria. The Communist capture of an important railway and manufacturing centre occurred during the protracted negotiations between Kuomintang, Communists and Americans over supervision of a cease-fire. This strengthened the hand of the 'ultra-reactionaries' in the Kuomintang.[186] The Nationalists recaptured the city and despite Marshall's appeals, continued to march north. (In order to put pressure on the Kuomintang, first to continue negotiations, then to undertake reforms, an embargo was put on US military aid in July 1946. It was lifted, when civil war could no longer be averted, in May 1947.)[187]

At this time the Nationalist Army consisted of three million men —the Communists one million, nearly half of them irregulars.[188] Government forces made impressive gains: the Communist stronghold of Kalgan was taken in October 1946 and the Communists retaliated with vicious propaganda attacks against American 'interference'. Marshall felt he could no longer continue as mediator. In January 1947 he returned to Washington and was appointed Secretary of State.

In China, the year 1947 opened with Chiang Kai-shek determined to launch an all-out campaign against the Communists before financial deterioration made this impossible. The influence of the extreme right in the Kuomintang—notably the 'CC clique' of Chen Li-fu and Chen Kuo-fu controlling the party machine—became increasingly felt.[189] The US Military Attaché reported lack of morale among government troops faced with a seemingly endless civil war. Government lines were by now seriously extended, but the Army Chief of Staff confidently promised to defeat the Communists in six months.[190]

The final breakdown of negotiations between the Communists and the Kuomintang occurred in March 1947. That month the latter occupied the Communist capital of Yenan, but it was a hollow victory. In July the 'People's Liberation Army' went over to the offensive, forcing the Yellow River, thrusting into Shantung and deep into Manchuria. 'Attack dispersed, isolated enemy forces first . . .,' Mao recommended; 'attack strong enemy forces later. Take medium and small cities and extensive rural areas first; take big cities later. Make wiping out the enemy's effective strength our main objective. . . . Be sure to fight no battle unprepared, fight no battle you are not sure of winning. . . .'[191]

In the Kuomintang areas students demonstrated for an end to the civil war and for better economic conditions; the rice situation was particularly bad because of civilian hoarding and military requirements. The strategic initiative was passing to the Communists. Their drives in the North East, reported the American Consul-General in Mukden in May 1947, met no Nationalist resistance; 'apathy, resentment and defeatism are spreading fast' causing surrenders and desertions.[192] The American Ambassador, John Leighton Stuart, for many years a prominent missionary teacher at Yenching University, reported a 'picture of government corruption, inefficiency and aimlessness in the face of a major disaster'.[193]

Chiang Kai-shek did propose, in July 1947, 'all-out efforts in effecting national reforms and improvements', but Leighton Stuart could only report a 'general feeling of hopefulness and impending disaster'.[194] General Wedemeyer then arrived on a fact-finding mission for the US President. America, he said, could assist the Nationalists only if effective measures for recovery were taken under US supervision. He strongly criticized military and administrative corruption and inefficiency, adding that 'military force in itself will not eliminate Communism'.[195] In his report General Wedemeyer advocated United Nations' trusteeship for Manchuria with the Soviet Union as one of the five trustees; a five year assistance programme for China; and 'continuing evidence' that 'urgently required political and military reforms are being implemented'.[196] Chiang Kai-shek in September 1947 denounced his Party for failing to solve China's problems; but in October he outlawed the Democratic League. Two months later the Communist offensive in Manchuria cut off rail supplies to Mukden. It was the beginning of the end.

The Communists by then had captured or destroyed 80 per cent of the railway lines in Manchuria and about 40 per cent of those in the rest of China. General Barr, the American military adviser, stated that the US could not supply forward troops indefinitely by air and he urged, in March 1948, a 'progressive withdrawal from Manchuria'. But Chiang Kai-shek, he reported, was 'aghast at this proposal, stating that no circumstances would induce him to consider such a plan'.[197] Barr later criticized the 'strategic blunder' of occupying Manchuria: 'The Government attempting to do too much with too little, found its armies scattered along thousands of miles of railroads, the possession of which was vital in view of the fact that these armies were supplied from bases in central China. In order to hold the railroads, it was also necessary to hold the large cities through which they passed.'[198] This led to a disastrous 'wall strategy': Nationalist troops dug in within the city walls were unable to manoeuvre and not prepared to withdraw. Government fears of further defections tended to constrict the forces even more deeply in their defensive positions; the troops degenerated and lost their offensive spirit.

Ambassador Leighton Stuart reported in March 1948: 'Political and military disintegration is now rapidly approaching the long-expected climax. . . . There is most definitely accelerated demoralization, dismay and frantic search to save something from the wreckage, coupled with a psychological inability to do anything.'[199] The US Embassy at Nanking noted further 'disintegration and decay', with only tenuous government control over 1 per cent of Manchuria and 10 to 15 per cent of all China north of the Yellow River. Strong Communist elements had penetrated even to the Yangtse.[200] 'It should be possible to wipe out the entire Kuomintang army in about five years (counting from July 1946),' Mao himself observed.[201]

Against Chiang Kai-shek's opposition, General Li Tsung-jen was elected Vice President; he tried to rally the liberal and reforming elements, but received no encouragement from Chiang. The latter 'seems incapable of change,' commented Leighton Stuart in May, 'and gives every evidence of intention to persist in personal rule.'[202] He was enabled to do this by the 'Kuomintang machine' which, the Embassy reported, 'had rigged the elections to the National Assembly and had thus retained an almost solid bloc of delegates which could be strictly controlled, and which included politically experienced individuals well able to stir the Assembly and to control its deliberations. Also it had at its disposal a disciplined corps of political workers skilled in such minor political arts as bribery and intimidation. It had a controlled Press . . . and it had in its service, at least so most delegates thought, the secret police. Finally . . . it had with it the bulk of the Army High Command.'[203]

Students again demonstrated in May 1948. In June 'the government's inability to control food prices, which has led to rice riots in Chungking, Ningpo and the Yangtse delta towns is greatly increasing popular discontent'.[204] Government armies, reported the American Ambassador in July, 'can no longer be counted on to fight. . . . We are asked with increasing frequency why we adopt the policy of perpetuating in power a government seemingly bent on its own destruction.'[205] By August the Communists were occupying most of north China, except for a few urban centres. In central China and even south of the Yangtse, 'scattered Communist bands operate throughout the countryside creating confusion and disorder'. Though less active in the south, 'Communist guerrilla units operate more or less at will'. Everywhere, 'prices have become astronomical. . . . The all-consuming urge of the people today . . . is for peace.'[206]

Communist troops took Loyang in April, Kaifeng in June, Weihsien and Tsinan in September; at Tsinan alone they captured 50,000 rifles and much ammunition. The American Consul-General at Tsingtao reported 'outright defection to the Communists, immediate surrender and failure to stand and fight'—despite good fortifications, ample ammunition and food and up to 100,000 troops.[207]

Chinchow, supply base for Manchuria, fell in October and the great city of Mukden in November. Chiang Kai-shek, the Generalissimo, flew to Peiping to direct field operations. In Washington, the US Secretary of State warned: 'The United States must not assume responsibility for underwriting the Chinese Government militarily and economically . . . [which] would be impossible over so vast an area.' Yet the US Government, General Marshall added, 'will certainly continue to support the Nationalist government as long as it remains an important factor on the Chinese scene'. Decisions would be made 'in the light of US interests', if the Government moved from Nanking, collapsed or merged in a coalition with the Communists.[208]

'Recent military reverses in the North East,' announced in November 1948 the *Chung Yang Jih Pao,* an organ of the Kuomintang, 'are facts which the government no longer tries to hide and everybody is suffering terribly from the new high prices. The masses of people live under a feeling of fear and are pursued relentlessly by difficult living conditions . . . [but] the special privileged classes still enjoy their privileges.'[209] Peiping fell in January 1949. In four and a half months, from the fall of Tsinan to the fall of Peiping, the Government lost about one million men and 400,000 rifles. Seventy per cent of the US-equipped forces (seventeen divisions) had been lost by the previous November.[210]

The Generalissimo was now willing to enter peace negotiations with the Communists. 'What is the use of peace,' Mao sarcastically observed, 'if the war criminals and the classes to which they belong cannot preserve their freedom to oppress and exploit?'[211] Now the Chinese Foreign Minister asked America, Britain, France and the Soviet Union to act as intermediaries, but they all refused. Communist troops were massing on the north bank of the Yangtse: Chiang Kai-shek withdrew and Li Tsung-jen became acting President.* Li declared that 'the three years' civil war that followed the eight years' War of Resistance [against Japan] . . . has spread ruin everywhere north and south of the Yellow River, devastating innumerable farmsteads and houses, killing and wounding thousands upon thousands of innocent people'.[212]

A tentative draft by the Soviet Embassy now put forward three proposals: strict Chinese neutrality in case of international conflict; elimination of US influence as much as possible; establishment of a real basis for co-operation between China and Russia. Li agreed in principle and even asked for American support to Leighton Stuart's amazement.[213] But peace feelers with the Chinese Communists only

* Li returned to China in July 1965 after sixteen years of exile, mostly in the United States. In Peking he admitted his 'guilty past' and his 'mistaken' efforts to promote a third force between the Communists and the Kuomintang.

brought stern demands: punishment of 'war criminals', abolition of the Constitution, 'reorganization' of Nationalist troops 'on democratic principles', confiscation of 'bureaucratic capital', land reform and the establishment of a democratic, coalition government.

In March 1949 the American Ambassador reported that the Communists were ready to cross the Yangtse and advance to the south or south-west 'overcoming without too much difficulty any regional resistance they may encounter'. The acting President had 'increased tremendously in stature', he wrote, but 'centripetal forces' were too strong: it was every man for himself.[214] The Nationalist peace delegates left for Peiping in April and were given five days to accept Communist demands. At the last moment Li refused. Next day Communist troops crossed the Yangtse, which was made possible, the Ambassador said, by defections at key points.[215] The Nationalist capital Nanking, was quickly occupied, followed by Hankow (whither the Government had withdrawn) and Shanghai in May. On October 1, 1949, The Chinese People's Republic was proclaimed.

REFERENCE NOTES TO CHAPTER II

1. Lin Piao, 'Long Live the Victory of People's War' (*Peking Review,* September 3, 1965).
2. 'On New Democracy', *Selected Works of Mao Tse-tung* [hereafter *Selected Works* (Foreign Language Press, Peking, 1965), Vol. II, pp. 336-7.
3. 'Problems of Strategy in China's Revolutionary War', *Selected Works,* Vol. I, p. 245.
4. 'Problems of Strategy in Guerrilla War against Japan', *Selected Works,* Vol. II, p. 101.
5. 'On Protracted War', *Selected Works,* Vol. II, p. 172.
6. 'Oppose Stereotyped Party Writing', *Selected Works,* Vol. III, p. 61.
7. 'On Protracted War', *Selected Works,* Vol. II, pp. 168-9.
8. 'On Correcting Mistaken Ideas in the Party', *Selected Works,* Vol. I, p. 106.
9. Edgar Snow, *Red Star over China* (Gollancz, 1937), pp. 175-6.
10. Jerome Ch'en, *Mao and the Chinese Revolution* (Oxford Univ. Press, 1965), p. 165.
11. 'Problems of War and Strategy', *Selected Works,* Vol. II, p. 224.
12. 'On Protracted War', *Selected Works,* Vol. II, pp. 154-5.
13. Sir Robert Thompson, *Defeating Communist Insurgency: Experiences from Malaya and Vietnam* (Chatto and Windus, 1966), pp. 63-4.
14. David Galula, *Counter-Insurgency Warfare: Theory and Practice* (Pall Mall Press, 1964), p. 14.
15. *Ibid.,* pp. 71-2.
16. *Ibid.,* pp. 73.
17. Snow, *op. cit.,* p. 284.
18. 'On New Democracy', *Selected Works,* Vol. II, pp. 360-1.
19. Vladimir Dedijer, *Tito Speaks,* p. 331, quoted in Ch'en *op. cit.,* pp. 263-4.

20. 'The Chinese Revolution and the Chinese Communist Party,' *Selected Works,* Vol. II, pp. 316-7.
21. Cited in 'Resolution on Certain Questions in the History of our Party', adopted April 20, 1945, *Selected Works,* Vol. III, p. 184.
22. 'The Struggle in the Chingkang Mountains', *Selected Works,* Vol. I, p. 100.
23. Benjamin I. Schwartz, *Chinese Communism and the Rise of Mao* (Harvard Univ. Press, 1951), p. 183.
24. 'Resolution on Certain Questions . . .', *Selected Works,* Vol. III, pp. 189, 191.
25. Harold R. Isaacs, *The Tragedy of the Chinese Revolution* (Stanford Univ. Press, 2nd revised edit., 1961), p. 21.
26. *Ibid.,* Chap. 4, 'The New Awakening'.
27. C. P. Fitzgerald, *The Birth of Communist China* (Penguin Books, 1964), pp. 52-3. Revised edition of *Revolution in China* (Cresset Press, 1952).
28. *The Question of Agricultural Co-operation* (Foreign Languages Press, Peking, 1956).
29. Snow, *op. cit.,* p. 127.
30. *Ibid.,* pp. 131-2.
31. Ch'en, *op. cit.,* p. 98. But see S. Schram, *Mao Tse-tung* (Pelican, 1966), pp. 80-7.
32. Snow, *op. cit.,* p. 157.
33. 'Report on an Investigation of the Peasant Movement in Hunan', *Selected Works,* Vol. I, pp. 23-4.
34. *Ibid.,* p. 27.
35. Isaacs, *op. cit.,* p. 162.
36. Chen, *op. cit.,* p. 108.
37. Comintern message, October 1929. Schwartz, *op. cit.,* p. 135.
38. Schwartz, p. 128.
39. Isaacs, pp. 273, 277.
40. Schwarz, p. 137.
41. Snow, *op. cit.,* p. 165.
42. 'Struggle in the Chingkang Mountains', *Selected Works,* Vol. I, pp. 97-8.
43. *Ibid.,* p. 73.
44. *Ibid.,* pp. 73-4.
45. 'On tactics against Japanese Imperialism', *Selected Works,* Vol. I, p. 159.
46. Vo Nguyen Giap, *People's War People's Army* (Foreign Languages Publishing House, Hanoi, 1961), p. 28.
47. 'A Single Spark can start a Prairie Fire', *Selected Works,* Vol. I, pp. 117-20.
48. *Ibid.,* pp. 117-18.
49. Schwarz, *op. cit.,* pp. 138-9.
50. 'A Single Spark . . .', *Selected Works,* Vol. I, p. 118.
51. Giap, *op. cit.,* pp. 47, 78-9.
52. 'A Single Spark . . .', p. 121.
53. 'Problems of Strategy in China's Revolutionary War', *Selected Works,* Vol. I, pp. 196-8.
54. *Ibid.,* p. 199.
55. Snow, *op. cit.,* p. 288.
56. 'Problems of Strategy . . .', *Selected Works,* Vol. I, pp. 215-16. (Two other conditions were a favourable terrain and concentration of forces.)
57. 'Be Concerned with the Well-Being of the Masses, Pay Attention to Methods of Work', *Selected Works,* Vol. I, p. 147.

58. Snow, *op. cit.*, p. 285.
59. 'Be Concerned . . .', pp. 147, 149.
60. 'Report on an Investigation of the Peasant Movement in Hunan', *Selected Works,* Vol. I, pp. 27, 31-3.
61. Snow, *op. cit.*, pp. 163, 166.
62. *Ibid.*, p. 169.
63. Agnes Smedley, *The Great Road: The Life and Times of Chu Teh* (Monthly Review Press, New York, 1956), pp. 256-7.
64. *Ibid.*, p. 216.
65. *Ibid.*, pp. 256-7
66. 'The Chinese Revolution and the Chinese Communist Party', *Selected Works,* Vol. II, p. 316.
67. '. . . Investigation of the Peasant Movement . . .', *Selected Works,* Vol. 1, p. 28.
68. *Ibid.*, p. 28.
69. Snow, *op. cit.*, p. 173.
70. Smedley, *op. cit.*, p. 237.
71. 'China Weekly Review', August 20, 1927. Cited in Isaacs, *op. cit.*, p. 272.
72. Snow, *op. cit.*, p. 186.
73. 'The Struggle in the Chingkang Mountains', *Selected Works,* Vol. I, pp. 87-8.
74. *Ibid.*, p. 98.
75. *Ibid.*, p. 89.
76. 'Our Economic Policy', *Selected Works,* Vol. I, pp. 142, 144.
77. 'Spread the Campaigns to Reduce Rent, Increase Production and "Support the Government and Cherish the People" in the Base Areas', *Selected Works,* Vol. III, pp. 132-3.
78. J. K. Fairbank, *The United States and China* (Viking Press, 1962), p. 243.
79. 'Why is it that Red Political Power can Exist in China?', *Selected Works,* Vol. I, pp. 64-5.
80. 'The Struggle in the Chingkang Mountains', *Selected Works,* Vol. I, p. 99.
81. *Ibid.*, pp. 89-90.
82. Smedley, *op. cit.*, pp. 235-7, 252.
83. 'A Single Spark can Start a Prairie Fire', January 1930, *Selected Works,* Vol. I, p. 118.
84. *Ibid.*, p. 127. (emphasis added.)
85. Giap, *op. cit.*, p. 104.
86. *Ibid.*, p. 21.
87. 'Problems of Strategy in China's Revolutionary War', *Selected Works,* Vol. I, pp. 240-1.
88. *Ibid.*, pp. 240-1.
89. 'A Single Spark . . .', p. 124.
90. 'Problems of Strategy . . .', p. 237.
91. *Ibid.*, p. 231.
92. Giap, *op. cit.*, pp. 158-9.
93. 'Problems of Strategy . . .', p. 215.
94. *Ibid.*, p. 217.
95. *Ibid.*, p. 216.
96. Smedley, *op. cit.*, pp. 233, 296.
97. Snow, *op. cit.*, pp. 285-6.
98. *Selected Works,* Vol. I, pp. 246-8.
99. 'Problems of Strategy in Guerrilla War against Japan', *Selected Works,* Vol. II, p. 86.

100. 'On Protracted War', *Selected Works,* Vol. II, p. 119.
101. 'Problems of Strategy . . .', p. 91.
102. *Ibid.*, p. 85.
103. 'On Protracted War', p. 172.
104. *Ibid.*, pp. 137-8.
105. *Ibid.*, pp. 138-40.
106. *Ibid.*, p. 140.
107. Snow, *op. cit.*, p. 106. (See also *Selected Works,* Vol. II, p. 120.)
108. 'On Protracted War', p. 166.
109. 'The Tasks of the Chinese Communist Party in the Period of Resistance to Japan', *Selected Works,* Vol. I, p. 277.
110. *Ibid.*, pp. 269-70.
111. 'On Tactics against Japanese Imperialism', *Selected Works,* Vol. I, pp. 153, 161, 164.
112. *Ibid.*, p. 165.
113. *Ibid.*, pp. 163-5.
114. Giap, *op. cit.*, p. 44.
115. 'On New Democracy', *Selected Works,* Vol. II, pp. 358, 361.
116. Chalmers A. Johnson, *Peasant Nationalism and Communist Power: The Emergence of Revolutionary China, 1937-1945* (Stanford Univ. Press, 1962), p. 41.
117. *Ibid.*, p. 86.
118. *Ibid.*, p. 90.
119. *Ibid.*, p. 31.
120. *Ibid.*, p. 55.
121. *Ibid.*, p. 49.
122. *Ibid.*, p. 195, note 8.
123. *Ibid.*, pp. 53-4.
124. See, eg., *ibid.*, p. 110.
125. Fairbank, *op. cit.*, pp. 221, 225.
126. 'For the Mobilization of All the Nations's Forces for Victory in the War of Resistance', *Selected Works,* Vol. II, pp. 24-5.
127. Robert C. North, *Moscow and Chinese Communists* (Stanford Univ. Press, 2nd ed., 1963), pp. 204, 206.
128. 'On Protracted War', *Selected Works,* Vol. II, p. 158.
129. Johnson, *op. cit.*, p. 39.
130. *Ibid.*, p. 43.
131. *Ibid.*, p. 61.
132. *Ibid.*, pp. 62-3.
133. *Ibid.*, p. 63.
134. *Ibid.*, pp. 66-7.
135. *Ibid.*, p. 65.
136. 'The Question of Independence and Initiative within the United Front', Selected Works, Vol. II, p. 215.
137. 'On Policy', *Selected Works,* Vol. II, p. 444.
138. 'Current Problems of Tactics in the Anti-Japanese United Front', *Selected Works,* Vol. II, pp. 421-5.
139. *Ibid.*, pp. 426-7.
140. *Ibid.*, p. 423.
141. *Ibid.*, pp. 427-8.
142. *Ibid.*, p. 429.
143. US War Department, Military Intelligence Division, in US Senate Committee on the Judiciary, 'The Chinese Communist Movement', *Institute*

of Pacific Relations (Washington, 1952); cited by Johnson, *op. cit.*, p. 197, note 20.

144. 'On New Democracy', *Selected Works,* Vol. II. p. 344.
145. *Ibid.*, p. 350.
146. 'On Policy', *Selected Works,* Vol. II, p. 444.
147. 'The Role of the Chinese Communist Party in the National War', *Selected Works,* Vol. II, p. 196.
148. *Ibid.*, pp. 197-8.
149. 'Freely Expand the Anti-Japanese Forces and Resist the Onslaught of the Anti-Communist Die-Hards', *Selected Works,* Vol. II, p. 435.
150. 'On Policy', p. 445.
151. *Ibid.*, p. 446.
152. 'Recruit Large Numbers of Intellectuals', *Selected Works,* Vol. II, p. 301.
153. 'On Policy', p. 446-7.
154. *Ibid.*, pp. 448-9.
155. 'Conclusions on the Repulse of the Second Anti-Communist Onslaught', *Selected Works,* Vol. II, p. 467.
156. 'Our Study and the Current Situation', *Selected Works,* Vol. II, pp. 171-3.
157. Letter of April 1929 to the Party Central Committee, *Selected Works,* Vol. I, p. 122.
158. US Department of State, *United States Relations with China: With Special Reference to the Period 1944-1949* (Department of State Publication 3573, Washington, August 1949), p. xiv.
159. North, *op. cit.*, p. 210.
160. *Ibid.*, pp. 230-1.
161. *United States Relations with China,* p. 64.
162. *Ibid.*, pp. 64-5.
163. *Ibid.*, p. 896.
164. *Ibid.*, p. 898.
165. *Ibid.*, pp. 686-8.
166. 'Problems of War and Strategy', *Selected Works,* Vol. II, pp. 223-4.
167. *United States Relations with China,* p. 688.
168. 'On New Democracy', *Selected Works,* Vol. II, pp. 364-5.
169. John P. Davies Jr. (November 7, 1944) in *United States Relations with China,* pp. 566-7.
170. John Stewart Service (June 20, 1944) in *ibid.*, pp. 568-9.
171. *Ibid.*, pp. 311-3.
172. *Ibid.*, pp. 131-2.
173. 'On Coalition Government', *Selected Works,* Vol. 11, pp. 259, 264.
174. *Ibid.*, pp. 269-70.
175. *Ibid.*, pp. 274-5.
176. *Ibid.*, pp. 279-81.
177. *Ibid.*, pp. 286-8.
178. *Ibid.*, pp. 276-7.
179. 'Problems of War and Strategy', *Selected Works,* Vol. II, p. 223.
180. 'On Some Important Problems of the Party's Present Policy', *Selected Works,* Vol. IV, p. 187.
181. 'The Present Situation and Our Tasks', *Selected Works,* Vol. IV, p. 174, note 4.
182. *Ibid.*, p. 164.
183. Hiroshi Johno, Director of the China Consolidated Research Institute, in *Chuo Koron,* December 1965.
184. *United States Relations with China,* p. 380.

185. *Ibid.*, p. 358.
186. *Ibid.*, p. 149.
187. *Ibid.*, p. 155.
188. *Ibid.*, p. 313.
189. Despatch by Leighton Stuart (March 3, 1947) in *ibid.*, p. 235.
190. *Ibid.*, pp. 236, 238.
191. 'Strategy for the Second Year of the War of Liberation', *Selected Works*, Vol. IV, pp. 144-5.
192. *United States Relations with China*, p. 316.
193. *Ibid.*, p. 242.
194. *Ibid.*, p. 253.
195. *Ibid.*, pp. 257-8.
196. *Ibid.*, pp. 260-1.
197. *Ibid.*, p. 325.
198. *Ibid.*, p. 336.
199. *Ibid.*, p. 844.
200. *Ibid.*, p. 267.
201. 'A Circular on the Situation', *Selected Works*, Vol. IV, p. 225.
202. *United States Relations with China*, p. 282.
203. *Ibid.*, p. 909.
204. *Ibid.*, p. 869.
205. *Ibid.*, p. 873.
206. *Ibid.*, pp. 885-6.
207. *Ibid.*, pp. 319-20.
208. *Ibid.*, pp. 285-6.
209. *Ibid.*, p. 880.
210. *Ibid.*, pp. 323, 357.
211. 'On the War Criminal's Suing for Peace', *Selected Works*, Vol. IV, p. 311.
212. Statement as acting President, January 22, 1949; cited in *Selected Works*, Vol. IV, p. 353.
213. *United States Relations with China*, p. 293.
214. *Ibid.*, p. 301.
215. *Ibid.*, p. 305.

III SUCCESS

The situation in China was, in many ways, a model for the Vietnamese. The Chinese Communists, like the Vietminh, were able to rally the people against an alien force. In so doing the Chinese Communists transferred their limited appeal on social and economic grounds—chiefly affecting the poor tenant farmers and landless peasants of south-east China—into a 'national' appeal: that is, it extended 'vertically' to other groups and classes as well as 'horizontally' over a wider and indeed a different area.

With the Chinese Communists' reversal of policies—the 'national democracy' of the united front against Japan replacing the 'worker-peasant' dictatorship—occurred a reversal of support: northern China, hitherto largely 'immune' to the Communists, became their major stronghold, while the original base areas of the south-east only with difficulty revived after suppression at the hands of the Kuomintang.

Above all, the Japanese invasion and brutal occupation, especially of northern China, aroused an intense national consciousness among the people. The ardent nationalism swept away both the prevalent attitude of warlord 'self interest' (ready for a deal with the Japanese so long as their own 'feudal' interests were not adversely affected) and of northern peasant apathy (problems of tenancy were not so acute as in the centre and south). In their desperate state of insecurity the northern peasants rallied to the organization which could best protect them.

Struggle for Vietnam

Nationalism was also the major factor in Vietnamese resistance to the French. But the struggle in Indo-China developed in quite a different manner to the way it had in China. Sporadic 'hunger' revolts organized both by Nationalists—the Vietnamese equivalent of the Kuomintang—and by Communists were suppressed by the French in 1930 and again in 1940 with great severity: and no protracted warfare from liberated bases developed. It was not until the Japanese occupation of Indo-China in 1940 and especially after the overthrow of the French administration in March 1945 that the Vietminh—

operating from China—was able to set up bases in the mountainous border areas. In the confusion of the sudden Japanese surrender in August 1945 the Vietminh—best organized of the nationalist forces, as even the Kuomintang acknowledged—seized control. Abdicating in favour of Ho Chi Minh's republican régime, the Emperor Bao Dai epitomized the situation in these words: 'I would prefer to be a private citizen of an independent State than king of a subject nation.'[1] And President Ho resolved in his declaration of independence—starting with the 'immortal' words of the US Declaration, 'all men are created equal . . .'—on September 2, 1945:

'The French have fled, the Japanese have capitulated, Emperor Bao Dai has abdicated. Our people have broken the chains . . . and have won independence. . . . The whole Vietnamese people, animated by a common purpose, are determined to fight to the bitter end against any attempt by the French colonialists to reconquer their country. . . .'[2]

But independence was shortlived. British forces, responsible for disarming the Japanese in southern Vietnam, handed over the administration to the French. In the North, Chinese occupation armies similarly handed over large areas to Nationalist parties under their supervision. Finally the French Government reached agreement in March 1946 with the Chinese, after renouncing French concessions in China, and French troops took over the role of occupation. Ho Chi Minh's provisional government at Hanoi, broadened to include Nationalist representatives, proposed negotiations for an independent Vietnam within the 'French Union'. But the French would neither accept independence—though in March 1946 they recognized 'the Republic of Vietnam as a free State . . . forming a part of the Indo-Chinese Federation',[3]—nor the unity of Vietnam, which was divided by the French into Tonkin (north), Annam (centre) and Cochin-China (south).

In the ensuing negotiations, as with the parallel Communist-Kuomintang talks in China, all was to founder on an insuperable distrust. French officials and settlers were determined to secure Cochin-China—now the heart of South Vietnam—from the Vietminh.* The latter insisted that it was an integral part of Vietnam.

* A French settler's motion, passed in July 1946, by the Council of Cochin-China, resolved to 'fight by all means' for the 'autonomy' of Cochin-China in the Indo-Chinese Federation. By this time the Vietminh was controlling practically three-quarters of the region (virtually all but the urban areas). Devillers, *Histoire de Viet-Nam de 1940 à 1952*, pp. 318-19.

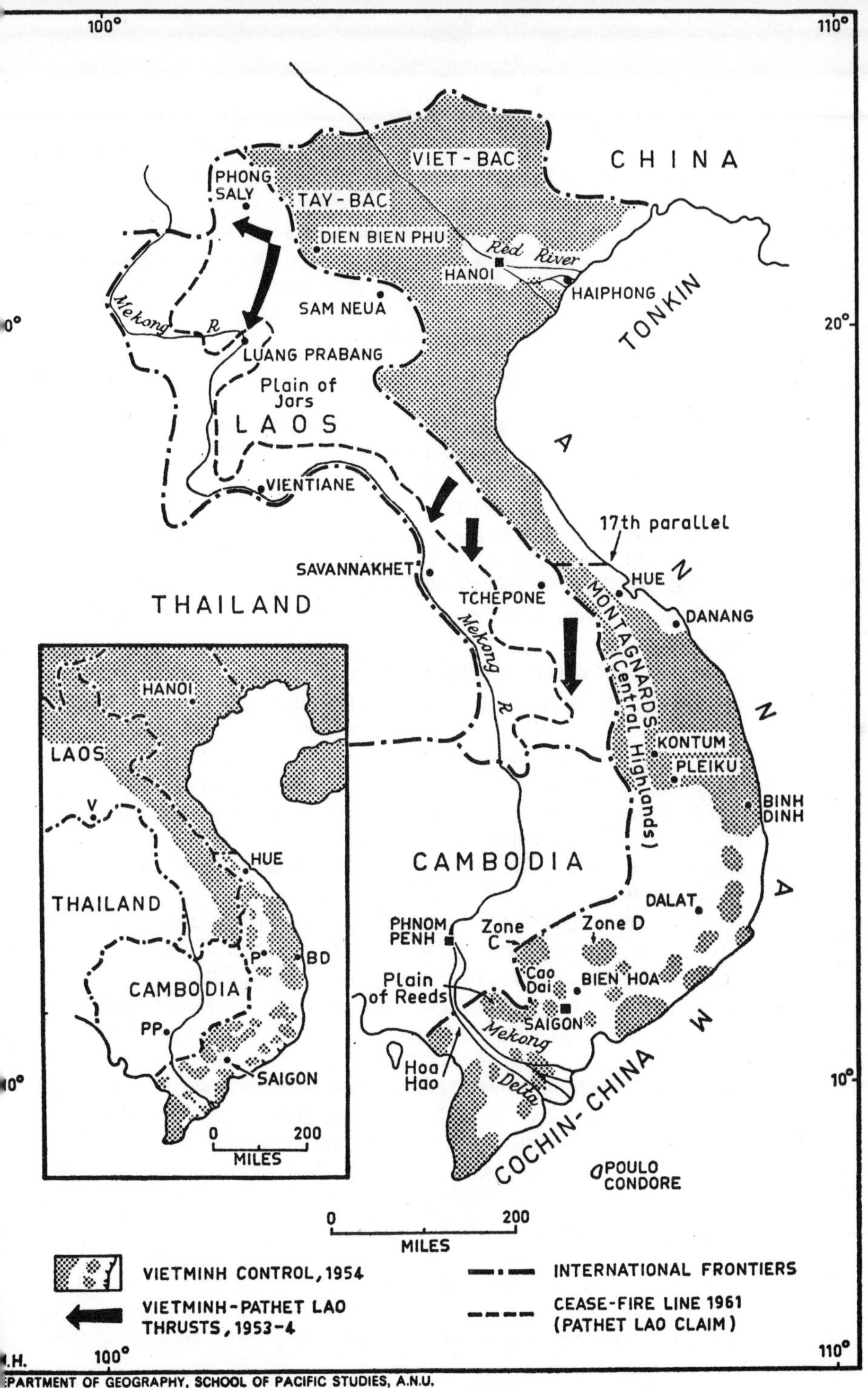

ndo-China: North and South Vietnam, Laos, Cambodia. Inset, 1965. Sources: Vo Nguyen Giap, *People's War, People's Army*. Hugh Toye, *Laos: Buffer State or Battleground*. Inset: *New York Times*, February 11, 1965.

The March 1946 cease fire agreement soon broke down in the south. The unhappy cycle of Vietminh assassination of village notables, separatists and collaborators of the French, followed by French reprisals, arrests and shooting of suspects, terrorization of villages by both sides, followed by more attacks and reprisals, began.[4] This was to be the pattern of the next twenty years. And the end is not yet in sight.

AUGUST INSURRECTION

Unlike the gradual accumulation of strength by the Chinese Communists, leading eventually to a change in the balance of forces with the Kuomintang, the initial Vietminh take-over in August-September 1945 was as complete and sudden as that which the early Chinese Communists had dreamed of. It was a revolutionary insurrection, an upheaval, a rapid and total change of authority: the new 'Mandate of Heaven', as the French scholar, Paul Mus, puts it. This swing from one side to the other, 'proceeding not by compromise as in the West . . . but by a total replacement, is the precise way in which the Confucian spirit, still living in the heart of the Vietnamese countryside, is accustomed to represent history and to anticipate it. It can be seen as the cosmic or climatic concept of revolution. . . . At times of crisis, institutions, doctrines and the men in power change altogether, just as one season replaces another.'[5]

The French, overthrown by the Japanese, had lost the Mandate of Heaven. The Vietminh, 'succeeding like a miracle . . . almost without firing a shot, a whirlwind sweeping away Japanese, foreigners of all kinds and even the national dynasty', had taken their place.[6] According to Chinese conceptions of society, deeply rooted among the Vietnamese—the only people in South East Asia to come under Chinese cultural and political domination—the Vietminh had shown itself destined to rule. This conviction that the Vietminh was the 'true' successor to the French was to prove extremely important throughout the long years of resistance that were to follow the outbreak of war in December 1946.

The Vietminh, by its thorough preparation, organization and leadership, had established its supremacy over all rival nationalist groups. Indeed it represented, for the Vietnamese, the spirit of resistance to renewed French occupation and of the historic determination of the people to be free. The fact is, as Bernard Fall states, 'given French policy in 1945-46, Ho Chi Minh could scarcely have acted differently if he had been a nationalist of the extreme Right!'[7] The Vietnamese Communists, like their counterparts in China, were not *acting* as Communists, but as Nationalists: they were the embodiment of the desires of the nation. If the French, despite their humiliating overthrow by the Japanese early in 1945, had given the Vietnamese what they wanted—independence and unity—as they later were compelled to give it to Bao Dai (but with reluctance, gradually and too late to win approval); if this had been done in 1946 they might still have cut off the Vietminh from its basis of popular support. Instead, as Paul Mus observes, 'the war created against us [the French] an alliance of nationalism with a moderate Marxism on a programme of socialization—at a time when we were offering this nation, imbued with a sense of unity, no more than a division into three [Tonkin, Annam and Cochin-China were officially considered by the French to be 'separate' regions] within a union of five [with Laos and Cambodia in the Indo-Chinese Federation] under our direction and our sovereignty. We have seen what the national reaction was . . .'[8]

* * *

The Vietminh, like the Chinese Communist Party, was a movement based on the villages. 'In a backward colonial country such as ours where the peasants make up the majority of the population,' pointed out General Giap, 'a people's war is essentially a peasant's war under the leadership of the working class. Owing to this fact, a general mobilization of the whole people is neither more nor less than the mobilization of the rural masses. The problem of land is of decisive importance. . . .'[9]

Again like China, the land problem in Vietnam was more one of overpopulation than of 'feudal' oppression.* The misery of the Vietnamese peasants in contrast to the wealth of the French settlers and officials and of the gallicized Vietnamese landowners is amply attested. But it was essentially the result of the increasing density of population—inheriting land in ever smaller strips—throughout the small fertile delta regions of Vietnam. The Red River delta in the North—nine million people living in an area of 12,000 square kilometres—has one of the highest population densities in the world. In the North, nearly a million small holders owned only 40 per cent of the cultivated area; 20 per cent was in the hands of 180 landowners; the rest was owned by middle farmers or was communal land. As the Vietnamese historian Le Thanh Khoi argues, how could a family of four or five people live on an average holding of just over one acre?[10]

Cochin-China—southern Vietnam—by contrast is a region of relatively recent settlement, less crowded than the North, but with

* However, peasant indebtedness to large landowners was a major evil in Vietnam, as in China.

a far higher proportion of large estates and correspondingly of landless labourers and share-croppers. Nearly three-quarters of those who did own some land in the French period were small holders (the average holding was less than five acres) but they owned only 15 per cent of the total area.* A small number of big landowners ($2\frac{1}{2}$ per cent) owned 45 per cent of the cultivated area. More than half of the rural population in Cochin-China had been reduced to the status of 'share cropper'—often handing over half or more of the crop to the landlord—compared to only a quarter of the population in Tonkin. Moreover, the village communal lands, amounting to a quarter of the area in the North, had virtually disappeared in the South.[11] 'One of the gravest errors of French colonial policy,' writes Bernard Fall, 'was to let the communal lands fall into the hands of speculators and dishonest village chiefs, despite the advice of experts on the importance of maintaining, even increasing, the communal rice fields.'[12]

Economic problems were greatest in North Vietnam, social problems in the South. The North, despite its industrious population, is a deficit area: it needed a quarter to half a million tons of rice a year from the South. When the supply failed to arrive—as in 1944 with the disruption of communications by US bombing against the Japanese—the North faced starvation. Half a million to a million people (two million, according to the Vietminh) are said to have died. When Giap urged in March 1946 the need to negotiate with the French for independence—rather than to fight it out—one of his main arguments was that the recent agreement with the French did provide for internal autonomy, which would lead to independence. He frankly explained:

'Above all, we have negotiated to protect and reinforce our political, military and economic position. . . . We have the power and the time to organize our internal administration, to strengthen our military means, to develop our economy and to raise the standard of living of the people. Soon the three *ky* [regions] of the country will be united. The rice of Cochin-China will arrive in Tonkin, the spectre of famine will disappear. . . .'[13]

The complementary nature of Vietnam—the agrarian surplus in the South, the industrial raw materials in the North—is undoubtedly a compelling reason for Hanoi's continuing drive for unity, under its leadership.

* In Thailand, by contrast, 90 per cent of cultivated land was owned by the cultivator, according to the 1950 agricultural census. See Robert J. Muscat, *Development Strategy in Thailand* (Praeger, 1966), p. 172.

Famine conditions in the North and a dispossessed peasantry in the South: these were explosive conditions. The Indo-Chinese Communist Party, founded in 1930, organized a few months later the march of 6,000 starving peasants, which the French authorities suppressed, arresting hundreds of militants. 'For the first time,' Philippe Devillers records in his history of Vietnam, 'a [political] party had been able to mobilize the rural population, hitherto aloof from all political activities.... The traditions of nationalism, the disappointed hopes of the humiliated intellectual élite and the social aspirations of the proletariat had combined.'[14]

In 1940, a revolt of even greater magnitude broke out in Cochin-China. 'In the towns as well as in the countryside, agitation zones were to be prepared, while Communist-organized Committees were to instigate demonstrations and a general strike, leading finally to the "armed insurrection which would enable the seizure of power".' The movement spread rapidly from around Saigon to western Cochin-China (the area of large estates), taking the form of a vast peasant uprising. Again, the French intervened with police and military forces and air bombardment of rebel villages. The revolt was suppressed and some six thousand of the insurgents were arrested.[15]

Almost a year later, in September 1941, Nguyen Ai Quoc (soon to be known as Ho Chi Minh) announced in southern China the formation of the Viet-Nam Doc Lap Dong Minh, or Vietminh, the 'Front for the Independence of Vietnam'. Ho had strongly disapproved the premature outbreak of revolt in Cochin-China. His objective, working with the Chinese authorities against the Japanese in Indo-China (and against the Vichy régime), was to infiltrate the mountainous areas of northern Vietnam, win over the tribal peoples inhabiting the greater part of the country, organize resistance bases and prepare for the correct moment to launch a nation-wide insurrection. In all these objectives, thanks to the Japanese *coup* against the French administration, followed soon after by their surrender, the Vietminh was brilliantly successful. The 'August Revolution', as it was called, is a model for the rapid and effective take-over of a country, virtually without bloodshed—the result more of political than military action.

According to Giap's analysis in *People's War, People's Army*:

'Our [Communist] Party continued [in the early 1940s] to do its utmost to step up propaganda and agitation among the people, to gather all patriotic forces into the Vietminh, to build guerrilla bases, set up revolutionary armed forces and make preparations for armed insurrection....'[16]

'Only on the basis of strong political organizations could semi-armed organizations be set up firmly, guerrilla groups and guerrilla units organized which have close connection with the revolutionary masses. . . . In the early years, as the political mobilization among the masses was not strong enough and the enemy's forces still stable, the political mobilization among the masses had all the more to be considered as the main task for the preparation of armed insurrection. The propaganda and organization of the masses carried out everywhere in the country, particularly at the key points, was of decisive importance. Viet Bac [north-eastern Tonkin, bordering China] mountain regions were soon chosen by the Party Central Committee as the armed bases. . . .

'In the then conditions, the armed bases must be held secret, must be localities where the revolutionary movement was firm and the mass organizations strong. . . . Underground operating cadres' teams, underground militarized teams, armed shock teams and local armed groups and platoons gradually appeared. The most appropriate guiding principle for activities was *armed propaganda; political activities were more important than military activities, and fighting less important than propaganda*. . . . Once the political bases were consolidated and developed, we proceeded one step further to the consolidation and development of the semi-armed and armed forces. . . .'[17] [See p. 156.]

'Our Party had drawn bloody experience from the Nghe-Tinh [1930] and Nam Ky [1940] insurrections. All these spoke out the decisive importance of the right opportunity for uprising. . . . The instruction on the *preparations for the Insurrection* issued by the Vietminh Central Committee in May 1944, also pointed out clearly the moment the people should rise up:

1. The enemy's ranks at that moment are divided and dismayed to the extreme.

2. The organizations for national salvation and the revolutionaries are resolved to rise up and kill the enemy.

3. Broad masses wholeheartedly support the uprising and determinedly help the vanguard. . . . We must always be on the alert to feel the pulse of the movement and know the mood of the masses. . . .'[18]

'Basing ourselves on the powerful political forces of the people, backed by military and para-military forces, and on our skill in neutralizing the Japanese army then in dismay, the [August 1945] insurrection cost little blood and rapidly gained success from North to South. . . . Availing itself of the right opportunity, our Party led the August General Insurrection to victory. Had the insurrection broken out sooner, i.e. when the French were still in control, it would have certainly met with numerous difficulties. It would have been in a dangerous situation had it broken out later, when the Chiang Kai-chek and British [occupation] armies had arrived in our country. The Party led the people to seize power immediately after the Japanese capitulation and before the allied forces arrived in Indo-China. The splendid victory of the insurrection was due to its timely launching.'[19]

This was a classic example of the revolutionary seizure of power. All the factors of success were operating at the decisive moment: the break-up of the enemy régime and the demoralization of its supporters; the ardent desire of the people for independence; the existence of widespread mass poverty and discontent; the organization of an effective political and military instrument; and an experienced, flexible and skilful leadership. All the factors, except one —protracted resistance. For by an extraordinary combination of circumstances, a decisive blow—rather than the gradual and remorseless change in the balance of forces between weak and strong, as was occurring in China—this alone was needed. But protracted war—after the failure to reach an effective compromise between the Vietminh demands for independence and a unified Vietnam on the one hand and the French determination to reassert their authority on the other—this was to come in full measure.

RESISTANCE WAR

In November 1946 the French bombarded Haiphong; in December the Vietminh attacked the French in Hanoi. Just as in the South, more than a year before, so French forces quickly mastered the capital and occupied the towns; but the countryside fell into the hands of the Vietminh. Even in the northern Delta region, where the French were to establish a ring of fortifications, the Vietminh within a few years infiltrated thousands of troops within the French lines; the Delta was French by day, Vietminh by night. 'The reversal of sovereignty at dusk, even where we [the French] are so near,' concluded Mus, 'gives to the conflict this cosmic guise, this appearance of an interregnum—when the mandate [of heaven] is in reserve. . . .'[20]

French forces had at first driven the lightly armed and inexperienced Vietminh into the mountainous areas north and west of Hanoi, where 'resistance bases' had been organized; these were to be Ho's headquarters until the end of the war. 'We must win time,' Ho emphasized. 'In military affairs, time is of prime importance. Time ranges first among the three factors for victory, before the terrain conditions and the people's support. . . .'[21] Time was needed to develop, train and organize the instrument of victory, Giap's 'main force'. Just as Mao had decided, when faced with an overwhelmingly more powerful enemy, so Truong Chinh,* the Secretary-General of the Indo-Chinese Communist Party, also pointed out that the 'guiding principle of the strategy of our whole resistance must be to prolong the war'.[22]

'Why must the war be protracted? Because if we compare our forces with those of the enemy, it is obvious that the enemy is still strong, and we are still weak. The enemy's country is an industrial one—ours is an agricultural country. The enemy has planes, tanks, warships; as for us, we have only rudimentary weapons. . . . If we throw the whole of our forces into a few battles to try and decide the outcome, we shall certainly be defeated and the enemy will win. . . .'[23]

This was precisely the French objective: in Giap's words, 'the enemy's strategic principle was to attack swiftly and win swiftly. The more the war was protracted, the lesser would be his strong points and their [French] weak points would grow weaker.'[24] The French were confident of success. A few well-timed blows could 'vaporize' both Ho and his armed rabble.[25] The French commander, General Valluy, expected to reimpose peace in two months.[26] Infantry battalions, armoured squadrons and parachutists were massed towards the end of 1947, to throw back the Vietminh from its mountain bases, capture Ho and his Government, destroy the Vietminh regular army and close the frontier with China. The Vietminh was taken by surprise by the strength and mobility of the French assault, losing a vast amount of territory, 8,000 dead and 1,000 rifles.[27]

Truong Chinh, writing in 1947 *The Resistance Will Win,* showed a realistic appreciation of the facts of power. He noted then that even if the strategy were correct, if 'tactics are consistently wrong, the numerous errors in tactics may lead to strategic failure. . . . After all . . . if command is weak and suffers continual losses in all battles, how can strategy succeed? Again, due to a single heavy defeat, which shatters the army's strength and destroys the morale of the troops, strategy may be confronted with danger. . . .'[28] This is a

* Truong Chinh, considered to be pro-Peking (in contrast to Giap, who exemplified traditional Vietnamese distrust of the Chinese) was appointed Secretary-General of the Vietnamese 'Workers' Party in 1951—the successor to the Indo-Chinese Communist Party, dissolved in 1945. After the widespread abuses of 'land reform' carried out in North Vietnam in 1956, Truong Chinh was dismissed as Secretary-General of the Party; but he remains one of its most influential members.

useful corrective to the Marxist determinism which assumes that if the basic revolutionary strategy is sound the means of victory are assured.

Truong Chinh, despite his doctrinaire reputation, actually underlines the importance of the 'talent and subjective efforts of man, which may exercise a great influence on objective conditions'. This, he writes, explains why even a country with objective advantages over another may still lose, because it 'did not try hard enough, underestimated its enemy and lacked skill'.[29] In the war against the French, the enemy's weaknesses were 'moral' ones—the lack of a good cause—but 'most of his strong points are material ones. . . . Material conditions are quite necessary to victory—even a temporary victory—in any military action, whether in war, or in an armed uprising.'[30] And if the Vietminh sought to use the enemy's disadvantages against him, Truong Chinh conceded that the French were not so stupid as to forego the same tactics in return. Other 'eventualities' considered in 1947 were these:

'In the course of the resistance war, some disadvantages may come our way, created by efforts made by the enemy, by our own errors, or by circumstances unforeseen either by us or the enemy. For instance: natural calamities, or famine might occur, there might be intervention by a third country which would first help the French colonialists to fight us and then oust them; again, the loss of a number of our cadres and outstanding men could have a considerable effect on the leadership of the resistance; or grave errors by our officers could lead to serious losses. . . .'[31]

This is a prophetic statement. More than six years later the United States was on the point of intervention—Dulles's call for 'united action' to save the French. And in a further year or two it had 'ousted' France as the new 'protector' of Vietnam. Moreover, twenty years after Truong Chinh's statement, the loss of 'cadres and outstanding men' in the South did call in question the entire strategy of the 'second resistance war'.

In 1947 these circumstances were still far from being realized. The French were fighting what they called 'a handful of prisoners escaped from Poulo Condore' [the island prison off South Vietnam]; the struggle had not yet been transformed into a war for the defence of the Free World against Communism.* The French still hoped, in

* The French were more concerned to stop the spread of *nationalism* than of Communism. French official circles saw the need to prevent nationalism coming to power in Indo-China in order to prevent it coming to power elsewhere, especially in Africa, and thus breaking up the French 'Empire'—an early example of the 'domino theory'.

Giap's words, 'to end the war by a quick victory'. As for the Vietminh, 'facing an enemy who temporarily had the upper hand . . . time was needed to mobilize, organize and foster the forces of the Resistance, to wear out the enemy forces, gradually reverse the balance of forces, turning our weakness into strength . . . eventually to triumph over the enemy'.[32]

Four Factors

Vietminh survival and growth depended on four factors: national unity—the 'moral' advantage stressed by Truong Chinh; and three 'material' factors: the organization of (mountain) resistance bases; the mobilization of the Vietnamese peasantry; and the transformation of guerrilla fighting into mobile warfare. Balancing the advantages and disadvantages, in the manner of Mao Tse-tung, Truong Chinh established the Vietminh's 'strong points':

'(a) The aim of the war is just. (b) The entire people are united. (c) The morale of the army and people is high. (d) Our troops fight on their native soil to defend their people's interests, and they thus enjoy three advantages: They are used to the climate (*Thien Hoi* the climate is favourable to them), well acquainted with the natural features (*Dia loi* the terrain is favourable to them) and supported by the people (*Nhan Lao* the population is favourable to them).'[33]

This owes nothing to Marxism-Leninism. The three advantages enunciated are—as an editorial note to Truong Chinh's work observes—'the three classic principles of Sun Tsu, a great Chinese strategist'. Sun Tsu is the third century B.C. Chinese writer so often quoted with approval by Mao Tse-tung.

Vietminh weaknesses were the obverse of French strength. While the French had numerous modern arms, Vietminh weapons were 'few and rudimentary'; the French had numerous well-trained troops, the Vietminh forces were 'not numerous and not yet inured to war'. The French had achieved a high level of organization, while the Vietminh's—especially in military and economic affairs—was low; finally, the French were directing 'large-scale propaganda' to foreign countries, while Vietminh propaganda abroad was poor. But French weaknesses, Truong Chinh considered, overcame this strength. Their war had 'reactionary' and aggressive aims 'which arouse hatred for them'; there was 'internal division' in France; low morale of the troops 'waging an aggressive war in a foreign county'; French finance and economy were in a 'state of exhaustion' after the Second World War: and lastly, French 'forces are limited and must be scattered throughout the French Union'.[34]

Morale

Morale inside France and the limited number of French forces were among the deciding factors. The confusion of French public opinion resulted from the fact that the French Government had been compelled in 1949 to concede to Bao Dai the principle of the independence and unity of Vietnam, which it had refused in 1945-46 to Ho Chi Minh. Having 'given up' the reason for starting the war, there was no valid motive for continuing it. Opinion in France, disgusted at the corruption of the Bao Dai régime, the scandalous fortunes made by French and Vietnamese out of the war and the irresponsible manoeuvrings of the French parliamentary parties, inevitably influenced the French troops fighting the *sale guerre* in Vietnam. The lower the morale of the 'enemy', including the Bao Dai régime, the higher became that of the Vietminh. Militarily, moreover, the French found themselves insufficiently strong to garrison all the towns and lines of communications against guerrillas and mobile forces; the latter avoided open confrontation but attacked secretly and swiftly at points of their own choosing. The French were never able to master this unconventional war. It was not from lack of skill or judgement—in fact, the French also tried out guerrilla tactics and deployed mobile columns and airborne troops—but because the advantages of this kind of war lay heavily with the 'home side'.*

Vietminh strategy, like that of the Chinese Communists, was based firmly on what was possible. The lightly armed and poorly trained Vietnamese troops had no chance of winning a frontal assault against the cream of the French Union forces, equipped with tanks, artillery and airplanes. In the first desperate months it was all the Vietminh could do to escape destruction. As they had done in Cochin-China, so in Tonkin they simply 'merged' into the countryside or regrouped in almost inaccessible mountain and forest regions. The 'popular' forces reverted to their civilian life, as peasants or artisans, until the immediate danger had passed. They formed a nucleus of resistance in the villages and towns—resistance to the enemy which had suppressed their independence. Not as Communists, pledged to Socialist revolution, but only as leaders of the national struggle could the Vietminh retain the allegiance of the people.

* For a good account of the war as experienced by a Vietminh military 'cadre', see Ngo-Van-Chieu, *Journal d'un Combattant Viet-Minh* (Editions du Seuil, 1955). And from the point of view of the other side, Bernard B. Fall, *Street without Joy: Indochina at War, 1946-54* (The Stackpole Company, 1961).

Tribes

Safe in their mountain hideouts, the Vietminh leaders gained time to train and equip their 'main force'—the regular troops, protected by guerrilla and regional forces, which probed the weaknesses of the French, struck and rapidly dispersed. Even more than the loyalty of the Vietnamese peasants, it was the support of the mountain tribes that enabled the Vietminh to hold out during those early years, since its base areas were in tribal territory. French intelligence reported in 1953 that an entire Vietminh division was largely recruited from among the half-million Tho tribespeople, two more regiments were composed of Tho and one of Muong tribesmen.[35] Chu Van Tan, a Tho leader, was a general in the Vietnamese People's Army and in 1953 was appointed to the Central Committee of the Lao Dong—Workers'—Party of Vietnam.[36]

Despite the historic antagonism between the rice-farming, lowland Vietnamese and the roaming mountain tribes, the Vietminh had in the early 1940s won over a number of influential tribal leaders, some of whom were already at odds with the French administration.[37] The Vietminh promised to respect their autonomy in an independent Vietnam. The tribes, though few in number—some three and a quarter million compared to nearly thirty million Vietnamese—inhabited the greater part of the country. Strategically, the mountain areas dominated Tonkin, almost surrounding the thin wedge of the densely populated Red River delta. Southern tribes—though far more primitive than the Tho, Meo, Thai and other tribes living in northern Vietnam and in Laos, north Thailand, Burma and Southern China—occupied an almost equally strategic area: the Annamite mountain chain extending to within about sixty miles of Saigon. The French statutorily protected the 'Mountain People of the South'; and throughout the war they retained much support from these tribes. But in 1955 their French-protected special status was abolished.[38] Thereafter, tribal support for the Vietminh—labelled by Saigon as 'Vietcong'—played an important part in the disintegration of the Diem régime.

Bases

On Mao-ist principles, Truong Chinh noted that 'there are many kinds of bases: mountainous areas, in the delta and in marshy areas'. Favourable natural features were important for the safety of the bases. But Truong Chinh, like Mao, laid more stress on 'regular troops ready to make sacrifices . . . to stay the enemy's advance, to safeguard the base and defend the leading organs and the population'; and above all, on an 'active, widely organized' people 'ready to support the army in every field'. The existence of these two factors contradicted the opinion held by some 'people'—unspecified, though Mao Tse-tung himself had held this view—that 'because our territory is small, it is impossible for us to establish resistance bases'.[39]

Land

In addition to tribal support, which could hardly be acknowledged on Marxist lines, the Vietminh 'relied on the countryside to build our bases, to launch guerrilla warfare in order to encircle the enemy in the towns. . . . Therefore it was of particular importance to pay due attention to the peasant question. . . .'[40] And in Ho Chi Minh's words, reminiscent of Mao's dramatic appeal to the Communist Party to lead the peasant revolution over twenty years before:

'Our forces lie in millions of peasants who are ready to wait for the Government and Party to organize and lead them in order enthusiastically to rise up and smash the feudal and colonial yoke. With skilful organization and leadership, these forces will shake heaven and earth, all the colonialists and feudalists will be swept away. . . .'[41]

The resistance war, as both Giap and Truong Chinh asserted, was a peasant's war. 'Nearly all the fighters of our regular, militia and guerrilla forces are also peasants. . . .' This, Truong Chinh insisted, was because 'they love their native soil, their Fatherland. They are deeply attached to their villages, their rice fields and the graves of their ancestors. . . . We see that the people constitute the source of manpower for the army; and for the militia and guerrilla forces we recruit and train our regular forces.'[42]

Vietminh agrarian policy played a decisive role—according to Giap—in the building of rural bases, the reinforcement of rear areas and the 'impulse' given to the resistance. 'In a colony where the national question is essentially the peasant question the consolidation of the resistance forces was possible only by a solution to the agrarian problem.'[43] Vietminh reduction of land rent and rates of interest after August 1945 'bestowed on the peasants their first material advantages'. Land 'monopolized' by the 'imperialists and the traitors'—i.e. Vietnamese collaborating with the French—was confiscated and shared out. 'Communal land and ricefields were more equitably distributed.'[44]

Yet the Vietminh could not press ahead with a thorough-going programme of land reform, during the early years, from fear of alienating those landowners who were supporting the struggle for independence. Like their Chinese comrades, the Vietnamese Communists veered from radical policies of outright seizure of 'large' estates—'to confiscate the whole of the plantations and property belonging to the imperialists and the Vietnamese reactionary capitalist class and distribute them to poor peasants', according to the inaugural programme of the Communist Party of Indo-China in 1930[45]—to a 'postponement' of the agrarian revolution when the 'Vietminh Front' was established in 1941. Again following Chinese Communist policy, with the mounting tempo of war and the need for the utmost support from the hard-pressed peasantry, the Vietminh leaders revived the campaign for land reform. The peasants are the 'eyes and ears of the army, they feed and keep our soldiers. It is they who help the army in sabotage and battle,' Truong Chinh declared.[46] Ho Chi Minh himself acknowledged in December 1953 that 'in former times we were biased against [*sic*, presumably it should be 'in favour of'] unity with landlords for the sake of the resistance war, and have not attached due importance to the peasant question. . . .'[47] Yet, as Ho had pointed out a year before, 'the peasants make the biggest contribution to the Resistance'—providing soldiers, guerrillas, taxes—and thus the greatest sacrifice to the Fatherland. 'Nevertheless, they are the poorest people, because they have not enough land to till. . . . This is a most unjust situation.'[48]

In Ho's view, the peasants accounted for almost 90 per cent of the people, but owned only 30 per cent of the arable land, worked hard 'and suffer poverty all their lives'. The goal set for land reform, Ho declared in his Report of December 1953 to the National Assembly, 'is to wipe out the feudal system of land appropriation, distribute land to the tillers, liberate the productive forces in the countryside, develop production and speed up the Resistance war'. Ho frankly believed, at a time when the enemy was doing its 'utmost to deceive, divide and exploit our people', that 'land reform will exert an influence on and encourage our peasant compatriots in the enemy rear to struggle more enthusiastically against the enemy in order to liberate themselves, and more enthusiastically to support the Democratic Resistance Government; at the same time it exerts an influence on and disintegrates the puppet [Bao Dai] army because the absolute majority of the puppet soldiers are peasants in enemy-occupied areas.'[49]

Land confiscated or 'requisitioned', Ho went on, must be 'distributed definitely to the peasants who have no land or are short of it. The peasants have the right to ownership of the land thus distributed'.[50] There is no doubt that Vietminh distribution of land to poor peasants, though in the long run no real solution (for the problem is one of overpopulation rather than the existence of large landowners), did greatly inspire them to help the Vietminh.

Popular support

'The people are the water and our army the fish'[51]—this echo of the Chinese Communist slogan was no empty phrase. As Truong Chinh explained, 'guerrilla warfare is the method of fighting in partisan units or with relatively small groups of the regular army disguised as civilians and mingling with the people. . . .' Their task was to 'cut communication lines, harass the enemy while he is eating or sleeping, wear out his strength, cause him weariness and distress. . . .'[52] Further,

'Experience has taught us that to avoid disintegration [as a result of enemy encirclement], our troops should quickly abandon their uniforms, combine with the people, distribute a part of their arms to them, organize militia forces, arm the entire people, using every means to fight the enemy. They should cling to their ricefields and struggle against the enemy to win the right to live. . . .'[53]

The very fact that the Vietminh was able in 1953 to infiltrate units of up to division strength, altogether a total of about 35,000 men, *within* the Tonkin 'redoubt'—tying up three times their number of French troops[54]—indicates the effectiveness of peasant support for the Vietminh. Although French 'pacification' was more successful in Cochin-China—the reason why the 1954 settlement divided Ho's North from a non-Communist South—even there the swampy terrain and mountainous or forested regions made French operations 'exceedingly slow and difficult' and Vietminh skill at disappearance and infiltration frequently foiled these efforts. In his illuminating study of Vietminh tactics, George Tanham points out that 'French intelligence was poor and most Vietminh areas seemed to have prewarning of the enemy's armies'. He adds, and this was to characterize the régime to follow, that 'French soldiers frequently conducted themselves in a manner that alienated the native population, and did not seem to realize the importance of winning the local people to their side through positive acts'.[55]

The Vietminh, by contrast, laid great emphasis on soldierly discipline and the need to assist the villagers. This is not to deny Vietminh terrorism, which certainly existed, and was even a potent factor in creating insecurity and the disruption of administrative links with the countryside. But terrorism for the Vietminh, as for the Vietcong, was not indiscriminate violence—as it is sometimes portrayed in the West—but an instrument selectively applied to attain specific objectives: it was a means of war used against the civil population, or that part of it considered to support the 'enemy'. This is what is meant by the term 'people's war'—the involvement of the people, like it or not, on one side or the other.

Terrorism apart, the Vietminh (like the Chinese Communists) took great care to conciliate the villagers, whether tribal or lowland peasants. In 1948 Ho Chi Minh issued 'Twelve Recommendations' to his soldiers: e.g. '1. Not to do what is likely to damage the land and crops or spoil the houses and belongings of the people. 2. Not to insist on buying or borrowing what the people are not willing to sell or lend. . . . 3. [Not to offend mountain peoples.] 4. Never break our word. 5. Not to give offence to people's faith and customs. . . .'[56] The positive recommendations were: '1. To help the people in their daily work (harvesting, fetching firewood, carrying water, sewing, etc). 2. Whenever possible to buy commodities for those who live far from markets (knife, salt, needle, thread, pen, paper, etc). 3. In spare time, to tell amusing simple and short stories useful to the Resistance, but betraying no secrets. 4. To teach the population the national script and elementary hygiene. 5. To study the customs of each region. . . . 6. To show to the people that you are correct, diligent and disciplined.'[57]

Guerrillas

The Vietminh guerrillas depended on the country people: 'More than 90 per cent of soldiers in the National Defence Army, local guards, militia men and guerrillas are of peasant stock. Most of the taxpayers and volunteer workers are peasants. The peasants make the biggest contribution to the Resistance,' as Ho acclaimed.[58] 'When the enemy comes we fight, when he goes, we plough,' as Truong Chinh put it. Actually this refers to the basic level, the village 'self defence' militia, or part-time soldier. The middle level—and the same applies to the 'Vietcong'—consists of regional troops who 'do not participate in production any longer and move about in a specific region'. Their task, according to Truong Chinh, is to defend a region or district, supporting the villagers in their farm work, 'carrying out armed propaganda, repressing traitors and bandits, laying ambushes to attack the enemy, and launching sudden attacks on his isolated posts'.[59]

The regular army or 'main force' forms the highest level; it is recruited from the best elements of the regional forces (themselves recruited from the 'most enthusiastic and thorough-going' of the village militia). This 'endless process of development', in Truong Chinh's words, from peasant auxiliaries to regional forces to regular troops, exactly matched the development of strategy; 'people's war, long-term war, guerrilla warfare developing step-by-step into mobile war', as Giap described it.[60] The different types of warfare were designed for the three stages of revolutionary war: 'defensive, equilibrium and offensive'—the Vietminh equivalent of Mao's 'strategic defensive, consolidation and counter-offensive', outlined in his 1938 lecture *On Protracted War*.

Three stages

Vietminh practice was exactly in line with Mao's celebrated advice: *The enemy advances, we retreat*—the first stage of protracted war. In Giap's words, the bulk of Vietminh forces were ordered to 'fall back towards our rear in order to keep our forces intact with a view to a long-term resistance'.[61] *The enemy camps, we harass*—the second stage: This is the period of consolidation, when the enemy, having occupied the towns and major lines of communication, launches 'mopping up operations', seeking to re-establish order in the occupied zones. 'He strives to encircle and raze our guerrilla bases . . . or chop up our free zones into many parts. . . . Their [the enemy's] political aim is to set up a puppet national government . . . at the same time fostering the puppet power in the localities and the organizations of reactionary notables [traditional village leaders] in order to divide and deceive our people. . . . They count on this puppet power and its "armed forces" to repress our movement for liberation. . . .' The Vietminh response was to 'wear out the enemy forces, annihilate them piecemeal; sabotage, disturb, give the enemy no peace . . .', Truong Chinh declared.[62]

The second stage is also one of guerrilla warfare developing into mobile war: 'guerrilla war must multiply', as Giap put it, it must keep up its momentum. 'If guerrilla warfare did not move to mobile warfare, not only the strategic task of annihilating the enemy man-power could not be carried out but even guerrilla activities could not be maintained and extended.'[63] Vietminh tactics were to operate 'in small pockets, with independent companies penetrating deeply into the enemy-controlled zone to launch guerrilla warfare, establish bases and protect local people's power. . . . We gradually formed a network of guerrilla bases. . . . The soil of the fatherland was being freed inch by inch right in the enemy's rear lines.'[64]

During this time Giap's 'main force'—secure in the resistance bases—was being trained for mobile war: *The enemy tires, we attack*. This is still the second stage, but it is the 'key' period when the balance of forces gradually changes and the revolutionaries prepare for the final stage of counter-offensive: *The enemy retreats, we pursue*. As Giap described the sequence of events:

'In 1947, with the plan of independent companies operating separately and concentrated battalions, we began to move to more concentrated fighting, then to mobile warfare. In 1948, we made relatively great ambushes and surprise attacks with one or several battalions. In 1949, we launched small campaigns not only in the

North but also on other battlefields. From 1950, we began to launch campaigns on an ever larger scale enabling mobile warfare to play the main part on the northern battlefield while entrenched camp warfare [positional warfare, the last stage] was on the upgrade. This fact was clearly manifest in the great Dien Bien Phu [April-May 1954] campaign.'[65]

After 1950* when the Vietminh overran most of the garrisons along the frontier with China, the French were faced with an insoluble problem. 'The enemy found himself face to face with a contradiction: without scattering his forces it was impossible for him to occupy the invaded territory; in scattering his forces he put himself in difficulties. His scattered units would fall easy prey to our troops. . . . On the other hand, if he concentrated his forces to . . . cope with us with more initiative . . . it would be difficult for him to hold the invaded territory.'[66] Trying to protect 'thousands of posts and garrisons' all over the country from guerrilla raids, the French inevitably had to disperse their troops; but this left them dangerously exposed to Giap's 'main force'. Once the latter had been organized, trained and augmented—the first Vietminh divisions appeared in 1950[67]—the French found themselves with insufficient troops to meet both the guerrilla and the regular army threat.

By mid-1951 there had been a striking increase in the number of *regular* Vietminh battalions, especially in Tonkin (seventy-eight battalions, largely the result of the 'transformation' of regional forces) and to a lesser extent in Annam (twenty-one battalions) and Cochin-China (eighteen regular, twenty-five regional battalions).[68] This indicated, in a period of just over two years, a nearly *four-fold* increase in regular strength. General Navarre, the French Commander-in-Chief during the latter stages of the war (French C.-in-C.s changed almost as rapidly as French Governments), estimated in mid-1953 that he was facing some 125,000 full-time regular Vietminh troops, organized in six divisions, actively supported by over 75,000 regional troops and backed by 200,000 to 350,000 village militia. The French Expeditionary Force amounted to 189,000 men—just over a quarter being French troops, the rest were Legionnaires, Vietnamese and North Africans. About half of this Force was tied down in a static defence role. The untried Vietnamese national (Bao Dai) army nominally amounted to 150,000 men but could deploy less than 100,000 in the field.[69] With local

* Giap launched a premature 'counter-offensive' in 1951 and suffered a serious reverse. Thereafter the Vietminh *avoided* any major engagement with French forces—which the French tried in vain to bring about—until the advantage was clearly on the Vietminh side, as at Dien Bien Phu.

superiority, Vietminh mobile forces could strike almost at will, as they demonstrated in the 1953-54 campaigns in Laos, Tonkin and the central highlands, culminating in the battle of Dien Bien Phu. Trying both to stave off the constant guerrilla depredations and to confront the main thrust of the Vietminh divisions, the French met disaster.

Undoubtedly Chinese aid *contributed* to the Vietminh success. It has been estimated that up to 40,000 Vietminh soldiers received training in China by the time of the cease-fire in mid-1954.[70] The Chinese supplied 3,000 to 15,000 tons a month of war material,[71] notably rifles, machine guns, mortars and field artillery (used with devastating effect at Dien Bien Phu). But there were no supplies of tanks, aircraft or heavy artillery. It has been suggested—and this would be similar to the presumed Soviet attitude towards the Chinese Communists—that 'the main objective of Chinese policy seemed to be not so much to enable the Vietminh to win a military victory as to maintain it at fighting strength'.[72] An important Lien Viet* official, who fled to the Bao Dai zone late in 1952, related the existence of an agreement providing for Chinese intervention only in the case of the Vietminh suffering a decisive defeat.[73]

UNITY AND ORGANIZATION

'In the face of an enemy as powerful as he is cruel,' wrote Giap, 'victory is possible only by uniting the whole people within . . . a firm and wide national united front.'[74] The 'factors of success', he continued, were these: first, 'it was a just war, waged for independence and the reunification of the country'; second, the 'revolutionary armed force . . . adopted the tactics and strategy of a people's war'; third, the national united front comprised 'all the revolutionary classes, all the nationalities living on Vietnamese soil'; fourth, 'people's power [was] established during the August Revolution and thereafter constantly consolidated . . . it devoted its efforts to mobilizing and organizing the whole people for the Resistance'; fifth and 'above all', the war was 'organized and led by the Party of the working class: the Indo-Chinese Communist Party, now the Vietnam Workers' Party'.†[75]

* The Vietminh was absorbed into the Lien Viet—National United Front—in February 1951.

† The Communists were the strongest, the most skilful and ruthless element in the Vietminh Front. The longer the war continued, the more powerful that element became. Even within the Communist Party, which although 'voluntarily dissolved' in November 1945 'continued to lead the administration and the people', according to Ho Chi Minh (Vol. III, p. 248), the bitterness of the war favoured the extremists and the doctrinaires. [See also p. 156.]

This was the order in which Giap analysed the factors of success. To put them in another way: first, it was a national struggle; second, it had to be fought by guerrilla methods; third, the Vietminh, putting nationalist objectives first, attracted the support of Vietnamese and tribal peoples, of peasants and townsmen, Buddhists and Catholics: 'by force alone', writes Hammer, 'the Vietminh, at best a small minority in the country, could never have remained in power; the strength of the Vietminh in the fall of 1945 lay in the wide popular following it commanded among non-Communist Vietnamese'; for example, the 'majority of the two million Catholics made common cause with the Vietminh Government and the four Vietnamese bishops appealed to the Pope to support Vietnamese independence'.[76] Fourth, an independent Vietnamese Government, sanctioned by the ex-Emperor Bao Dai himself, had been established in September 1945. Though it had been physically removed from power by the French—first in Southern Vietnam, a year later in the North—its authority remained. Moreover, if the French were nominally in control of the institutions of the State, it was the Vietminh—through the countryside—which possessed much of the reality. Finally, the Vietminh was led, not just by ardent patriots, but by men whose dedication, ability and disciplined restraint far outclassed their anti-Communist rivals in the various 'nationalist' parties and groups.

Ho Chi Minh's practical disposition,* his organizational skill and his years of revolutionary experience had deeply impressed the Kuomintang military government of Kwangsi province, during the war against Japan. Although the Chinese preferred the VNQDD (Nationalist Party) leader to Ho—who was even imprisoned for a time—the former, however trustworthy, was old and ineffective. It was Ho who was appointed in 1943 leader of the Chinese-sponsored 'Revolutionary League', thereby taking over the Kuomintang subsidy of 100 Chinese dollars a month for spying and sabotage in Tonkin.[77] It was under Nationalist Chinese auspices—the local Kuomintang leaders hoped to use Ho for their own purposes against both Japan and France—that the Vietminh organized and established resistance bases in northern Vietnam.

Similarly it was with the Vietminh, rather than with the fanatically anti-French Nationalists, that the French, early in 1946, sought to reach agreement on the future of Vietnam. There is no doubt that the Vietminh was genuinely prepared to accept a compromise at that time, provided it led to the independence and unity of Vietnam, which all nationalists were demanding. To secure what was possible,

* Ho Chi Minh's *Selected Works* reveal little of the brilliant analytical studies of society characteristic of Mao's 'Thought'.

this was the Vietminh objective. Thus, despite vehement popular opposition, the Vietminh accepted in March 1946 the stationing of French forces in northern Vietnam in return for French recognition of the 'free State' of the Republic of Vietnam, within the Indo-Chinese Federation and the French Union (France and her overseas possessions). Under the agreement, French forces were to be replaced each year by Vietnamese—one-fifth at a time—thus leaving the Vietnamese army in full control at the end of five years.

The conciliatory attitude of the Vietminh could hardly be better shown than in Giap's explanation, before a huge crowd in Hanoi, of the reasons for signing the agreement. Giap pointed out that some aspects were satisfactory—recognition of Vietnam's internal freedom, 'though it is not yet independence'—while others were not: the return of French troops. But he went on:

'Those who are not satisfied consider total independence as if it were only a slogan or word of command, either spoken or on paper. They do not understand that the country's independence is the result of objective conditions and that in our struggle to achieve it there is a time when we must be firm and a time when we must yield.

In present circumstances, there were three possibilities: long-term resistance; a shorter resistance; and negotiation, when the time came. We did not choose long-term resistance because the international situation was no longer favourable to us. France had signed a treaty with China, America had joined France's side. . . . Thus we were practically isolated. . . . By continuing a military struggle we would have lost our forces and our land. We could only have held certain regions. To resist in this way would have been very heroic, but our people would have endured terrible sufferings. . . . Equally we would have succumbed if we had attempted a few months' resistance, because France is armed with modern weapons. Therefore we chose the third way, that of negotiations. . . . In this way, we have the ability and the time to organize our internal administration, strengthen our military means, to develop our economy and to raise the standard of living of the people. . . . The agreement [with France] opens the way to total independence, which is not far off, and this remains our aim.'[78]

This spirit of realism was shared by the French negotiators at that time—Jean Sainteny and General Leclerc, Commander of the French forces. Leclerc, according to Devillers, who was a member of his staff, realized that French reconquest of Vietnam was impossible with the limited means available. He could seize the cities and ports, but to penetrate further would require a major effort by France, resulting in an exhausting war, whose length could not be foreseen and which would absorb the French Army for years.* Moreover, a Vietnamese Government—led by Communists, it is true, but representing a powerful national movement according to all the evidence—this existed in Hanoi.[79] Leclerc believed that Vietnamese nationalism was a real force—not merely the propaganda creation of the Vietminh, as local French officials and settlers claimed.[80] French interests could best be served by negotiating with Ho—and Leclerc even urged the French Government to recognize Vietnam's 'independence'[81]—rather than risk losing all in a long-drawn-out war.

These views were not shared by the French High Commissioner, d'Argenlieu, a former Carmelite monk, later admiral in the Free French Navy, enthusiastic supporter of de Gaulle and a man, as Devillers describes him, 'imbued with the traditions of French grandeur'.[82] It was d'Argenlieu who, convinced that the Vietminh leaders were no more than a bunch of Communist agitators, complained in March 1946 to General Valluy (later to command French forces against the Vietminh) that he was 'astonished that France has such a fine expeditionary corps in Indo-China and yet its leaders prefer to negotiate rather than fight'. D'Argenlieu's tactics, on his return to France a few months later, were to sound the alarm that if Indo-China were lost, the whole French Union would be threatened. This gloomy prediction had its effect on the French deputies of the Right and Centre who were haunted by the spectre of France's weakness—political, military and financial.[83] In their view, France could only reassert her authority by standing up to the Vietminh; by 'teaching it a hard lesson',[84] as General Valluy put it, before the French bombardment in November 1946 of the port of Haiphong.

Even when the war broke out, a month later, the French were confident that they could quickly disperse the 'handful' of Vietminh supporters, who were deemed totally unrepresentative of Vietnamese opinion. 'The immense majority of the Vietnamese people fears and rejects the oppression of the Vietminh'; 'against us [the French] there are only a handful of prisoners escaped from Poulo Condore [the convict settlement] and who impose their role by terror': this was the constant refrain of the French Press, from the

* After six months of fighting, the French War Minister reported in May 1947 the complete success of French arms, the occupation of major cities and control of communications. But, he added, 'it is evident that the greater part of the country remains in the hands of the Vietminh. I do not think we should undertake the conquest of French Indo-China. It would necessitate an expeditionary corps of at least 500,000 men [in 1947, it was only 115,000 strong]'. Ellen Hammer, *The Struggle for Indo-China 1940-1955*, p. 207.

centre-Left all the way to the Right.[85]

The French Government simply could not envisage any genuine demand for independence. Cut off from Indo-China by the occupation, the Gaullists were unaware of the growth and intensity of Vietnamese nationalism, encouraged as it had been both by the Vichy administrators and still more so by the Japanese. Thus all the de Gaulle Government could bring itself to offer in 1945 was autonomy, not independence. But these illusions were also shared by French vested interests within Indo-China. 'They [the Vietnamese] only await our return,' was the opinion of Albert Torel, legal counsellor to the High Commissioner, expressing the common attitude of French officials and settlers.[86]

Similar to the evolution of Japanese policy in central China during the war, the French discovered to their cost that Vietminh resistance and the evidence of widespread nationalist support for it necessitated a change of tactics. Their aim therefore became to rally the Vietnamese people to the 'authentic' national leader Bao Dai (Wang Ching-wei had been the Japanese choice). The French conceded the principle of Vietnamese nationalism—rather than continued colonial rule—but they still would not concede the practice. The 'Elysée Agreements' of March 1949 confirmed the 'internal sovereignty' of the Vietnamese Government under the Head of State, Bao Dai, but French permission was required for any change in status of French property and enterprises, French forces were given the right to circulate freely among the bases and garrisons assigned to them, and French nationals retained special legal privileges.[87] The continued presence of French troops on Vietnamese soil and of French officials in the Vietnamese administration,' writes Hammer, 'was enough to convince the average Vietnamese and the Emperor [Bao Dai] that they all had still to achieve independence. . . . As a result most of the intellectuals and young people either continued to work with the Vietminh or remained aloof from politics.'[88] Their attitude was epitomized by the Right Wing nationalist Ngo Dinh Diem, who in 1949 refused offers to head Bao Dai's Cabinet:

'The national aspirations of the Vietnamese people will be satisfied only on the day when our nation obtains the same political status which India and Pakistan enjoy. . . . I believe it is only just to reserve the best posts in the new Vietnam for those who have merited most of the country: I speak of the resistance elements.'[89]

The unhappy experience of the Bao Dai 'solution'—independent in theory, but under French military and administrative control in fact—prevented any rallying of the people against the Vietminh. On the contrary, the scandals, corruption and incapacity of the Bao Dai régime repelled and disgusted the majority of non-Communist Vietnamese. 'In Vietnam, where political office and economic advantage were inevitably linked, the resultant profiteering helped further to discredit the regime . . . and to raise the prestige of the Vietminh. . . . Not only was there no national assembly in the zones nominally ruled by Bao Dai, but there were no political parties—merely self-interested groups, like the Cao Dai and Hoa Hao in the South or the newly-formed Dai Viet in the North, which carved out their own zones of influence in exchange for lending their support to Bao Dai.'[90] This disunity and fragmentation of non-Communist forces in Vietnam was to prove of major significance, not only in the downfall of the Bao Dai régime, but of its successors.

As Ho Chi Minh realized, the only effective way of competing with the Vietminh would be the achievement of true independence and the implementation of political and economic reforms. In December 1953, Ho had to warn his followers against the Franco-American 'policy of deceit' which took the form of: 'Declaring sham "independence" and "democracy", holding fraudulent elections. Pretending to carry out land reform to deceive the peasants in temporarily occupied areas. Setting up "yellow" trade unions to mislead the workers. Advancing a fable of peace . . . to deceive our people.'[91]

In other words, Ho was denouncing the French and the Bao Dai régime for carrying out—or rather stating that they would carry out—precisely the policy the Vietminh was advocating: independence, parliamentary elections, land reform, establishment of trade unions, and proposals for a peaceful settlement. There is nothing 'Communist' about this programme;* what 'saved' the Vietminh was that the French authorities, first of all, and their Vietnamese supporters, secondly, never got beyond the initial stage—independence—and even this was hedged with practical limitations. The most important of these, of course, was that Bao Dai was dependent on the French Army for his survival. Moreover, the Bao Dai régime could not, or would not, proceed to the stage of 'democratic' reforms, because it was equally dependent for political support on gallicized Vietnamese, wealthy landowners, traditionalist village notables and the virtually autonomous Hoa Hao and Cao Dai sects, who would not accept any drastic change.

The way Truong Chinh saw the situation—as early as 1947, before

* Paul Mus points out that from 1946 [but why not before?] the French administration in Cochin-China tried to carry out agrarian reform and create a class of small and middle peasant proprietors. This, he writes, seemed 'very near' to Vietminh proposals. *Viet-Nam: Sociologie d'une Guerre*, p. 242.

the French had even conceded independence—was like this: 'This resistance war is a revolutionary war of the entire people led by our government. It is not a private war concerning only the Communists or the Vietminh Front. The Communists or the Vietminh Front have the sole aim of gaining freedom and independence. . . .'[92] Now, we know, of course, that this was not their 'sole' aim: but it was, like Mao Tse-tung's attitude to the Japanese in China, their *main* aim; and in this they were unrivalled.

It was the same with the Vietminh programme of reforms, intended to achieve what Mao called 'national democracy'. What is important in this regard is not so much that the Communists had ulterior motives —they were not simply 'agrarian reformers'—but that their reform policy was based on what the people—the majority of people—wanted; and it was the only policy that was. It was not even a very 'radical' policy. Take, for instance, the Vietminh attitude to the land. Only French property and that of Vietnamese 'traitors' (opponents of the Vietminh) was actually confiscated and distributed to poor peasants: this was hardly a revolutionary move. Even in 1953, the land reforms proposed and carried out by the Vietminh went no further—except for confiscation instead of purchase—than the successful programmes sponsored by the Americans in post-war Japan and Taiwan. It is true that when the Communists achieved undisputed power in North Vietnam, they revealed their real aims in a merciless parody of land reform, a prelude to collectivization. This should surely have given their 'democratic' opponents in the South the opportunity to show that they could do better. The tragedy is that they did not. Diem's 1956 land reform only affected properties above the absurdly high figure of nearly 250 acres, compared to an *average* holding of less than five acres; and even this reform was only carried out in part. After 1961 land reform remained virtually a dead letter; as it still does, up to the present day.

Thus, it is not a question of comparing the merits of a democratic and a totalitarian system; but of two types of authoritarian régime—one of which, at a certain period of time, achieved something for the people, while the other did not.

VIETMINH-VIETCONG

Diem and his entourage were good nationalists; so were the supporters of the Vietminh. This was not an important issue between them. What was important was the huge difference between their social and political attitudes and ability. The Vietminh, dependent on peasant support, distributed land to the tenants; after 1954 this land was handed back to the original owners. The Vietcong's subsequent appeal to the villagers centred on the right of the farmers to own their land. Diem, himself, recognized the need for reforms. But his measures were inadequate, improperly executed, easily thwarted and soon overtaken by events.*

The Vietcong promised a 'social revolution' to the people of Vietnam; Diem, creating new administration on the wreckage of French rule, 'turned back' to old mandarin traditions. The thorough, well-planned organization of the Vietcong made a remarkable contrast to the personal confusion and bureaucratic ineptitude characteristic of the Diem régime (and still more so of its successors). Despite an overwhelming technical superiority and massive American economic (and later military) assistance, the government was unable to make headway against a few thousand rural guerrillas. Once the insurgency had started in earnest in 1959 it was only three years before the régime was in serious trouble. The paratroopers' *coup* of November 1960 was a portent. According to the Army rebels, 'the Ngo Dinh Diem Government has proved itself incapable in the national salvation and reconstruction work. While the Communists have daily increased their pressure, Ngo Dinh Diem has applied a blind dictatorial, feudal and family rule policy. He has placed the family interests above the national interests. . . .'[93]

In 1963, in an access of folly, the régime turned against the Buddhists and indulged in wholesale arrests of students and high-school children—sons and daughters of civil servants and army officers among them. Tran Van Chuong, Vietnamese Ambassador to the United States and father of Madame Nhu, resigned from his post in protest. He voiced the common opinion of disillusioned ex-supporters (strikingly reminiscent of the views of people in responsible positions about Chiang Kai-shek): 'There is no possibility at all of victory over the Communists under the present régime . . . which has become the greatest asset of the Communists and the greatest obstacle to victory.'[94]

What is surprising is not that the Diem Government should have collapsed 'like an empty shell' in 1963, but that it should have lasted so long. Credit for this should perhaps be given to the United States, which propped up the 'family régime' diplomatically, politically, economically and militarily—until finally it was virtually the only prop that was left. When President Kennedy at last recognized that the war could not be won with Diem—though the American

* '. . . Diem went through the motions of a leader interested in the living conditions and the opinions of those he led. But his heart was not in social reform. . . . The land reform programme was the classic example: it lasted but three years and aided only about 10 per cent of the landless.' Douglas Pike, *Viet Cong* (M.I.T. Press, 1966), p. 60.

military still believed that the 'shooting war' was 'going well'[95]—the régime could no longer survive against the mass of opponents it had rallied against itself. All the fissiparous forces of South Vietnam, too long repressed, were now released: resulting in religious disputes, regional rivalries, army ambitions, political intrigues, student indiscipline, trade union unrest, tribal revolt—and in the background the Vietcong, infiltrating demonstrations, exploiting administrative anarchy (thanks to the successive purges of officers and officials), and launching ambushes and attacks on an ever-larger scale. Thus by early 1965, according to the Americans, Vietcong units were advancing 'with total freedom' in Central Vietnam and 'moving unimpeded' between their 'war zones' just north of Saigon and the 'critical delta areas'.[96] Again there is the resemblance to the last days of Nationalist China—though not yet to the point of mass defections from the armed forces—when the US Embassy in Nanking reported that 'scattered Communist bands operate throughout the countryside creating confusion and disorder' and 'guerrilla units operate more or less at will'.[97]

Two quotations indicate the rooted strength of the Vietcong and the flawed nature of the régimes it faced. Denis Warner writes:

'Out in the remote villages of mud and wattle, the Government was identified as the man in uniform who came on a punitive raid, or with a heavy bodyguard, and who always wanted something—money, labour, or even those suspected, sometimes incorrectly, of working for the Vietcong. The Vietcong cadre, on the other hand, was barefooted and dressed in black like every other peasant. He made tax demands, but they were not excessive. He was meticulous about paying for food and lodging. . . . To begin with, he did not talk Communism, or Marxism, but exploited local grievances.'[98]

And from the Vietnamese editor, Ton That Thien:

'[Vietcong] cadres were drawn mostly from the peasant milieu, and they lived and worked in the countryside. . . . The Communist cadres were constantly reminded that they must stay close to the people, and live and work among them. Another habit instilled into the Communist cadres was that they must keep away from the corrupting influence of the cities. . . . In a sense, the Communist leaders and cadres had replaced the Confucian mandarins. . . .'[99]

Two 'worlds' were involved—either apart or in conflict: the world of the peasants, the great majority of the Vietnamese people, more or less remote in their villages. 'The Emperor's laws,' in the traditional saying, 'yield to the customs of the village.' And the world of the wealthy Western-educated urban or land-owning elite, often barely touched by the war being fought in the countryside. In fact, 'to villagers in Vietcong villages,' as an American scholar has noted, 'the Vietcong is the protection association against the government.' Elsewhere in the country, 'the choice is not whether to get involved but merely on which side to do so. Young men know that they are going to be drafted on one side or the other.'[100] Even the Vietcong cadres represent a rural response to the urban-based administration: 'The cadres are village-based active competitors to the civil servants recruited on the basis of education. Their concern is for the protection of their village community against exploitation from the city.' These 'cadres . . . understand politics among villagers in a way the GVN [Government of Vietnam] never will. . . .'[101] As the struggle intensified, so villagers became increasingly caught up in the clash between the two sides. 'Without battle lines, without an identifiable enemy,' writes Gerald Hickey, 'the war was everywhere. . . . Although most villagers did not take sides actively, accusations of being on one side or the other were rampant. . . . [The] effect has been to turn many villagers inward. They now are primarily concerned with survival for themselves and their families.'[102]

From the Communist point of view—authoritatively expounded by the North Vietnamese party theorist Truong Chinh in September 1963—the 'armed struggle' in South Vietnam is characteristic of the 'outbreak of national liberation revolution', similar to the Vietminh uprising against the French:

'In a country like Vietnam, which was a backward agrarian country dominated by foreign imperialism, an uprising for seizing power must, in general, be launched in the countryside and then in the cities. . . . [This was] because the enemy was weaker in the countryside than in the cities, and the peasants of our country were ardently revolutionary and warmly supported the slogan of national independence and of land to the tiller. . . . Under the circumstances . . . an armed uprising may be launched by stages, guerrilla bases or even liberated areas may be set up and then, in accordance with the situation, the uprising may be expanded into a national one for the seizure of State power. . . .

In the countryside ['a vast expanse of mountains, forests' and regions with poor communications] it was difficult for the enemy to concentrate his forces and his administration was weaker. Therefore the countryside provided easy concealment for the revolutionary cadres and facilitated the building up of the revolutionary forces; moreover it had favourable conditions for guerrilla activities. From the point of view of the distribution of population, the countryside possessed the enormous strength of the people and a very reliable ally—which is the main force of the revolution—the peasant. . . .'[103]

The point is not so much that all or even most of the peasants were 'ardently revolutionary', but that a sufficient number were—for good reason. Before the Vietminh war, two-thirds of the rural population in Southern Vietnam (Cochin-China) were tenants, paying some 40 per cent of their crop to the landlords.[104] Of the one-third or less who owned rice land, a tiny proportion (2½ per cent) owned nearly half of it (altogether over two and a half million acres); the 183,000 small-holders (averaging under five acres of land a family) owned about one-seventh.[105] According to Diem's 1956 land reform programme, less than two million acres were to be expropriated—that is, properties of over 100 hectares (247 acres), with some exceptions. About one million acres were actually expropriated (over half this amount was in French-owned estates, for which compensation was provided by the French Government). By the time the land reform had been officially 'completed' in 1961, some 580,000 acres had been distributed.[106] A quarter of a million tenants had expected to become owners; by 1961 those who became new owners numbered 109,000[107] and five years later only another seven thousand had received their titles to land.[108] 'In short, of an estimated 1 to 1.2 million tenant households existing in 1955, about 10 per cent obtained land under the government's land transfer programme.'[109]

Given these circumstances, it is not surprising that the 'land policy of the [National] Liberation Front is: to confiscate the land belonging to the imperialists and their agents and distribute it to the labouring peasantry: to purchase land from the patriotic landlords [i.e. those who co-operate with the Vietcong] . . . to be distributed to the poor peasants without payment. . . .'[110] The N.L.F. claimed that by early 1965 two million hectares (nearly five million acres) of cultivated land had been distributed among the peasants[111] out of eight million acres in all—three times more land than was distributed 'during the war of resistance against the French'.[112] The N.L.F. claim is certainly exaggerated; the total amount of cultivated (if not cultivable) land in South Vietnam, 84 per cent of which is under rice, is only six and three-quarter million acres,[113] not eight. But what is significant is that the land distributed by the Vietminh—over one and a half million acres*—is nearly *three times* the amount distributed by Diem and his successors. In other words, something like two in every three of the peasants who had been given land by the Vietminh found it

* This figure is probably accurate, given that nearly two million acres were *subject* to expropriation under Diem's reforms.

taken away from them after 1954, handed back to the former owners and not subsequently returned. Indeed, from the record of the past fourteen years, observed a US Congressional committee in March 1968, there is 'scant hope' that the Government of Vietnam will 'institute a meaningful programme of land reform in the near future'. Since 1962, it pointed out, the Government had acquired no land for the land reform programme and only limited distribution of Government-held land had taken place. Yet 'perhaps more than any other single programme, land reform offers the opportunity for the Government of Vietnam to secure the allegiance of the Vietnamese people'.[114]

The Vietcong readily linked the 'peasant land problem' with the 'basic problem of the present revolutionary tasks in the South'. In October 1963, the N.L.F. argued, 'a solution [to the land problem] could not only mobilize the people in the liberated areas to participate in the struggle for . . . revolutionary results but could also mobilize the masses in the oppressed [i.e. government-controlled] areas to rise up and struggle . . . to liberate themselves'.[115] By May 1965 the People's Revolutionary Party—the 'Marxist-Leninist' vanguard of the N.L.F.—was declaring that 'this year, all our armed forces and people must exert every effort to liberate the greater part of the rural areas, to destroy the [remaining] network of strategic hamlets, to abolish the landlords' ownership of rice fields and to restore all lands to the toiling peasant. . . .' In this 'May Day Letter' to the peasants of South Vietnam, the P.R.P. hammered away at the four '*valuable* lessons' they had been taught:

'(1) Backed by . . . the US imperialists and puppet [Saigon] army and administration, the landlord class has increased the land rents and has struggled to restore its ownership of rice fields. . . . If our peasants want to own a piece of land and to lead a happy life . . . they must struggle to exterminate the imperialists and overthrow the landlords. . . .
(2) Thanks to their solidarity and unity, our peasants have managed to win back their rice fields in the past. . . . [To preserve their ownership and strengthen themselves] our peasants must unite very closely in the peasant associations and work exchange teams. . . . They must neglect neither the struggle for class liberation nor their duties to their country. . . .
(3) We must constantly step up violent action, carry out armed revolution and resolutely crush the enemy if we want to recover our rice fields and our right to live. If we lay down our weapons we shall lose all our rice fields and live in poverty. . . . If our peasants

do not encourage their children to join the liberation army to kill the enemy, if they do not work for our military recruitment . . . they will be failing in their sacred duty. . . . They will have neither land nor freedom. . . .
(4) [Peasants must have] confidence in the Party and revolution . . . only the Communist Party, the party of the working class, is loyal to the interests of the peasant class. . . .'[116]

'The key to peasant loyalty,' as Ton That Thien wrote from Saigon two years later, is simply this: 'The Vietcong tell the peasants that the land they till is still theirs and they will get more after victory . . . the peasants therefore tend to believe that a Government victory is not to their advantage . . . because under their [Government troops] cover the landlords may come back and wrest the land from them.' He referred to landowners 'co-operating with local authorities' to delay the disposal of land 'while enforcing the collection of rent in "secure" areas'. As a result, 'the peasants often look upon the troops and police agents in their areas as allies of the landlords'. The new Constitution of 1967, upon which the Americans have set such hope, pledges (in Article 18) to 'recognize and guarantee private property', but as Ton That Thien rightly states, no land reform if it is to be capable of winning over the peasants can avoid taking drastic expropriation measures against the landlords.[117] Where land reforms were successful—in Taiwan and Japan—Wolf Ladejinsky points out: 'Reforms were not designed to satisfy the claims of both contending parties: the tenant was to gain at the expense of the landlord.'[118]

In Nationalist China and Japan, however, the ruling classes had suffered a catastrophic defeat. Those who remained, or who replaced them, realized the vital need for reforms if the new régimes were to survive. This situation faces the South Vietnamese authorities; but spared the shock of disasters (thanks to American intervention) they have not been forced into an awareness of the problem —that is, the drastic nature of the sacrifices required of them. Without having this desperate sense of urgency, the 'old order' cannot be expected to carry out fundamental improvements. This is because reforms, if they are to be effective, are bound to strike at the vested interests on which the régime depends for its (limited) support. If the régime were more widely based it could afford to take such measures: but a more representative government does not usually face these problems. Nor can the existing 'system' be changed without violence (from one quarter or another) since an authoritarian régime normally does not encourage the possibility of peaceful change: it is at the top and intends to stay there. Any outside appeal for reforms—unless the régime can understand, or be made to understand, that these are the only alternative to destruction—is so much wasted effort. (Since it is the régime's own policies which are chiefly responsible for getting it into such a precarious position in the first place, it is unlikely that the leaders of the régime will have the capacity to take the enlightened point of view required of them.)

Thus in wartime Nationalist China, Chiang Kai-shek had thwarted General Stilwell's plan to train and reform the Chinese armies to meet more effectively the Japanese threat. To Chiang the Chinese armies were political forces. He owed his power to armies commanded by his supporters; these were not the most efficient—indeed, successful commanders were considered dangerous rivals—and would have been displaced in any thorough-going reform. Chiang Kai-shek, like Diem, 'looked upon loyalty to himself rather than effectiveness in fighting the war as the most important criterion in allocation of equipment and supply and in promotion and advancement'.[119] This attitude may work if the régime is not under pressure; but if it is, it is likely to prove fatal.

Towards the end of the Diem régime the US Administration realized that it was losing ground. But Washington still clung to the belief (a) that if the 'sinister' influence of Ngo Dinh Nhu were removed all would still be well, and (b) that Diem could be persuaded to get rid of his brother. Yet, as Nguyen Thai, a senior official who broke with the Diem régime in 1961, pointed out at that time: 'All the talk of having Diem reform his régime by getting rid of Mr and Mrs Nhu is just wishful thinking.' The Nhus were by then inseparable from Diem; they were 'three sides of a triangle'.[120] In the 'family régime', Nhu, the Political Counsellor to the Presidency, was the 'organizer and decision-maker': 'Whereas Diem remembers vaguely, Nhu has facts and documents.' These were provided by the 'Political and Social Research Service of the Presidency' managed by Nhu—the 'miniature real government which guides, directs, supervises and controls the official government appointed by Ngo Dinh Diem'.[121] Nhu was French-trained, more methodically organized than Diem; he worked more efficiently, got things done faster. As a result the senior administrators often channelled important documents to Nhu instead of to the President, knowing that they would be dealt with. Thus, Nhu, given 'valuable information which serves him well', more and more acted as a screen between his brother and the administration,[122] effectively isolating the President (who was by nature stubborn, proud and heedless of 'outside' advice) from all but narrow and distorted views.

By 1963 the policies of this régime—the constant manipulation of army commands, the 'blind eye' turned to Communist infiltration in the delta region, the frenzied pace of the strategic hamlet programme, the senseless attack on the Buddhists—all indicated that it was heading for disaster. President Kennedy, in September 1963, publicly urged 'changes in policy and perhaps with personnel' on the Vietnamese Government; unless it regained popular support, he doubted that the war could be won.[123]

There were fundamental weaknesses in the Diem régime. Politically it restricted freedom, not extended it. In 1956 the elected village and municipal councils were abolished and replaced by appointed officials.[124] National election campaigns were subject to strong Government pressures,* particularly in the countryside where, as Scigliano writes, 'candidates were screened and undesirable ones pressured to withdraw . . . the government did not hesitate to tamper with the ballots' and 'waves of civil servants were sent out in each election to propagandize in the countryside'.[125] The National Assembly, composed almost entirely of pro-government members, was 'excluded from meaningful action' in important financial matters.[126] Legally, no opposition party was allowed; there were no opposition newspapers after 1958.[127] Ex-Northerners and those from the centre predominated in senior levels of the administration;[128] one result was that almost all the 'information and civic action agents who serve as spearheads in the central government's effort to win the [Southern] villagers to its side' were Northerners—many of them Catholics.[129] The military was trained in conventional warfare;† but it also began to take over the provincial administration: by 1962, there were thirty-six military officers and only five civilians left as province chiefs.[130] However, personal loyalty to Diem remained the chief criterion in military appointments; capable commanders were frequently shifted to less important, but safer (for the régime) positions.[131] Most of the leading military plotters, who eventually overthrew Diem, had been treated in this way. The Diem régime had 'amply proved' that it could be as oppressive as the Communists, Nguyen Thai observed; where they differed was in the 'political spirit and zeal' of the Communists compared to the 'haze of imprecise lipservice and external obedience' proffered by a demora-

* Right from the beginning: 'The campaign preceding this referendum [on Bao Dai or a Republic in October 1955] was conducted with such a cynical disregard for decency and democratic principles that even the Viet Minh professed to be shocked.' Donald Lancaster, *The Emancipation of French Indochina* (Oxford Univ. Press, 1961). p. 398.

† The adverse effects are brilliantly discussed in Dennis J. Duncanson, *Government and Revolution in Vietnam* (Oxford Univ. Press, 1968) pp. 304-7.

lized bureaucracy and in the lack of 'political substance' in Diem's régime.[132]

In contrast to the fragmented nature of Diem's support—which his policy of playing off military, police and provincial administrators one against the other (and against themselves) did little to improve—the Vietcong developed on the mass basis founded by the Vietminh. An estimated two million (of 14 million) Southern Vietnamese had lived under this system, Pike states, while another five million lived in areas contested with the French.[133] The Vietminh—which 'attempted to solve local land tenure problems and to improve living conditions for the people' with 'fair and just' administration in many areas—however failed to achieve an alliance wth Southern nationalists, particularly the Cao Dai and Hoa Hao religious sects, which came to terms with the French.[134] Ironically, Diem's obstinate refusal to seek a reconciliation with the sects (after breaking their power in 1955-56) drove their followers, in self defence, to join ranks with the Vietcong. The most ardent supporters of the original N.L.F., Pike points out, were, in addition to the sects and the Vietminh, 'a scattering of minority group members, primarily ethnic Cambodians and Montagnards [hill-tribes]; idealistic youth, recruited from the universities and polytechnic schools; representatives of farmers' organizations from parts of the Mekong delta, where serious land tenure problems existed; leaders of small political parties or groups . . . intellectuals who had broken with the [government] . . . military deserters; refugees of various sorts from the Diem government . . .'; and they were soon joined by Southern members of the Vietminh who had gone North after 1954 and infiltrated back. Some 90 per cent of these were Vietnamese from the poor areas, especially in Central Vietnam—'some of the most desolate land and destitute people in all of Indo-China'.[135]

Four years of tireless effort, from 1959 to 1962, converted the N.L.F. organizational structure from a loose collection of dissident groups, often with nothing more in common than hostility to the Diem régime, into a 'tightly knit movement able to demonstrate a co-ordinated efficiency rare in a developing nation'. From 1960 the N.L.F. 'grew into a structure that reached to some degree into virtually every village in the country'.[136] This is illustrated by simple, basic information on the N.L.F. leadership in some twenty Mekong delta districts and provinces, captured by the South Vietnamese army in 1962, which identified as chairmen of provincial central committees: eight Marxists (i.e. cadres or officials of the Vietminh organization), five Cao Dai, five intellectuals and two notables (the traditional village ruling group). The vice-chairmen were: eight farmers, four Buddhists monks, three women, two teachers and one each Marxist, Cao Dai and businessman. The secretaries-general were ten youths, four farmers, three workers, two Cao Dai and a woman. Pike comments: the chairman was either a Communist or an experienced member of a non-Communist nationalist group. Notables and intellectuals, mostly teachers, held postions of status in the village—as did Buddhist monks. The Cao Dai and the intellectuals were the first major social groups to be alienated by Diem. Above all, the 'N.L.F. placed heavy emphasis on youth, entrusting them with great responsiblities. In the secretary-general the N.L.F. sought the eager, the zealous, the dedicated, the hard-working, the young.'[137]

'In today's war,' reaffirmed a North Vietnamese journal in 1964, 'political factors have a decided significance; the side that can hold the people . . . is the victor.'[138] The Vietcong sought to win the people by providing them with 'material benefits'; and to hold them by engaging them in 'struggle'. A widely-used cadre handbook entitled *Needs of the Revolution,* dated July 1962, points out:

'. . . Set clear purposes and realistic goals for the struggle in terms of the people's interests. Use realistic slogans that reflect the people's demands. . . . Choose the right moment to launch [the struggle, such as] . . . the enemy committing a mistake and the population being in a state of preparedness . . . or when the people's rights have been endangered . . . by corruption, high taxation, forced money donations, land robbing, building strategic hamlets, forced membership in reactionary organizations, terror or killing, military draft [conscription]. . . . Struggle movements can also be launched in favour of freedom to travel and work, freedom of trade, freedom to move to a new part of the country, and for village council elections. . . . Use every form of struggle to create public opinion . . . the demonstration, petition, complaint. The demonstration may use small or large groups, a few persons, several villages, or tens of thousands of people. . . .'[139]

The criteria for a struggle, another N.L.F. document declared, was that it must be justified; it must be profitable; and it must be 'kept within bounds'.[140]

The early years of the N.L.F. were dominated by two major activities: propaganda to 'advertise' the Front and the existence of the 'Revolution' to the villager; and agitation to convert grievances into organized hostility.[141] The objective was to paralyse government administration at the village level: local officials were driven out (or neutralized by agreements to 'live and let live'[142]), troops were harassed, and government efforts were sabotaged. The N.L.F. goaded the government into increasingly repressive measures, which widened the gulf between it and the villagers.[143] Military activity formed a relatively small part of the day-to-day work of the 'liberation armed forces', whether village guerrillas or 'main force' units. Vietnamese government officials estimated that a main force unit in the 1962-63 period spent an average of only one day a month on military missions; much of the rest of the time was taken up with training, indoctrination and propaganda work, and food production.[144] 'Army political tasks are fundamental,' emphasized an indoctrination booklet captured in 1963; it is of 'prime importance' that 'military action is subordinated to political action'.[145]

In the three great crises faced by the Vietcong—in 1961, 1963 and 1965—this was shown to be the case. The first and last were military crises brought about by American intervention; but the effects of both were nullified by political developments. The second was the unexpected overthrow of Diem, which for a time left the N.L.F. at a loss. A notorious régime was replaced by one which was, at least momentarily, popular; moreover, the N.L.F. had badly underestimated the strength and appeal of the Buddhist movement. But the opportunity for Saigon to create a viable political alternative to the N.L.F. soon foundered in a welter of rivalry and suspicion, while the administrative framework established under Diem, inadequate as it might be, was almost completely destroyed in the purge of Diemists. As US Defence Secretary McNamara reported, thirty-five of the forty-one province chiefs were replaced; nine provinces had three chiefs in three months; one province had four. Almost all major military commands changed hands twice. 'The confidence of the peasantry was inevitably shaken by the disruptions in leadership and the loss of physical security. Army and para-military desertion rates increased and the morale of the hamlet militia . . . fell.' The Vietcong exploited the 'confusion'; and it 'regained the initiative'.[146] As Nguyen Thai had predicted before the fall of Diem, echoing Dean Acheson's sombre warning on Nationalist China:

'Massive injections of military equipment and foreign technical help can only produce a temporary morale-boosting effect on the Vietnamese population; it cannot be a long-range substitute for adequate political and administrative leadership.'[147]

REFERENCE NOTES TO CHAPTER III

1. Philippe Devillers, *Histoire du Viet-Nam de 1940 à 1952* (Paris, Editions du Seuil, 1952), p. 140.
2. Ho Chi Minh, *Selected Works* (Hanoi, Foreign Languages Publishing

House, 1961), Vol. III, p. 20.
3. Devillers, *op. cit.*, p. 225.
4. *Ibid.*, pp. 251-2.
5. Paul Mus. *Viet-Nam: Sociologie d'une Guerre* (Paris, Editions du Seuil, 1952), p. 26.
6. *Ibid.*, p. 31.
7. Bernard Fall, *Le Viet-Minh: La République Démocratique du Viet-Nam 1945-1960* (Paris, Librairie Armand Colin, 1960), p. 37.
8. Mus, *op. cit.*, p. 270.
9. Vo Nguyen Giap, *People's War, People's Army* (Hanoi, Foreign Languages Publishing House, 1961), p. 27.
10. Le Thanh Khoi, *Le Viet-Nam: Histoire et Civilisation* (Paris, Editions de Minuit, 1955), p. 422.
11. *Ibid.*, pp. 422-3.
12. Fall, *op. cit.*, p. 265.
13. Devillers, *op. cit.*, p. 230.
14. *Ibid.*, p. 61.
15. *Ibid.*, pp. 79-80.
16. Giap, *op. cit.*, p. 71.
17. *Ibid.*, pp. 78-9 (Giap's italics).
18. *Ibid.*, pp. 82-3 (Giap's italics).
19. *Ibid.*, p. 85.
20. Mus. *op. cit.*, p. 291.
21. Ho Chi Minh, Vol. III, p. 224.
22. Truong Chinh, *The Resistance Will Win* (written in 1947, published in Hanoi, Foreign Languages Publishing House, 1960), p. 35.
23. *Ibid.*, p. 36.
24. Giap, *op. cit.*, p. 99.
25. Mus, *op. cit.*, p. 301.
26. Devillers, *op. cit.*, p. 405 (n. 10).
27. *Ibid.*, pp. 413-14.
28. Truong Chinh, *op. cit.*, p. 104.
29. *Ibid.*, p. 95.
30. *Ibid.*, p. 96.
31. *Ibid.*, p. 100.
32. Giap, *op. cit.*, pp. 100-1.
33. Truong Chinh, *op. cit.*, p. 88.
34. *Ibid.*, pp. 88-90.
35. Fall, *op. cit.*, p. 90.
36. *Ibid.*, p. 91.
37. Devillers, *op. cit.*, p. 102.
38. Fall, *op. cit.*, p. 90.
39. Truong Chinh, *op. cit.*, p. 112.
40. Giap, *op. cit.*, p. 94.
41. Ho, Vol. III, p. 428.
42. Truong Chinh, *op. cit.*, pp. 116-17.
43. Giap, *op. cit.*, p. 31.
44. *Ibid.*, p. 31.
45. Ho, Vol. III, p. 148.
46. Truong Chinh, *op. cit.*, p. 40.
47. Ho, Vol. III, p. 419.
48. *Ibid.*, p. 378.
49. *Ibid.*, pp. 421-2.

50. *Ibid.*, p. 423.
51. Truong Chinh, *op. cit.*, p. 40.
52. *Ibid.*, p. 38.
53. *Ibid.*, p. 65.
54. George K. Tanham, *Communist Revolutionary Warfare: The Vietminh in Indochina* (Praeger, 1961), p. 102.
55. *Ibid.*, p. 99.
56. Ho, Vol. III, p. 146.
57. *Ibid.*, p. 147.
58. *Ibid.*, p. 378.
59. Truong Chinh, *op. cit.*, pp. 116-17.
60. Giap, *op. cit.*, p. 49.
61. *Ibid.*, p. 19.
62. Truong Chinh, *op. cit.*, pp. 74-5.
63. Giap, *op. cit.*, p. 108.
64. *Ibid.*, p. 21.
65. *Ibid.*, p. 107.
66. *Ibid.*, p. 159.
67. Tanham, *op. cit.*, p. 41.
68. *Ibid.*, p. 49.
69. Edgar O'Ballance, *The Indo-China War 1945-1954: A Study in Guerrilla Warfare* (Faber and Faber, 1964), p. 195.
70. Tanham, *op. cit.*, p. 63.
71. Fall, *op. cit.*, p. 196.
72. Ellen Hammer, *The Struggle for Indochina 1940-1955* (Stanford Univ. Press, new ed. 1966), p. 253.
73. *Loc. cit.*
74. Giap, *op. cit.*, p. 33.
75. *Ibid.*, pp. 34-5.
76. Hammer, *op. cit.*, p. 140.
77. Devillers, *op. cit.*, p. 105.
78. *Ibid.*, pp. 228-30.
79. *Ibid.*, p. 207.
80. *Ibid.*, p. 208.
81. *Ibid.*, p. 214.
82. *Ibid.*, p. 149.
83. *Ibid.*, pp. 340-1.
84. *Ibid.*, p. 336.
85. Mus, *op. cit.*, p. 55.
86. *Ibid.*, pp. 50-1.
87. Hammer, *op. cit.*, p. 235.
88. *Ibid.*, p. 245.
89. *Loc. cit.*
90. *Ibid.*, p. 273.
91. Ho, Vol. III, p. 417.
92. Truong Chinh, *op. cit.*, p. 43.
93. Nguyen Thai, *Is South Vietnam Viable?* (Carmelo and Bauermann, Manila, 1962), p. 157.
94. John Mecklin, *Mission in Torment: An Intimate Account of the* US *Role in Vietnam* (Doubleday, 1965), p. 235.
95. Roger Hilsman, *To Move a Nation: The Politics of Foreign Policy in the Administration of John F. Kennedy* (Doubleday, 1967), p. 502.

96. General Earle Wheeler, Chairman of US Joint Chiefs of Staff, January 17, 1967, *Department of State Bulletin,* February 6, 1967.
97. *United States Relations with China* (State Department, Washington, 1949), pp. 885-6.
98. Denis Warner, *The Last Confucian: Vietnam, South-East Asia and the West* (Angus and Robertson, 1964), p. 32.
99. Ton That Thien [editor-in-chief *Vietnam Guardian,* later suspended], 'Vietnam: a Case of Social Alienation', *International Affairs,* London, July 1967.
100. Ithiel de Sola Pool, 'Political Alternatives to the Vietcong', *Asian Survey,* August 1967 (Vietnam: A special issue), p. 559.
101. *Ibid.,* pp. 560, 564.
102. Gerald Cannon Hickey, *Village in Vietnam* (Yale Univ. Press, 1964), p. 279.
103. Truong Chinh, *Hoc Tap,* September 1963, reported in *New China News Agency,* October 29, 1963.
104. Douglas Pike, *Viet Cong: The Organisation and Techniques of the National Liberation Front of South Vietnam* (M.I.T. Press, 1966), p. 62.
105. Le Thanh Khoi, *Le Viet-Nam: Histoire et Civilisation* (Edits. de Minuit, 1955), pp. 422-3.
106. Bernard B. Fall, *The Two Viet-Nams: A Political and Military Analysis* (Praeger, 1964), p. 311; and Ton That Thien, 'The Key to Peasant Loyalty', reprinted in *Canberra Times,* May 10, 1967.
107. *Loc. cit.*
108. Ton That Thien.
109. Robert Scigliano, *South Vietnam: Nation under Stress* (Houghton Mifflin, 1964), p. 123.
110. *Vietnam News Agency,* Hanoi, July 3, 1964.
111. *Ibid.,* July 22, 1965.
112. *Ibid.,* March 30, 1966.
113. South Vietnamese Government figures of 1964, in Pike, *op. cit.* p. 277 note.
114. Government Operations Committee (US House of Representatives) reported in *International Herald Tribune,* March 4, 1968.
115. Liberation radio [N.L.F.] October 16, 1964, monitored in B.B.C. *Summary of World Broadcasts* (Far East).
116. Liberation radio, May 2, 1965, in B.B.C. *Summary of World Broadcasts.*
117. Ton That Thien, 'Key to Peasant Loyalty'.
118. Wolf Ladejinsky, 'Agrarian Reform in Asia', *Foreign Affairs,* April 1964.
119. Tang Tsou, *America's Failure in China 1941-50* (Univ. of Chicago Press, 1963), pp. 50, 76.
120. Nguyen Thai, *op. cit.,* p. 180.
121. *Ibid.,* pp. 197, 207.
122. *Ibid.,* pp. 198, 201.
123. J. F. Kennedy, September 2, 1963, D.S.B. September 30, 1963.
124. Scigliano, *op. cit.,* p. 32.
125. *Ibid.,* pp. 94, 96.
126. *Ibid.,* pp. 42-3.
127. *Ibid.,* p. 80.
128. *Ibid.,* p. 51.
129. *Ibid.,* pp. 53-4.
130. *Ibid.,* p. 166.
131. *Ibid.,* p. 203.

132. Nguyen Thai, *op. cit.*, p. 265.
133. Pike, *op. cit.*, p. 47.
134. *Ibid.*, pp. 48-9.
135. *Ibid.*, p. 83.
136. *Ibid.*, p. 44.
137. *Ibid.*, p. 222.
138. Thong Nhat, June 26, 1964, in *ibid.*, p. 90.
139. Pike, *op. cit.*, p. 97.
140. *Ibid.*, p. 98.
141. *Ibid.*, pp. 154-5.
142. Wilfrid G. Burchett, *Vietnam: Inside Story of the Guerrilla War* (International Publishers, New York, 1965), pp. 59, 198.
143. Pike, *op. cit.*, p. 155.
144. *Ibid.*, p. 238.
145. *Ibid.*, p. 232.
146. Robert S. McNamara, March 26, 1964, D.S.B., April 13, 1964.
147. Nguyen Thai, *op. cit.*, p. 18.

Extra notes

1. 'Armed propaganda' (p. 122): a sinister term, but one which covers a variety of forms from assassination and intimidation to making a show of force and demonstrating authority; but the political aspect is most important.
2. 'Led by . . . the working class' (p. 135): paying lip-service—as in China—to Marxism-Leninism. The working class in Vietnam was minute; most Vietminh leaders were of landlord or bourgeois origin or of mandarin descent like Pham Van Dong and Ho Chi Minh.
3. Catholics (p. 136): most wanted independence; later, many went over to the Bao Dai 'solution' in return for the virtual autonomy of Catholic regions in the North (similar to the autonomy given the 'Buddhist' Hoa Hao and Cao Dai sects in the South). After 1954 over 600,000 Catholics moved or fled to the South, and became President Diem's main source of support. But their influx—and the preferential treatment they received— introduced a further element of discord into an already divided society.

IV. FAILURE

*China in Maphilindo**

LESSONS FROM MALAYA AND THE PHILIPPINES

In both countries the early insurgent situations were ominous; they bore striking resemblance to insurgencies which had succeeded or were to succeed. Revolt against colonial rule in Malaya could be likened to the Vietminh struggle for independence; peasant revolt against the corrupt and incompetent government of the Philippines could be likened to the Communist struggle against the Nationalists in China—or to the Vietcong struggle against the Saigon régime. Yet the differences proved to be even more important—and a large factor in these differences (in the Philippines, thanks to a change in leadership, the decisive factor) was the 'enlightened' nature of the government under attack: that is, it assessed the situation realistically and worked out effective remedies for existing weaknesses. This is in contrast to the obstinate pursuit of selfish interests by Chiang Kai-shek and the dominant reactionary wing of the Kuomintang in China; by the French settlers, officials and some soldiers in Indo-China; and by Diem and his successors in Vietnam. For the insurgent situation involves the people, most of whom are peasants. The struggle is a *competition* for their loyalty (the active support of a minority, the acquiescence of the majority); but if one side realizes this and the other does not, the latter is half way to losing the battle.

In the Philippines the basis for popular support through democratic constitutional government had been prepared for many years by the Americans and had not been eroded; it was not being observed, but it could be reactivated. But in China, especially in the last degenerate stages of the Empire and during the anarchic years of warlord rule, there was no sort of nationally representative government (despite Sun Yat-sen's assertions, his party in practice was only one clique among many). French rule in Indo-China had not prepared the people for independence, while it had bred among those

* 'Maphilindo' was coined by President Macapagal of the Philippines and President Sukarno of Indonesia in 1963 to symbolize co-operation between their countries and Malaysia—the three 'Malay' States of South East Asia. Here it is used to encompass Mao-ist, rural insurgencies in Malaya and the Philippines and Aidit's attempt to follow Mao's course in Indonesia.

working for government a 'fonctionnaire' mentality (following the rules and avoiding responsibility) which, combined with the suppression of political movements, had either demoralized or decapitated the country's natural leaders—except for those who later joined the Vietminh. Diem continued, and even intensified, this process.

Ramon Magsaysay (Secretary of Defence in 1950, elected President of the Philippines in 1953) actually carried out what the Huk (rebel) slogans promised: 'Land for the landless', 'equal justice for all' and an end to 'inefficiency and corruption in government'.[1] He was able to do this because a sufficient number of the Filipino people, although disgusted by the previous régime, were not hopelessly alienated from the system of rule; they were more than willing to support a government which was adopting good measures. Magsaysay himself was a 'man of the people'—not a mandarin like Diem or a militarist like Chiang. He had started work as a mechanic, later became manager of a provincial bus company, was a prominent guerrilla leader in the war against the Japanese and in 1945 was elected an independent congressman. Appointed—almost at the last hour—as Secretary of Defence, Magsaysay and his followers within fifteen months had broken the back of the Huk insurgency. Resigning as Secretary in 1953, when he was no longer allowed to act freely, Magsaysay wrote to the President:

'You must realize that we cannot solve the problem of dissidence simply by military measures. It would be futile to go on killing Huk, while the Administration continues to breed dissidence by neglecting the problems of our masses. . . . The need of a vigorous assault on these problems I have repeatedly urged upon you, but my pleas have fallen on deaf ears. . . .'[2]

Magsaysay went on to stand as President and was elected by an overwhelming majority.*

In Malaya the absence of feudal and political abuses which were prevalent in the Philippines more than offset the anti-colonial stimulus to revolt. Moreover Malaya, with its small population (under five million in 1947 compared to twenty-five million in the Philippines) and its rich tin and rubber resources, was by far the most prosperous country in South East Asia.

There were conditions in Malaya making for revolt, but they were not 'sufficient' conditions. Nationalism played a part, but it was the

* But the 'problems of our masses' continued to be neglected. No effective attack on the landlord-tenancy system was undertaken by Magsaysay (who died in an air crash in 1957) or his successors: and there has been a resurgence of the Huk movement in Central Luzon.

nationalism of a minority—the 40 per cent of Chinese in Malaya. Even then, as an observer pointed out in 1949, a year after the 'Emergency' had been proclaimed, 'the Chinese population, by and large, sat on the fence during the early stages of the rising. Some Chinese gave active co-operation to the insurgents, but nearly all withheld co-operation from the government.' However, the Malays, 'seeing in this Communist rising a threat by the Chinese as a whole to their position in Malaya, flocked to the aid of the government'. The United Malay National Organization—later the ruling party in the 'Alliance' with its Chinese and Indian associates—supported the call for Malay recruits, particularly in the police forces. These were special constables defending the estates and mines, auxiliary police patrolling with the regulars (also largely Malay) and many thousands of *kampong* (village) guards.[3]

There were economic grounds for unrest. But again they affected chiefly the Chinese, or rather that proportion of it (about half the rural Chinese) who were 'squatters', nearly half a million people in all. These were Chinese who had either fled to the jungle fringes to avoid persecution by the Japanese or poor people who had no other way of making a living. But the Malays, over 80 per cent of whom were villagers (and therefore much the largest element in Malaya's rural population) were hardly affected by Communism[4]—unlike the Chinese squatters, whose support for the revolutionaries was initially far stronger than it was, for example, among the South Vietnamese peasants.[5]

Finally there were administrative weaknesses—but again nothing like the paralysis which developed in large parts of rural Vietnam, and in much of Central Luzon in the Philippines, which was effectively under Huk control. The weaknesses in Malaya sprang directly from the large number of squatters who, as the 'Committee to Investigate the Squatter Problem' reported in January 1949, were outside the normal processes of administration. Squatters' assistance to the rebels was not an indication of their commitment to the revolutionaries, the report noted, for most of them were without sympathies either way, but they 'necessarily succumb to the more immediate and threatening influence—the terrorist on their doorstep—against the vague and distant authority of the government'.[6]

The first two years, government forces thrashed about blindly trying to bring the terrorists to battle. 'The predilection of some army officers for major operations seems incurable,' comments General Clutterbuck, although neither the giant encirclement operations when a camp was known to be in the area nor the wide sweeps 'based on no information at all', had any success.[7] Meanwhile, the Communists were more than making up their losses by recruiting and they were murdering more than one hundred civilians a month with impunity. The Government was losing, Clutterbuck points out, because the guerrillas could get all the support they needed—food, clothing, information and recruits—from the squatters, whom it was impossible to police or to protect.[8]

A new strategy was needed—not just military operations but co-ordinated civil-police-military measures. This was the basis of the 'Briggs Plan' to resettle the Chinese squatters in carefully planned New Villages, where they would be brought under administrative control and be freed from the attentions of the guerrillas. The Plan set out these aims:

(a) To dominate the populated areas and to build up a feeling of complete security, which would in time result in a steady and increasing flow of information coming from all sources.
(b) To break up the Communist organizations within the populated areas.
(c) To isolate the bandits [guerrillas] from their food and supply organizations in the populated areas.
(d) To destroy the bandits by forcing them to attack the security forces on their own ground.[9]

These measures were successful. The number of police had already been rapidly expanded (9,000 to 45,000 in six months).[10] Police posts provided protection to the villages and they were backed up by army units. At the height of the insurgency there were twice the number of police (70,000 plus 40,000 on call from the much larger village Home Guard) to regular army forces—40,000 British and Commonwealth. (The ratio in South Vietnam was just the opposite.*) Resettlement brought law and order to the squatters—and a degree of prosperity they had previously lacked. The New Villages provided schools, dispensaries, better public services; the sites were defensible and were chosen to give sufficient opportunities for agriculture; a census of occupations was undertaken before resettlement to ensure continued employment.[11] (All these preparations were lacking with the strategic hamlet programme in Vietnam.) One factor was fortuitous: the boom in rubber and tin created by the Korean war which guaranteed high wages. But the clearest justification of the New Villages is that virtually none of the people have moved away from them, once they were free to do so.[12]

A Communist document captured in 1949 admitted: 'Our greatest weakness is that we have not sufficient strength to protect co-operative villages because our environment becomes more and more difficult, especially from the financial and provision [of] supply

* 85,000 police, 300,000 regular army, 15,500 air force (South Vietnam, April 1968).

aspects. *We suffer from unreliable information, non-co-operation of the people and difficulty of movement.*'[13] In other words, with the government providing good administration and security (and not the insurgents) the situation is reversed. This is when the 'war is turned round'—a situation the Americans hoped to achieve in Vietnam. Information increasingly flows to government forces, enabling them to lead more successful operations against the guerrillas, which in turn confirms villagers' confidence in the outcome, and thus encourages them to give still more information and co-operation.

Intelligence is vital if the security forces are to make contact with the guerrillas—otherwise it is hitting out in the dark. Intelligence is obtained at least partly through restrictions (registration of villagers, food controls in deficit areas, curfew and so on) which force the guerrillas' suppliers to take risks; thus they can not only be more easily captured (and often be persuaded to work secretly for the government side, to avoid punishment or to gain rewards[14]); but are given a valid excuse not to co-operate further with the guerrillas, because they say the chance of capture is too great. This throws all the more onus on the committed guerrilla supporters, who have to work far harder (to make up for the defection of their colleagues) and thus expose themselves to still greater danger in the process.[15]

Secondly, intelligence can be obtained because it is in the interest of at least the more prosperous villagers to co-operate with the government, provided either they can do so secretly or be protected from reprisals. The same applies to the bulk of the villagers (unless in real poverty) who simply want to be left alone—that is free from political pressure; material assistance is another matter. But villagers will not take sides, naturally enough, until they are sure who is winning.

Finally, intelligence is earned by patient, painstaking watching and waiting: again, more a matter of police methods than of military operations. Sir Robert Thompson underlines the disadvantages of entrusting internal security intelligence to the army (this was done in South Vietnam, but not in Malaya): 'The army will have had little concern with subversion before the open insurgency breaks out; [and] it will have had very limited experience of contacting the people, particularly rural communities, which are inherently suspicious of troops. . . .'[16] The army may indeed be clumsy—or even, as in South Vietnamese villages, indulging in 'operations and actions which might just have been excusable as acts of war if carried out in enemy territory'.[17] However, the police itself, in many countries, is hardly above suspicion. The latter may be an 'organization reaching out into every corner of the country' with 'long experience of close contact with the population', as Sir Robert says, but this contact may be far from appreciated by the villagers.*

The state of discipline, order and good administration among the police forces in Malaya may well be exceptional: it is one of the reasons why the 'turning point' was reached in a matter of only four years after the outbreak of the Emergency; and why in its absence the situation in South Vietnam instead grew worse. Yet the combination of local officials' corruption, social and economic abuses and government incapacity which alienated the South Vietnamese villagers undoubtedly faced the Philippines. In their noted counter-insurgency study, Colonels Valeriano and Bohannan confirm this from their description of the three areas where outbreaks of violence chiefly occurred. First, south of Manila, where half the people worked little farms and the rest were labourers on large estates, share-croppers and cottage industry workers, the 'region has been systematically victimized for 150 years by land reformers and demagogues, unscrupulous politicians and land racketeers'. In Manila itself the Communists had an 'easy success' in infiltrating labour unions and in appealing to intellectuals, students, the discontented and the unemployed. Finally, in Central Luzon, 'well over half the farmers in the rich rice lands are share-croppers, farming large estates, often held by absentee landlords. So keen is the competition for land . . . that the average farm runs from four acres in some provinces to eight in others. . . . The tendency is to borrow, often at ruinously high rates of interest. . . .'[18]

Altogether some 40 per cent of the cultivated land in the Philippines is owned by 10 per cent of the population. More than half the country's farmers are tenants.[19] Under Spanish rule—when huge estates were granted to the *Conquistadores* and their native collaborators—as under the Americans, the power of the local constabulary was used to support the interests of the landlords.[20] On top of continuing rural poverty and resentment came the brutal Japanese occupation of the Philippines. This met resistance by American and Filipino guerrillas and there was tremendous destruction. In the words of an American observer:

'Manila lay prostrate, a jungle of wreckage. . . . Looting and banditry made life and property unsafe. . . . War casualties had decimated capable leadership. Government bureaux were completely dis-

* In a number of developing countries the police are known more as bullies and extortionists than 'protectors of the people'. Poorly paid (like the army, which helps to explain why troops seize food without paying for it) the local police often harass the villagers at checkpoints or blackmail them with the threat of prosecution for the infringement of minor regulations.

organized. There was no equipment, no personnel and in many instances no records.'[21]

At the end of the war, Huk guerrillas moved out of their fastness They appeared as protectors of the people. They consolidated theii rule by collecting taxes and a share of the rice harvest, and they liquidated government officials and agents. From 1946 to 1950, the Huks had some 150,000 supporters and 12,000 armed soldiers.[22] But the Philippine Army had been reduced from a wartime strength of 132,000 to only 37,000:

'Government troops, poorly trained, underpaid and hardpressed were sent out to eradicate the Huk menace. Barrios [villages] shielding Huk units were shelled. In a desperate effort to secure information the troops were sometimes guilty of maltreating suspects in an attempt to make them talk. This indiscriminate terrorism turned the people against the government and strengthened the Huk movement. . . . Even in the area where the government troops patrolled during the day, the Huks took charge after dark.'[23]

The security the government offered to life and property in the rural areas was almost nil, recalls General Jesus Vargas, who was appointed Armed Forces Chief of Staff by Magsaysay. The toll exacted by Huk depredations continued to mount. Many people—caught up in the conflict—abandoned their farms and fled to the densely populated urban areas. This mass flight from the countryside wreaked havoc on the rural economy. Travel on the highways became perilous. The Huks stepped up their raids and occasional, scattered clashes with government forces did little to stop them. In 1949 the Huks envisaged that within three years they would have an active and armed strength of 173,000 and a mass base of two and a half million, at which time they were to seize national power.[24]

Parallel to the disintegration of authority in the countryside went the decay and corruption of government at the centre. The general election of 1949 was known as the 'dirty election'. Armed 'goons' guarded the voting places, according to Carlos P. Romulo, later Ambassador to the United States, and Marvin Gray, a Manila newspaper publisher, and by constant gunfire kept the cowed citizens from casting their ballots. Hundreds who had the courage to go to the polls were shot down and killed.[25] By 1950 the Huks had virtually taken over the city of Manila. Armed bands roamed the capital at will. President Quirino was a virtual prisoner in the Presidential Palace—advised by his generals not to leave the palace grounds lest he be liquidated by the Huks.[26] In many respects, Romulo and Gray observe, conditions were even worse than during Chiang Kai-shek's last hours on the Chinese mainland:

'Quirino's party—the party in power—was in hopeless disrepute. Army morale was so low that the soldiers were no longer interested in risking their lives for corrupt, lazy officers and politicians. The people, without whose effort the Huks could not subsist, had all but lost faith in the democratic way of life. The Filipinos feared pillaging army units more than they did the Communist bands. . . . The Filipinos did not want Communism. But they wanted agrarian reform. They wanted clean government. They wanted armed forces that could protect them, rather than steal from them. . . .'[27]

Many officers were grafting, accepting bribes or promoting one another to high rank in exchange for money or favours. 'They stayed in their homes while their soldiers were expected to go into the field and combat the Huks.'[28] In the face of such disinterest on the part of their superiors, soldiers saw no reason why they should emperil themselves hunting determined guerrilla bands. The civilians in their turn saw no reason why they should risk their lives by giving information concerning the Huks. The latter were winning by default.[29]

As a last hope, President Quirino appointed the 'obscure Congressman' Ramon Magsaysay in September 1950 Secretary of National Defence. Magsaysay vigorously cleaned up the army and police. Broad powers were given to field commanders to discharge or discipline their men. Frequent inspections were made by senior officers and by Magsaysay himself. He dismissed the chief of the Constabulary, discovered at a gambling party, followed by the armed Forces Chief of Staff, whom no one had previously been able to dislodge; because it was he who had provided Army 'co-operation' to Quirino's Party when it 'won' the last elections.[30] Within a month after his appointment, Magsaysay in a daring *coup* arrested the entire Communist Politburo in Manila—a devastating blow to the insurgents, as Communist sources later acknowledged.[31] From Magsaysay's own studies and experience the national policy of 'all-out force and all-out friendship' was evolved. He promised mercy and assistance to those who voluntarily renounced their allegiance to Communism and sincerely sought to live in peace. Resettlement of dissidents on their own land—the Economic Development Corporation (EDCOR) farms—was one of Magsaysay's most telling achievements for it effectively countered one of the main grievances exploited by the Huks.

Magsaysay also showed his determination to use 'all-out force' against those who continued to defy the government. The Army was expanded to 56,000; with superiority in numbers, equipment and renewed morale, it defeated the enemy wherever he could be found. On an average one soldier was killed for every eight Huks.[32] But as a result of these successes, it became more and more difficult to find sizeable concentrations of dissidents. Whereas formerly a hundred or more were grouped in a fairly well organized camp, afterwards they split up into wandering teams of from twenty to twelve men—and later into isolated bands of three to five men. By 1951 the tide of battle had turned and the State was reasonably secure against internal threats. But there was still the question of dealing with the guerrillas: 'Soon enough we realized,' General Vargas observed, 'that the enemy had superior knowledge of the terrain; that our forces were inadequate to achieve effective coverage of the area; and that real good intelligence was vital for success.'

It was the same process in Malaya. The large Communist bands, which were picking off police posts in overwhelming strength, were becoming increasingly vulnerable to jungle penetration tactics by small but experienced security patrols.* In fact Communist losses in 1951 were double those of 1950. Since the big jungle camps were no longer secure, the guerrillas were ordered to split up from regiments and companies into platoons.[33] They were safer, but they could not attack the villages so effectively; for the police posts could hold off a small number of attackers until relief came. As a direct result, monthly police losses dropped from one hundred in 1951 to twenty in mid-1952. In the same period, civilian losses fell from 90 a month to fifteen.[34] In both Malaya and South Vietnam there had been a rising trend in civilian casualties in the first three years of insurgency; but whereas in Malaya it then fell dramatically, in South Vietnam it continued to rise. As Clutterbuck points out: 'Once this kind of terror begins to get out of hand, it becomes progressively harder to restore confidence and reverse the trend.'[35]

* 'Patrols proved to be by far the most effective weapon for applying force to the Huk. . . . The most effective patrols were the smaller ones,' Valeriano and Bohannan, *Counter-Guerrilla Operations*, p. 130. As Clutterbuck rightly observes, the failure to apply this lesson in Vietnam is not because South Vietnamese soldiers are 'temperamentally unsuited for small scale raids against large enemy units', since they are of the same stock as the Vietcong, but 'it must be from lack of motivation and leadership', *The Long, Long War*, p. 73. He also points out that the 'effective *jungle* strength' in Malaya of army and police combined, at the turning point of the war in 1952, was only *2:1* over the guerrillas and was 'never anywhere near the 10- or 12- to -1 ratio so often quoted by commentators' (p. 43). Valeriano and Bohannan confirm that with civilian co-operation 'military forces need not greatly exceed the number of the guerrillas' (p. 104).

In Malaya two-thirds of the 8,000 to 10,000 guerrillas were wiped out in two years (1952-53);[36] it was much the same in the Philippines, a year earlier. But in South Vietnam the Vietcong nearly doubled its armed strength in one year (from 35,000 to 63,000 by the beginning of 1962) and doubled it again by the beginning of 1965.[37] This sizeable increase was *dependent* on the parallel growth of the Vietcong's village infrastructure, for as Sir Robert Thompson has reiterated, both insurgent growth and outside infiltration is limited by the 'absorptive capacity' of the area under insurgent control.[38] When this area expands the number of troops it can 'support' also expands. For this reason the 'government must give priority to defeating the political subversion—not the guerillas' (Thompson's 'Fourth Principle'*). 'Unless the Communist subversive political organization in the towns and villages is broken and eliminated, the insurgent guerrilla units will not be defeated';[39] otherwise as soon as government forces withdraw from an area the guerrillas will simply return (as they do repeatedly in South Vietnam) and the process will start all over again.

The fundamental importance of the village infrastructure to the insurgents was strikingly revealed during the Emergency in Malaya. By 1957, when heavy casualties had far outweighed recruitment, the number of fighting guerrillas was only 200 men, compared to 5,500 in 1951. But the strength of the political and supply organization was roughly maintained at the same level—it stood at 1,800 men compared to 2,500 in 1951. The fighting strength fell because General Templer (High Commissioner and Supreme Commander, 1952-54) 'so decimated the political and supply organization, particularly the M.C.P. [Malayan Communist Party] branches, that the fighting units had to be milked to keep the branches going'. By 1957, the M.C.P. was forced to employ 90 per cent of its men in branch duties.[40] The Party Central Committee had issued strict orders that while fighting platoons could be mobile, the M.C.P. branches *must* stay in their districts, whatever the pressure.[41] Only when the party branches were eliminated, through government 'priority operations' undertaken in concentrated strength after 'months of intelligence build up', could these areas be considered secure.[42]

Political achievements at the national level are needed to complement the patient work among the people undertaken at the village

* The others are: (1) A 'clear political aim: to establish and maintain a free, independent and united country. . . .' (2) Functioning in accordance with law. (3) Overall plan, including political, social, economic, administrative, police and other measures. (5) Security of base areas.

level.* When General Templer arrived in Malaya he brought with him the directive:

'The policy of the British Government is that Malaya should in due course become a fully self-governing nation. . . . To achieve a united Malayan nation there must be a common form of citizenship for all [i.e. Chinese and Indians] who regard the Federation or any part of it as their real home and the objective of their loyalty. . . . Malays must be encouraged and helped to play a full part in the economic life of the country, so that the present uneven economic balance may be redressed.'[43]

General Templer commented: 'I could win this war within three months if I could get two-thirds of the people on my side'.

The problem was not that of fighting a national movement, as in Indo-China or Vietnam, but of winning over the great majority of the people from a state of apathy, insecurity or discontent into positively supporting both the authorities and the new political leaders being thrown up among the Chinese and the Malays. Chinese loyal to Malaya were assured of their stake in the nation, while the Malays themselves were promised greater economic opportunities. Thus was formed the basis of the 'Alliance' between Tunku Abdul Rahman's United Malay National Organization and the Malayan Chinese Association (later to include the Malayan Indian Congress). At the 1955 elections the Alliance won all but one of the elected unofficial seats—i.e. just over half the total number of seats on the Legislative Council. The Alliance went on to win convincingly the 1959 general elections, the first to be held after Independence. A year later the Emergency was over.

INDONESIAN EXCEPTION

Armed struggle based on a supposedly revolutionary peasantry: this is the Mao-ist way now being advocated by Indonesian Communists in exile. But is this any more likely to succeed in Indonesia than Aidit's 'political' approach? This has yet to be proved. However, Aidit and his policies are certainly being made the scapegoat for the débâcle of 1965: the crushing of the Indonesian Communist Party (P.K.I.) and the mass slaughter of its followers; the extraordinary failure to mount any real resistance in the towns or to develop guerrilla warfare in the countryside.

* In the Philippines Magsaysay's crowning achievement was to guarantee free elections (in 1951) by using the Army to guard the polls. This finally convinced the people that 'the government was indeed their government, responsive to their will, effective in their interest. . . .' Valeriano and Bohannan, *op. cit.*, p. 240.

The 'Self-criticism' adopted by the P.K.I. 'Politburo' in 1966* blames Aidit's emphasis on 'peaceful' policies for not preparing the party or the masses to 'face the possibility of a non-peaceful road': 'The most striking proof of it was the grave tragedy which happened after the outbreak and the failure of the September 30th [1965] Movement. Within a very short space of time, the counter-revolution succeeded in massacring and arresting hundreds of thousands of Communists and non-Communist revolutionaries who found themselves in a passive position, paralysing the organization of the P.K.I. and the revolutionary mass organizations. Such a situation never would happen if the Party leadership did not deviate from the revolutionary road.'[44]

Paradoxically, the P.K.I. under Aidit, though given to revolutionary slogans (a weakness shared by others), was actually pursuing a reformist course: 'It gradually got bogged down in parliamentary and other forms of legal struggle', according to the 'Self-criticism'. Similarly, while violently hostile to 'Soviet revisionism' the P.K.I. itself followed revisionist practices from 1951 until the disastrous aftermath of the 1965 attempted *coup.*

There is no doubt that Aidit's policies deserved criticism, being tainted by the 'black line of Right opportunism'. The P.K.I. was the prisoner of the alliance with Sukarno and the 'national bourgeoisie' rather than the other way round. Not in control of the 'national united front'—Sukarno's *Nasakom* concept of nationalists, religious groups and Communists—but only a junior partner in it, the P.K.I. was subject to the 'penetration of the bourgeois ideology' both through its contacts with the dominant members and, more insidiously, 'through the bourgeoisification of Party cadres, especially the leadership, after the Party obtained certain positions in governmental and semi-governmental institutions'.[45] These were largely formal positions, lacking the substance of power. Thus Aidit and his deputy, Lukman, were made Ministers in 1962 (flanked by Army officers, nationalists and religious leaders) but they were Ministers without portfolio. They assumed part of the responsibility for government policy, which was Sukarno's intention, without being in a position to decide on policy. As the 'Self-criticism' argues, 'the Party lost its independence in the united front' and became an 'appendage of the bourgeoisie'.

Aidit's 'wrong political line'—the attempt to achieve socialism by peaceful means; by 'class collaboration' and not by class struggle

* Jusuf Adjitorop, who has been in Peking since 1964, is the only member of the Politburo to have escaped arrest or execution. Aidit was killed in Central Java in November 1965.

—was 'followed by the wrong line in the organizational field'. The creation of a 'mass Party' with 'as large a membership as possible' was basically intended to 'increase the influence of the Party in the united front with the national bourgeoisie'. As a result:

'The stress was no longer laid on the education and the training of Marxist Leninist cadres to prepare them for the revolution, for work among the peasants in order to establish revolutionary bases, but on the education of intellectuals to serve the needs of the work in the united front with the national bourgeoisie, and to supply cadres for the various positions in the state institutions that were obtained thanks to the co-operation with the national bourgeoisie. In the light of this policy, the slogan of 'total integration with the peasants' had become empty talk. What was being done in practice was to draw cadres from the countryside to the cities, from the regions to the centre, instead of sending the best cadres to work in the rural areas.'[46]

This is a damning indictment of Aidit's political course.. The consequence: a flabby, mass party, not a disciplined, revolutionary organization; leaders increasingly absorbed into the bourgois system and 'wallowing in the mire of opportunism'; advocating a peaceful, gradual approach, not stirring up the workers and the peasantry; collaborating in a bourgeois alliance led by Sukarno, not creating a 'revolutionary united front' led by the Party; finally, succumbing to the 'illusion among the people about bourgeois democracy' and not realizing the 'danger of attacks by the reactionaries who were constantly on the look for the chance to strike'. Hence, in the P.K.I. exiles' view, the Party's 'paralysis' when it came to a crisis.

This is largely true. The long period of revisionism from 1951 to 1965—had sapped the Party's revolutionary will. But what practical alternative did Aidit have? The brutal fact of the situation was that the Communists had been crushed in 1948 when they came out prematurely in revolt; that they were in a minority compared to nationalists and religious elements in Indonesia; and that the army leaders were not only in positions of power (though not the sole holders of power) under Sukarno, but were determined to use it to harass and if possible suppress their Communists rivals. Any resort to outright violence, as the 'Peking-P.K.I.' now advocates, would have been just as fatal as it turned out to be in 1965, but it would have been earlier.

Aidit's policy, in these circumstances, made sense: the gradual infiltration of political power—using the parliamentary process so long as this was possible; under Sukarno's patronage (since Sukarno needed the Communists as a counterbalance to army strength) when it was not; the organization of a base in the countryside, especially by supporting the landless and the poor peasantry; and the attempt to infiltrate the lower ranks—and subvert the higher ones—of the armed forces. This was a long-term programme which, if thoroughly prepared, promised the best chance of success when conditions were 'ripe': that is, when the work of organizing (and possibly arming) the peasantry and infiltrating the army was sufficiently advanced to have undermined the power and resistance of the anti-Communists. The weakness of Aidit's position was that several crucial factors were beyond his control—Sukarno's health, the attitude of the Army—and that, in addition, he increasingly came to believe in his own 'revolutionary' propaganda.

'The peasants,' Aidit announced after investigating the situation in Java early in 1964—a self-conscious emulation of Mao's famous 'investigation' in Hunan nearly forty years before—'are the source of food supplies for the revolution, the source of armed fighters for the revolution.'[47] Despite these fine phrases, the P.K.I. evidently neglected the organization of the peasants in favour of trying to influence the 'national front'; and it failed to take account of the fact that the peasants themselves, however poor and oppressed, 'are basically passive and conservative in their political outlook', neither militant nor revolutionary, as Donald Hindley observes in his study of the P.K.I. And he makes the point: 'Precisely by pursuing moderate non-revolutionary tactics since it gained control of P.K.I., the Aidit leadership has indeed succeeded in winning the support of a substantial segment of the peasantry. But by the same token it has failed so far to develop any significant degree of militancy among them.'[48]

Does the present reversal of Aidit's policies by the exile P.K.I.—the emphasis on 'armed agrarian revolution of the peasants under the leadership of the proletariat'—does this offer any better chance of success? The Politburo 'Statement' and 'Self-criticism', summarized by Peking, acknowledges that the 'way out' is not easy:

'At present, a severe white terror continues to reign over Indonesia. The Indonesian Communist Party is faced with an extremely difficult and complex task. The Party's struggle is undergoing a major change: a switch from the cities to the countryside, from peaceful struggle to armed struggle, from legal to illegal, from open to secret. For a Party whose main work over a long period of time was open and legal activity in the cities, this change is not easy indeed. It is bound to meet many difficulties. But the objective realities of the revolutionary situation compel people to make the change and compel them to learn armed struggle, and there is no alternative [but] for them to master it. . . .'[49]

There are two precedents for the success of armed struggle under such conditions: the guerrilla warfare conducted by the Indonesian Republicans against the Dutch; and Mao Tse-tung's protracted war against the Chiang Kai-shek régime after 1927. Indeed the latter has certain ominous parallels with the Indonesian situation. In both cases the Communists were the weaker partner in an alliance of convenience with the nationalists, led by an outstanding political personality—Sun Yat-sen and Sukarno. As the Communists developed their mass support, organizing trade unions and rousing the peasantry, so the military and the Right Wing nationalists became increasingly alarmed. The split widened with the removal of the great leader—the death of Dr Sun, the illness and (after 1965) displacement of President Sukarno. The Communists, who had been advocating moderate policies in order to maintain the alliance, were caught out by the violence and sweep of the military repression. Their political structure, their mass organizations and thousands of their supporters were destroyed. A few minor leaders escaped the massacre to organize guerrilla warfare among the desperate peasantry in remote areas. . . . But if history is to repeat itself, the military régime in Indonesia must (a) be incapable of solving the peasant problem—in both countries this centres on a limited amount of cultivable land for a dense population,* (b) permit soaring inflation to ruin the urban middle classes, (c) alienate, by its repressive measures, the political parties and the intellectuals, and finally (d) be subjected to—if the parallel is to be strictly observed—a devastating foreign occupation. This trend is discernible in Indonesia, but the conditions, as yet, are still far from fully realized.

Meanwhile present P.K.I. strategy is based on Mao's precept—shared by General Nasution, who has been both guerrilla and counter-guerrilla leader—that 'guerrilla warfare is the war of the weak against the strong'.[50] If the Indonesia Republicans could effectively harass the Dutch in this way—and ultimately win their objective cannot the P.K.I. expect to do the same against their military opponents? But, to quote Nasution again, 'the principal requirements for guerrilla warfare are a people who will give assistance, sufficient geographical room, and a war of long duration'.[51] A guerrilla movement has its base within the people: 'The people support, care for and conceal the guerrillas and spy for them,'[52] writes Nasution,

* Indonesia's population (1968) is some 112 million, two-thirds in Java. Java has a dense rural population of which about 50 per cent is landless (Hindley, *The Communist Party of Indonesia,* p. 5). Nearly 80 per cent of wet rice cultivators own less than half a hectare (just over one acre) of land (Bruce Grant, *Indonesia,* pp. 146-7). Redistribution, under the 1960 government land reforms, would only provide land for under 10 per cent of the landless.

drawing on his experience in fighting the Dutch. But, he points out: 'Only a strong ideology, a strong inner spirit, can make a guerrilla war explode. That spirit must be sufficiently courageous to tread the long and difficult road of suffering up to the moment when the enemy in power is finally defeated.'[53] Do the P.K.I. cadres have the 'devotion', their peasant followers the determination, to 'withstand difficult trials, such as enemy bombardments and all the cruel retaliatory measures to which the family is subjected, including the burning of villages and the torture of civilians'?[54]

Secondly, the terrain. As Nasution explains, it 'should consist of few highways, many mountains and hills, and if possible, forests and undergrowth'; these provide bases for the guerrillas which offset the 'enemy's superiority in technology and equipment'.[55] Confronting a powerful opponent, whose 'extremely intensive and active mopping up operations' were intended to 'break up and destroy' the guerrilla units and to demoralize their supporters—the aim of the Dutch in 1947 and 1948—the guerrillas made use of the favourable terrain 'to prevent annihilation in open battles, to retreat and hide'. As a result, 'the enemy was compelled to chase us until he became exhausted, the enemy was compelled to patrol everywhere'.[56] The Republican guerrillas had much popular support in the struggle for independence—Nasution indicates the widespread 'pockets' of rural resistance in Java.[57] But this would not necessary apply in a sectarian conflict. 'Significantly,' Hindley remarks, 'the few relatively extensive areas of mountains and forests, suitable for guerrilla warfare, are strongly *santri*' [the devout Muslims, opposed to the P.K.I.].[58] Outside Java there are rugged areas in abundance, but these are not, except in one or two cases, Communist strongholds.

'In order to fulfil the third condition, that of a long war,' Nasution continues, 'it is necessary that the people and the guerrilla army are truly determined and will patiently fight while suffering until victory is achieved.'[59] But as Nasution admits, the Republican guerrillas were only in the 'first stage' of the defensive phase and 'very seldom' could they destroy isolated enemy posts or patrols.[60] 'The reason that the Dutch were finally willing to withdraw their forces from Indonesia was not because they were defeated by our army, but because they were weakened and stymied by us so that there was no longer any hope for them to destroy the Republic. When their efforts to do this were frustrated, international pressure hastened the transfer of sovereignty [in 1949].'[61] 'Consequently, we did not have to prolong our guerrilla war. . . .'[62] Thus if the military struggle was important, it was the political context that proved decisive.

Such was the case—and to a still greater extent—in Algeria. The French army had actually broken up the 'National Liberation Front' into 'tiny ineffective bands' isolated from the people by the end of 1960, when French Government policy changed and de Gaulle agreed to Algeria's independence.[63] It seems unlikely that political or international pressures will operate to such effect in Indonesia, even if the P.K.I. suceeds in mounting its rural insurgency.

* * *

FAILURE:

United States in Indo-China

'The struggle in which the forces of the French Union and the Associated States [Cambodia, Laos and Vietnam] are engaged against the forces of Communist aggression in Indo-China is an integral part of the world-wide resistance by the Free Nations to Communist attempts at conquest and subversion'—United States-French joint communiqué, Washington, June 18, 1952.[64]

'The sending of men and arms across international boundaries and the direction of guerrilla war from outside a sovereign nation is aggression; and this is a fact which the whole international community must confront and whose consequent responsibilities it must accept. . . . The operation run from Hanoi against Viet-Nam is as clear a form of aggression as the violation of the 38th parallel by the North Korean armies in June 1950'—W. W. Rostow, Deputy Special Assistant to the President for National Security Affairs, June 28, 1961.[65]

'It is not a question of winning the South Vietnamese people's support for a government friendly to the United States, but of relieving them of the burden of North Vietnamese aggression and subversive insurgency'—Secretary of State Dean Rusk interviewed by *Dagens Nyheter,* Stockholm, July 2, 1967.[66]

Such is the melancholy process of misconception about Indo-China and its successor states—Laos, Cambodia, North and South Vietnam. Yet it is hard to tell whether the repeated emphasis on external aggression (as opposed to internal dissension) reflects a genuine belief that this is the case; or whether it is not largely an attempt to justify before American public opinion (and the 'international community') United States' participation in a conflict which, *pace* Rostow, is far from 'clear'.

For these successive statements of policy, which mark the deepening involvement of the United States in the Indo-China area, raise a number of important questions. Is it realistic to consider the situation of one small country, for example, in terms of a world-wide struggle for power? Does not concentration on the 'larger issues' entail a corresponding diminution of attention to the *specific* features of the country concerned—particularly if these do not conform to preconceived opinions? And if there is a growing divergence between the actual situation and what should be happening according to expectations, does this not eventually—when the discrepancy can no longer be ignored—create a crisis of policy? A crisis which may provoke far more dramatic and indeed agonizing reappraisals than if the particular situation had been faced and accurately assessed at the beginning?

Rostow's statement shares this element of unreality (though to a lesser degree than the French-US and Rusk statements). Rostow's view is that the 'sending of men and arms across international boundaries . . . is aggression'. Legally this is no doubt correct, but in practice it is almost meaningless unless we know the quantities and types of men and arms being sent and what *proportion* they bear to the forces already in conflict. If the amount is very small then perhaps 'interference' would be a better description than 'aggression'. The important point, which is obscured by emotional language, is that in 1961, and for several years thereafter, the North Vietnamese did not need to intervene with more than limited assistance: the Vietcong was doing well enough with its own forces recruited in the South and with the huge amount of weapons captured from army depots, police outposts and village supplies. Large-scale intervention by the North only began in 1965, the year the Americans themselves intervened in force.

To put it briefly, it is quite impossible to carry on for years an artificially incited insurgency. Protracted resistance against heavy odds in troops and equipment depends on indigenous support. The greater this support—and the weaker the machinery of government (this was and is the case in South Vietnam)—the less the need for external involvement. Conversely, the smaller the opposition and the more effective the government, the less the need for any form of Western assistance. To repeat: there was no need for Soviet intervention in China, for Chinese intervention (other than in training and equipment) in Indo-China and similarly for North Vietnamese intervention, until 1965, in South Vietnam. To speak of 'aggression' —the way the Kuomintang blamed 'Soviet aggression' in China or the Americans blamed 'Communist aggression' in Laos, Guatemala, Cuba and other trouble spots—is more than irrelevant, it is harmful. For it distracts attention, sometimes deliberately, sometimes unconsciously, from the real state of affairs. It is hard to know which is worse.

This attitude is revealed in the persistent attempts made during the Dulles era and revived as a result of the present *embroglio* in Vietnam to 'internationalize' the problem. The activities of every country and government were, and are now again, seen in terms of the 'world-wide struggle' between freedom and Communism. (Now, of course, it is Chinese rather than Soviet Communism.) According to President Eisenhower's (1953) Committee on International Information Activities, 'every significant act of virtually every department and agency of Government has its effect, either positively or negatively, in the global struggle for freedom'.[67] In the Far East 'the lines of the free world-Communism struggle are more clearly drawn . . .', stated a 1956 'Review of United States Policy',[68] and Taiwan was of 'key importance in the free world's island chain. . . .'[69] The Thai people were warned against Chinese attempts to 'overthrow their free government'[70] [the military had been in control since the 1947 *coup*]; however, 'the leaders of Free China and Free Korea . . . have bent every effort to build up their military strength'. In 1955 the only hope of survival for the 'Free Vietnamese' seems 'to be on a basis of continuing resistance to all forms of Communist power. . . .'[71] And in Dulles's own 'Threat of a Red Asia' speech of March 1954, 'if the Communist forces won uncontested control over Indo-China, or any substantial part thereof, they would surely resume the same pattern of aggression against other free peoples in the area'.[72] This is strikingly reminiscent of recent statements by President Johnson and Dean Rusk.

The same argument is reflected in Rostow's view that the 'whole international community' must 'confront' the fact of Hanoi 'sending men and arms' to the South and accept its 'consequent responsibilities'. Does this mean that it should send armed contingents to drive back the invaders, since North Vietnam's activities are 'as clear a form of aggression' as North Korea's 'violation' of the parallel? In that case, similar action would have to be taken against many countries of the 'free world' which are carrying on Hanoi's type of operation against their neighbours. Or does it only apply to Communists?

POST-WAR POLICY

Despite Dulles's attempt to seize the 'initiative'[73] in world affairs, the tendency of American foreign policy—as of most foreign policies—has been to react to events. Reaction to Soviet pressure on Europe brought forth the extremely successful countermeasures of the Truman era, notably the European Recovery Programme and the formation of the North Atlantic Treaty Organization. Reaction to the Soviet-inspired invasion of Korea also stimulated a series of measures, effective in halting aggression but far less so in dealing with the problem—and the consequences—of Chinese intervention. Least successful of all was the reaction to French defeat in Indo-China. The instrument with which Dulles hoped to gain the initiative —'massive retaliatory power' to deter aggression—could not be used in Indo-China. But the state of alarm engendered by Communist success in this area blinded Washington both to the specific conditions which had made this possible and to the general lack of success of Communist 'expansion' elsewhere.

As a result of the 'loss' of China and the conviction that stopping the Communists, first in Laos and then in Vietnam, was vital to America's security, there has been a marked shift in US foreign policy, away from Europe and towards Asia. During the Truman-Acheson era, America's main concern was to prevent the imminent economic collapse of Western Europe, which would render it an easy prey to Soviet pressure. Should this happen, in Acheson's words, 'the very survival of the United States would be more seriously at stake than at any other time in its history'.[74] Asian affairs were peripheral. Nationalist China was left to succumb to its own internal weaknesses (and to Communist assaults), while no figure of any influence in America, Republican or Democrat, was prepared to commit US troops to 'save' the foundering régime.

During the Eisenhower-Dulles era, Asian and European affairs were of equal concern. Agonizing reappraisal of European defence measures (after France's rejection of the integrated European army) was balanced by the 'deadly serious threat' of Communist 'encirclement' of the US which Dulles found particularly alarming in Asia and the Middle East.[75] By the end of this period, Laos—an 'outpost of the free world'[76]—was said to be almost as vital to US security as Berlin. After President Kennedy's brief interlude, which encompassed a political solution for Laos by international agreement, a climactic test of will with the Russians over the missiles in Cuba, renewed efforts at *rapprochement* with Moscow and the first direct involvement in the Vietnam crisis, the gloom deepened. Confronted with a desperate situation in South Vietnam the Johnson Administration, after first attempting to compel Hanoi to negotiate, intervened in massive strength. The inter-linked problem—bombing in the North, underpinning the South—came to absorb Washington's energies to the detriment of almost every other consideration.

The first stages in the US shift towards Asia, formally denoted by the change-over in 1953 to a Republican Administration, had actually been set in motion as a result of Stalin's 'invasion by proxy' of South Korea, nearly three years before. 'Communist imperialism' had turned, in Truman's words, 'from the familiar tactics of infiltration and subversion to a brutal attack.'[77] This came as all the greater a shock since the Truman Administration was convinced, early in 1950, that the 'greatest danger has receded—the possibility which faced us three years ago that most of Europe and the Mediterranean area might collapse under Soviet pressure'.[78] This hard-earned sense of relief was shattered by the North Korean attack. America's response was to insist on 'rapid building up of military strength at home and among our allies . . . [since] the period of greatest danger is before us'.[79] In December 1950 the President feared that Chinese intervention in Korea showed that the 'Communists . . . are now willing to push the world to the brink of a general war to get what they want'.[80] He annnounced that US armed forces, which in June 1950 were 1½ million men, had reached 2½ million and would be increased to nearly 3½ million.[81] It was decided, on the one hand, that 'German resources and manpower' were needed to contribute to Western Europe's defence;[82] on the other, that a peace treaty should be signed with Japan to complete 'special defence arrangements'.[83] By this time—late 1951—danger signs of 'further Communist aggression' were seen in Indo-China and Burma.[84]

'The same menace—the menace of Communist aggression—threatens Europe as well as Asia,' declared President Truman in December 1950. But he believed that the 'free nations' could present a common front.[85] Collective security methods, which had served so well in Europe, were to be employed by the Republican Administration in Asia. Ironically, while the Republicans were sweeping into power on a wave of anti-Communist militancy both at home and abroad, the target of their opposition, the Soviet Union, was already switching, even before the death of Stalin, from using brutal pressure and force to the pursuit of economic and political influence and 'friendship' instead. Thus the Republican drive to build up collective security in Asia—similar to that achieved in Europe and equally motivated by fear of Communist aggression—tended to confront an Asian opinion which was mostly indifferent or hostile. The concept of the 'free nations' of Western Europe was something of a reality on which to base an alliance. Unfortunately for the Republicans the free nations of Asia—those which had adopted and were carrying on democratic processes—were deeply suspicious of any attempt to make them take sides in the cold war. Those whom the Republicans called 'free' were almost invariably countries whose governments were least representative (the Philippines under Magsaysay was a notable exception) and for this very reason—from fear of popular opposition, whether or not the Communists were 'exploiting' it—chose to range themselves with the United

States. The protection they sought was as much internal—against the forces of change—as external. But to the Republicans such considerations were irrelevant in face of the overwhelming threat of Communism.

There were three main drawbacks to this attitude. First, it failed to take sufficiently into account the instability of narrowly-based autocratic régimes. Second, and following from this, it misconceived the situation: the chief danger to these régimes turned out to be—naturally enough—internal dissidence or subversion and not external aggression. And third, in these changed circumstances, the principal American means to preserve security—reliance on a military pact to deter aggression—was unsuited to the problem. Moreover Dulles, although far more alarmed than his predecessors about Communist expansion in Asia, wanted security on the cheap. If America's allies would provide the manpower, this would avoid the costly commitment of US combat forces which had taken place in Korea. 'It is not sound strategy,' Dulles argued in January 1954, 'permanently to commit United States land forces to Asia to a degree that leaves us no strategic reserves.' The Dulles solution was to *reinforce* local—and later collective—defence 'by the further deterrent of massive retaliatory power . . . able to respond vigorously [to aggression] at places and with means of its own choosing'. He also claimed, which was important to an economy-minded Congress, that the nuclear deterrent provided 'more basic security at less cost'.[86]

Unfortunately for the new doctrine the Asian situation did not develop along Korean-type lines. Although Dulles wished to 'respond vigorously' on behalf of the French during the seige of Dien Bien Phu—because 'the imposition on South East Asia of the political system of Communist Russia and its Chinese Communist ally, by whatever means, would be a grave threat to the whole free community'[87]—he was not supported either by his President or his allies. Belatedly, as the Geneva Conference was meeting on Indo-China, he recognized that the situation was 'not that of open military aggression by the Chinese Communist régime' which could call for the use of a massive deterrent. Rather it was a problem of restoring 'tranquility' in an area where 'disturbances are fomented from Communist China', but there was 'no open invasion'. And 'this task of pacification cannot be successfully met merely by unilateral armed intervention'.[88]*

* The Chairman of the US Joint Chiefs of Staff, Admiral Radford, argued that intervention to meet the threat was preferable to a negotiated 'surrender'. But General Ridgway, the Army Chief of Staff, believed that intervention could not succeed without committing ground troops—the minimum being ten divisions, or more than required in Korea. 'The military saw the appal-

The collective security system, patched up in South East Asia after 1954—Britain's *quid pro quo* to Dulles for accepting, however reluctantly, negotiations on Indo-China—may well have served its purpose in deterring 'overt military aggression'. But it was unable to cope with—indeed for a long time unable to recognize—the threat posed by political instability and internal unrest. And even though Dulles passed on, his rigid attitude to Communism left its mark. The logic of his commitment to prevent the tide of Communism from sweeping over Asia left his successors, in a deteriorating position, with little choice. When a 'free' government found itself unable to cope with its own internal problems the United States felt obliged to intervene—risking being embroiled, by definition, in an unfavourable situation—or else to back down, with consequent loss of face, and indeed, so it was believed, with danger to its own security. Both Kennedy over Laos and Truman over Nationalist China opted for the lesser evil—but the Democratic 'betrayal' of 'free China' itself created a backlash of American opinion, which clamoured for more effective, and hence more militant, action against Communism.

The hysterical attitude exemplified by the Republican Presidential campaign platform of 1952—

> 'We shall again make liberty into a beacon light of hope . . . it will mark the end of the negative, futile and immoral [Democratic] policy of "containment" [of Communism] which abandons countless human beings to a despotism and godless terrorism. . . .'[89]

exerted a baleful influence throughout the Dulles era. For it prevented the Republicans from assessing dispassionately the possible 'appeals' of Communism to Asians and from understanding the type of environment in which Communist methods and organizations could function to advantage. Instead, the new US Administration chose to confront the 'evil' force of monolithic Communism—'controlling all life and resources found between the Elbe and the Chinese sea', bent on world domination[90]—and believed that all right-minded peoples and nations must do likewise. Thus it failed to comprehend the reasoning of Governor Stevenson, the defeated Democratic Presidential candidate: 'When we think of Communism, we think of what we are going to lose. When many of the Asian peoples think of Communism, they think of what they are going to gain—especially if they believe they have nothing to lose.'[91]

ling prospect that the United States would either become bogged down in a jungle war that had little prospect of decisively affecting world Communist power' or be plunged into a full-scale war involving China: G. Arthur Dommen, *Conflict in Laos* (Pall Mall, 1966), p. 49. There was the same 'appalling prospect' ten years later. . . .

To Dulles, on the contrary, Communism was a 'gigantic conspiracy designed to overthrow our government by violence'.[92] This was a reflection of the 1950 US Congress resolution on internal security (passed by a two-thirds majority over Truman's veto):

'There exists a world Communist movement which in its origins, its development and its present practice, is a world-wide revolutionary movement whose purpose it is, by treachery, deceit, infiltration into other groups (governmental or otherwise), espionage, sabotage, terrorism, and any other means deemed necessary, to establish a Communist totalitarian dictatorship in the countries throughout the world through the medium of a world-wide Communist organization.'[93]

According to these views, the spread of Communism in the 'free' world could only be the result of 'artificial' incitement, force or fraud. Dulles himself spoke of a 'Bolshevik organization' working in every free country of the world to 'gain political control so as to add that country to the list of those who are subject to the will of international Communism'.[94] Moscow's world strategy, Dulles warned in his first speech as Secretary of State, was making 'very great progress'. The object was to 'encircle' the United States by picking up 'one country after another by getting control of its government, by political warfare and indirect aggression'. Already one-third of the peoples of the world were under 'complete domination'; and the (population) odds against America were seven to one.

This alarming picture of the forces of good and evil locked in global conflict—incidentally the way the Communists also saw the situation—bore little resemblance to reality. In Asia, at least, it would be difficult to demonstrate which leaders were 'good'—Chiang Kai-shek? Syngman Rhee?—if not which were 'bad'. Moreover the undifferentiated contrast between 'freedom' on the one hand and 'slavery' on the other (which had some point in North America and Western Europe, but was misleading, if not meaningless elsewhere) served to obscure two significant aspects of Asian insurgencies. These were applicable to China and Indo-China in the past and to Laos and Vietnam in the future. First, the great majority of the insurgents are not Communists (even if their leaders are). And second, they are fighting for popular, democratic reforms—land for the tiller, freedom from colonial rule, properly chosen representatives. It is a hard fact, but it must be faced, that in a number of Asian countries the Communists—whatever their ulterior motives—are closer to the peasants, who comprise after all the overwhelming majority of the population, than are the representatives or officials of an urban-based régime.

The unhappy paradox of the Dulles era is that those who were least democratic in Asia were considered the best allies of the United States. But, except where unconcealed abuses and blatant trickery were connived at, for the sake of larger ends, this attitude seems more the result of ignorance and illusion than of a deliberate attempt to deceive. President Eisenhower's Committee on Information Advisory Activities, for example, testified in 1953 to America's 'important advantages in the world conflict', which should receive greater attention. There were 'fundamental beliefs and values' shared by the people of America with the millions of others 'we are attempting to win to our side'. They included: 'belief in God, belief in individual and national freedom, belief in the right to ownership of property and a decent standard of living. . . .' Also common humanity, a peaceful world and the United Nations.[95] Apart from the fact that South East Asian Buddhists do not believe in God, the question of individual freedom and ownership of property—not to speak of a decent living—was precisely what was at issue between many of the Asian peoples 'to be won over' and their governments, backed by the United States.

Excessive fear of Communism and of strategic consequences of Communist takeovers undoubtedly contributed to Washington's distressing failure to distinguish between formal professions of democracy and freedom by anti-Communist leaders and the reality only too often of inequitable societies. As a result the US tended to become involved in disturbing situations which it could have avoided —or withdrawn from in good time—had it adopted a calmer and more rational approach. This was the advice of Dean Acheson in 1951, which was scorned by his successors as 'appeasement':

To avoid impatience; to realize that problems will be 'with us for a very long time'. The object is not to remove problems, which are not removable, but to reduce them to manageable proportions.

'To avoid over-dramatizing any particular problem or over-emphasizing it. That is always our danger.' Not to force a show-down—nor to let our opponents do so. In fact, a 'proper sense of proportion about the problems and difficulties which come before us'.

The 'need to match our strength with the interests which we must defend'. A balance between commitments and capabilities.

Not to rely solely on governments. 'The idea that we can make arrangements with this, that or the other government, without regard to popular support founded on free consent would all too probably involve us in excessively brittle alliances.'[96]

As Acheson warned, so it happened. Obsessed by the menace of Communism, US official efforts to repel it in Asian countries tended to go through three—or, in bad cases, four—successive stages. First was the decision to intervene, usually with varying degrees of economic and military assistance. Second came the period of adjustment between donor and client. Third, and overlapping the second, was the stage of appraisal and reappraisal, depending on the trend towards stability or instability. And fourth, in the event of deterioration, came the brutal choice between commitment to underpin a failing régime or extrication from an unsatisfactory and perhaps irredeemable position.

Much of the responsibility for America's 'physical' intervention in Asia, the Middle East or Latin America, was, moreover, simply the result of a misreading of Communist intentions and capabilities. Thus, even though the Soviet leaders had turned away from the aggressive posture of post-war Stalinism in favour of a more subtle and—as far as Afro-Asia was concerned—more effective policy of seeking to win over newly independent nations by friendship, trade and aid, the Republican Administration continued to act as if it were still fighting the cold war. To Eisenhower, as late as April 1959, 'the first and most important fact is the implacable and frequently expressed purpose of imperialistic Communism to promote world revolution, destroy freedom and communize the world'. And, he added, 'since the Communist target is the world, every nation is comprehended in their campaign for domination.'[97] Now, on this occasion, the President was trying to whip up domestic support for the US Mutual Security Aid programme by underlining the threat to America if money were not forthcoming to counter it. But the constant repetition throughout the 1950s of the 'Communist menace', its diabolical skill in manoeuvre and its apocalyptic aims, without serious qualification or interpretation, clearly came strongly to influence if not to dominate the formulation of US policy and, what is perhaps more important, US reaction to (presumed) Soviet policy.

Thus Dulles himself emphasized the danger to the peace and security of 'all American nations' if 'international Communism should gain control of the political institutions of any one of them'. This was to justify what was later revealed to be covert US intervention to overthrow a pro-Communist régime in Guatemala. In November 1954 Dulles claimed that 'international Communism had in fact got control of the government', but the 'Guatemalan people themselves backed loyal elements who cut out the cancer of Communism. The Communist-directed President [Arbenz] of Guatemala ignominiously fled, and the leader of the liberation movement is now the President of Guatemala.'[98]

This was surely a dangerous argument to use. To approve of a 'liberation movement' overthrowing the legitimate government of a country—let alone to finance and direct this movement, as the US

Central Intelligence Agency is reported to have done*—was later to backfire against America. What else is North Vietnam doing, although like the US Government it does not openly acknowledge this, in directing and supporting the National Liberation Front of South Vietnam? Moreover Dulles's attempt to justify America's reaction to Communism in Latin America could also be used to explain the Chinese reaction to US intervention in South East Asia. As Dulles put it, in a nation-wide radio and television address in June 1954, 'the master plan of international Communism is to gain a solid political base in this [Western] hemisphere, a base that can be used to extend Communist penetration to the other American governments. . . . If world Communism captures any American State, however small, a new and perilous front is established which will increase the danger to the entire free world.' It was in response to this threat that 'patriots arose in Guatemala to challenge the Communist leadership—and to change it'.[99]

Now as China and North Vietnam observed the growth of American influence in Laos in the late 1950s—with the same intermingling of ideological and strategic fears as the Americans watched the growth of Communist influence in Guatemala—they, too, reacted against what they called the US 'blueprint' in South East Asia, using Laos as a 'springboard for aggression'. And they also had 'patriots' available—in fact the Pathet Lao or 'Lao Patriots' —who successfully arose to 'challenge' the country's leadership.

CONFUSION IN LAOS

US intervention was effective in Guatemala. It was not effective in Laos. For American assistance, as Acheson recognized, could only be the 'missing component' in a situation which otherwise could be solved. The US itself could not furnish these other components: 'it cannot furnish determination, it cannot furnish the will, and it cannot furnish the loyalty of a people to its government. But if the will and if the determination exists and if the people are behind their government, then, and not always then, is there a very good chance. In that situation, American help can be effective. . . .'[100] In Laos, America's 'forward policy' went against the grain. The US opposed Prince Souvanna Phouma's attempts in 1956 and 1957 to live up to the

* Former President Eisenhower revealed on June 10, 1963: 'There was one time when we had a very desperate situation, or we thought it was at least, in Central America, and we had to get rid of a Communist Government which had taken over, and our early efforts were defeated by a bad accident and we had to help, send some help right away.' (David Wise and T. B. Ross, *The Invisible Government* [C.I.A.], Random House 1964), p. 166. (see also pp. 165-183).

spirit of the 1954 Geneva Agreements—by bringing in neutralists and pro-Communists (Pathet Lao) into a coalition government with the conservatives and by assuring China and North Vietnam that Laos would not be used as a base against them.[101] Washington feared the 'crumbling' effects of neutralism in Laos and on its 'committed' neighbour, South Vietnam. To prevent this, the US Administration covertly supported a vigorous anti-Communist movement.

Souvanna Phouma later protested that the US 'did everything possible to prevent the integration of the Pathet Lao with the government in 1957 and when, despite their efforts, I succeeded, the United States continued to sabotage me'. He said that Washington was responsible for his resignation as Prime Minister in 1958 and had 'planted the seeds for destruction' when it forced his successor, Phoui Sananikone, to be pro-West and strongly anti-Communist.[102] Phoui dismissed the Pathet Lao representatives from the government and inaugurated 'mopping up operations' against its supporters, notably in the tribal areas near North Vietnam. (Shaken by the reaction of Pathet Lao guerrillas in 1959 and the threat of intervention by North Vietnam, Phoui, at the prompting of the United Nations' Secretary-General, Dag Hammarskjold, proposed a return to neutralism. So he, too, was overthrown at the end of 1959.)

Washington's persistence in an anti-Communist course in Laos was marked by the emergence to power of the Right Wing 'strong man' General Phoumi Nosavan in 1959, his clash with the Neutralist Commander Kong Lae in 1960 and the disastrous defeats suffered by Phoumi's forces in 1961 and 1962. The US forward policy—and its failure—was the result of an extraordinary misconception of the importance of the country. 'The cold war is turning hot in the tiny Kingdom of Laos, strategic heart of South East Asia,' insisted a report by the United Press International as early as August 7, 1959. The US Administration saw the situation in Laos as part of the Communist drive for world domination: 'Laos Key to Defence of South East Asia' as the *New York Times* put it. The fall of Laos 'would have incalculable consequences, both psychological and strategic', US officials were reported as saying. 'It would give the Communists direct access to Thailand and Cambodia across an indefensible frontier, allow them to flank South Vietnam and possibly open the way to the rest of South East Asia.'[103] The 'international Communist conspiracy' theory was given free rein. The 'hand of Peiping' was visible, warned the US Assistant Secretary of State for Far Eastern Affairs, Walter S. Robertson, in September 1959.*

* Robertson's attitude, as Eden discovered at Geneva, was 'so emotional as to be impervious to argument or indeed to facts . . .'. *Full Circle, The Memoirs of Sir Anthony Eden* (Cassell, 1960), p. 113.

'The sudden attacks in Laos last month came on the heels of a lengthy visit to Communist China by Ho Chi Minh, Chief of the North Vietnamese régime.'[104] The US State Department 'demonstrated' evidence of 'outside Communist intervention' in this manner:

'(1) the assistance evidently being received by the Communist forces within Laos, including supplies and military weapons . . .
(2) the false—and ridiculous—Communist propaganda emanating simultaneously from Hanoi, Peiping and Moscow, to the effect that the Lao Government has been instigated by the United States to stir up a civil war within its boundaries;
(3) the continuing flow from Moscow, Peiping and Hanoi, of propaganda and false information about the situation in Laos aimed at confusing world opinion and stating that the United States is using Laos as a military base; and
(4) the fact that the military outbreak in Laos has followed conferences in Moscow and Peiping between Ho Chi Minh and Soviet and Chinese Communist leaders and also conferences in Moscow between two members of the north Vietnam Politburo and Deputy Prime Minister Anastas Mikoyan. . . .'[105]

To take the second and third points first: Phoui Sananikone's crack-down on pro-Communist elements, given the fact that until recently they were members (even if obstructive ones) of the coalition government of Laos, did suggest a 'civil war' approach. Moreover, Joseph Alsop, a well informed observer with close contacts in the US State Department and Pentagon at this period, commented with obvious approval that 'the American Government did everything possible to bring the [Phoui] Sananikone government into being. . . . The commitment [to defend Laos against Communist aggression] was then greatly deepened when American influence was also used to encourage the anti-Communist campaign rapidly launched by Prime Minister Sananikone.' The arrest of leading Communists and the summary execution of the 'more flagrant terrorists' in the provinces, Alsop went on, were measures 'taken with explicit American approval'.[106] And in a further report, he added: almost all these actions were taken with American approval and 'often as a result of American suggestions'.[107] A statement by Phoui Sananikone suggests that the 'rebels' may have had some cause for apprehension of Lao Government policy:

'Many inhabitants of the provinces on the northern border, especially former members of the Pathet Lao forces, have, since a group of the former Pathet Lao forces fled to join North Vietnam and later attacked our military posts and violated our territory, fled to the forest. Some have joined the rebels. It is believed that they have done so because they are ill-informed about the situation of the Kingdom and the Government's great concern for the people's welfare and because they blindly believe the propaganda of Hanoi and Peking radios and of the rebels. They fear that the authorities might arrest them if they stay at home. [Prince Souphanouvong and fifteen other former Pathet Lao leaders in Vientiane had been arrested at the end of July.] The Government greatly regrets this. The police and the army will arrest no one who is innocent. . . .'[108]

The 'main objective' of the Pathet Lao 'offensive', the Royal Lao Army General Staff reported on August 20, 1959, was actually to recapture its old base—the two provinces of Sam Neua and Phong Saly, adjoining North Vietnam—in order to 'force a return' of the International Control Commission for Laos, set up (as also for Vietnam) according to the 1954 Geneva Agreements. This was, of course, basically a political manoeuvre. In fact the Pathet Lao—or rather its newly formed party organization, the Neo Lao Hak Xat—*preferred a political approach,* since it stood more chance of coming to power in this way than by fighting. Fear of the consequences of the electoral success of the N.L.H.X. in May 1958[109] had prompted the Phoui Government, with American backing, to dismiss the Pathet Lao from the coalition; and it rejected Souvanna Phouma's conciliatory policy in favour of a 'hard line' against Communism.[110] Thus it was the Laotian Government, and not the Pathet Lao, which had excluded a political solution. It was in these circumstances that the Chinese and North Vietnamese urged the return of the International Control Commission (actually suspended by Souvanna Phouma before his fall) in order to ensure a measure of international protection for the supporters of the outcast Pathet Lao.

During the September 1959 'crisis'—the result of guerrilla fighting between Pathet Lao and Government forces*—the Soviet Union proposed the immediate recall of the Geneva Conference. But the US State Department turned this down, claiming that settlement of unrest in Laos 'is not to be found in international conferences but in the cessation of intervention and subversion of the Kingdom of Laos'.

* The Pathet Lao drew most of its support from the mountainous tribal areas (especially in regions near North Vietnam, partly because of the more conciliatory Communist policy towards minorities) while the Government was supported by the Lao people (not quite half the two or three million total population of Laos) living in the lowlands and valleys. See Hugh Toye, *Laos: Buffer State or Battleground* (Oxford Univ. Press, 1968), pp. xv, 116-17, 164.

(Two years later, when government forces were being defeated in Laos, Washington was to change its mind about the value of international conferences; there was a similar change of mind, after 1965, about negotiations on Vietnam.) The reason advanced by the State Department for its negative attitude was that a new Geneva Conference would 'inevitably suggest to the Royal Lao Government the imposition of new disabilities and new external interferences'. Precisely. For it would mean a return to the prohibition on reprisals and to the participation of 'all citizens' in the national community, through general elections, affirmed by the Governments of Laos and Cambodia in the Final Declaration of the 1954 Geneva Conference.[111] But the State Department saw no reason why the 'Lao Communists and their outside supporters' should further profit 'through the disruptive influences' of a new Geneva Conference.[112]

If the situation in Laos in 1959 was confusing, it was to become even more tangled in 1960. This was a result of the polarization of internal forces and the deepening involvement of both Russians and Americans, bringing the country to the verge of an international conflict. For although Washington had 'no doubt', in the words of a State Department official, that 'aggression had been taking place [in Laos] in a now-familiar pattern',[113] it was not quite as simple as that. As the perceptive American reporter Arthur Dommen noted, the initial American build-up in Laos was the result of a policy decision by the State Department contrary to the military advice of the US Joint Chiefs of Staff. Instead of reducing the Lao territorial Army from its wartime strength of 15,000 men to the level needed for routine internal policing, as the Joint Chiefs advised, the Army was actually increased in 1956 to 25,000 men[114] and three years later, to 29,000. To strengthen the Lao Army in its task of 'containment' of Communism, Dommen points out, 'the State Department set up an American military mission in disguise in Vientiane', known as the Programs Evaluation Office, attached to the US [aid] Operations Mission. The P.E.O. was headed by a US Army General, whose presence only became known in 1961, and its members were officially described as 'technicians'.[115] The 'P.E.O. not only controlled the bulk of the aid funds spent in Laos,' Dommen adds, 'but also possessed its exclusive channel of communication to Washington, through the Commander in Chief, Pacific Forces . . . and the Defence Department.'[116]

For a time all went well, until Kong Lae's neutralist *coup* of August 1960 threw into utter confusion the policy of building up Laos into an anti-Communist bastion. For the young paratroop captain turned on the 'unscrupulous' leaders who he said had been exploiting the struggle against Communism in Laos as a 'pretext for their own advantage'. 'Money which should have been spent on economic and social improvements has gone instead to pay for wars, and to a minority group of politicians. . . . If we adopt neutrality as declared to the Parliament . . . but never implemented, we shall certainly achieve peace,' Kong Lae declared. 'Otherwise we shall fall right in the middle of the cold war between two sides and find that we are fighting among ourselves as is happening now. . . .'[117]

The Americans were in a dilemma. Prince Souvanna Phouma had been re-appointed Prime Minister—to work for neutrality, a coalition government and negotiations with the Pathet Lao—a solution that Washington bitterly opposed. But the Prince's rival, and butt of Kong Lae's charges, General Phoumi Nosavan, echoed American (and Thai) policy when he accused the Prime Minister of exposing Laos to 'Communist aggression'. Phoumi then went into open rebellion, setting up his own 'revolutionary committee' to 'seize power and abrogate all constitutional rights of the present Government'.[118] The US Embassy in Laos decided to observe 'strict neutrality' and continued to act as paymaster to both parties. But since nearly all US aid went to the army and as most of the army was under Phoumi's control, this was rather one-sided. Moreover, while Washington still claimed to be striving for 'unity' in Laos it meant unity against the Communists. For Souvanna Phouma, however, unity meant an end to the civil war.

Divergent views within the various American agencies reflected the differences within Laos. The American Ambassador in Vientiane proposed that the US should support the Souvanna Phouma Government. The State Department 'felt that Kong Lae should be gotten rid of, but it had no means to achieve this'. And the Pentagon and C.I.A., 'consistent with their past efforts in Laos and with their interpretation of the current situation', immediately set to work to build up General Phoumi.[119] An agreement was reached with Souvanna Phouma that US military aid to General Phoumi would only be used against the Pathet Lao.[120] This did not deter Phoumi. In December 1960, heavily armed with American tanks and artillery, he forced his way into Vientiane. Souvanna Phouma fled to Cambodia, leaving behind one of his senior Ministers who made a deal with the Russians: the latter would arm and supply joint Pathet Lao-Neutralist resistance to Phoumi's forces.[121] The Soviet massive airlift in support of the 'legal' government of Laos—the Communist and non-aligned countries still recognized Souvanna Phouma—now matched American assistance to Phoumi, who set up his own government under a figure-head, Prince Boun Oum. Soon after the formation of the Right Wing government, combined Pathet Lao and Neutralist forces seized the heavily fortified Plain of Jars, the 'most important military complex in northern Laos'.[122] Phoumi's 'offensive' had crumbled.

In Washington the Republican Administration was at its last gasp. Faced with the disastrous consequences of its 'forward policy' in Laos all the State Department could do was to denounce, in familiar terms, 'Communist intervention . . . [and] determination to take over the country in line with the Communists' well-known and indeed oft-stated objective of ultimate global domination. . . .'[123] The Department continued to trot out a version of events in Laos made up of evasions and half-truths:

Despite Communist actions, 'Laos had been making *steady progress* in welding itself together as a nation'. The Lao Army was achieving a *capability* 'adequate to deal with domestic Communist guerrillas'. Successive governments from 1958 on had 'issued repeated statements' of the *intention* to follow a neutralist policy. The crisis in 1959 was the result of the Communists' 'evident' conclusion that opportunities to gain control of Laos by subversion, propaganda and small-scale guerrilla activity 'were being foreclosed by the country's increasing *stability*'. This 'progress towards domestic stability and tranquillity continued until August 9, 1960, when the Kong Lae *coup* plunged the country into chaos'. Initial doubts about Kong Lae's 'inspiration for action' were soon *'dispelled'* by his 'clandestine co-operation with foreign Communist governments'. 'This *series of events* [not retailed] culminated in the abandonment of the capital by the Prime Minister [Souvanna Phouma].' 'If Laos should be seized by the Communists, the effects would be far-reaching. . . .'[124]

The Kennedy Administration brushed aside this musty apologia for an abortive policy. Laos, President Kennedy declared, was the 'most immediate problem' he faced on taking office. He appealed to the Communists to agree to constructive negotiations—internationally as well as among the leaders of Laos—to help the country back to 'independence and genuine neutrality'. What we want 'is a truly neutral government, not a cold-war pawn'; a 'settlement concluded at the conference table, not on the battle-field'.[125] Two months later, in June 1961, Kennedy reported the 'sombre mood' of his famous meeting with Khruschev in Vienna. The one area which afforded some immediate prospect of accord was Laos. Both sides, he said, recognized the need to 'reduce the dangers' in the situation and endorsed the concept of a neutral and independent Laos.[126] This sensible agreement, formalized at the 1961-62 Genva Conference on Laos, averted the danger of an international conflict over Laos.

Both Russia and America realized that the land-locked, mountainous, sparsely populated country was not worth a war. They also agreed that neutrality offered Laos the best prospect of living in peace with its neighbours. What other choice was open?

Washington's 'abandonment' of Laos however, brought bitter reproaches from American advocates of a 'hard' line towards Communism. 'It is wrong to say that the [US] military do not want to fight in Laos,' a 'wise retired Army General of vast renown' told an American reporter in June 1962. 'They know in their minds that Laos is geographically vital and that we must fight rather than give up.' According to the General, 'it is doubtful that America would need more than two divisions in Laos, properly, gradually, perhaps stealthily, deployed. . . .'[127] What these divisions were supposed to do in Laos remains a mystery. Obviously they could control most of the little towns, villages and rice lands—at least in the day time—as the French did in Indo-China. But could they pursue the guerrillas into the mountains—and most of Laos is mountainous—find and defeat them and then prevent further infiltration? And would North Vietnam and China, with plenty of tribal warriors ideally suited for these conditions, stand idly by? If it took some 40,000 British and Gurkha troops—and 70,000 police—twelve years to drive 8,000 Communist terrorists out of Malaya—a country with an efficient administration, good system of communications and completely separated from any Communist state—how long would it take American troops, even with the doubtful aid of Phoumi, to pacify Laos? The idea of military intervention was an emotional response to an admittedly frustrating situation, but it never really faced the problem.

BACKING INTO VIETNAM

(1) *Commitment and . . .*

If, in Laos, US policy was both 'wrong'—because it was contrary to the Geneva Agreements—and unrealistic—given the nature of the country—in South Vietnam it was simply unrealistic. Washington could legitimately support an anti-Communist government in the South in answer to the Communist allegiance of the North. And if, despite the provisional nature of the Geneva settlement, a stable régime had emerged in the South, there would have been no problem. But North Vietnam, which in turn was 'wrong' to exploit Laos, also had a legitimate cause—reunification of Vietnam. The 1954 Geneva Agreements specified general elections in 1956 'which will bring about unification of Vietnam'; this was what the Vietminh had been fighting eight years of war to achieve. Moreover it was laid down at Geneva that the 'provisional military demarcation line' between the 'zones' of North and South 'should not in any way be interpreted as constituting a political or territorial boundary'.[128] Yet the US was entitled to salvage what it could from the wreck of Indo-China. Similarly, the Vietminh was entitled to work for the completion of its national aims. But once peaceful processes were barred—by the refusal of the Diem régime to accept nation-wide elections—it is not surprising that North Vietnam and Vietminh elements in the South should seek to attain their objectives by other means.

The Vietnam situation is a conflict of 'rights': the right to reunification; the right of one zone (or part of it) to resist domination by the other. The Diem régime never accepted the validity of the Geneva Agreements, whose provisions were broken—and repeatedly broken—by both sides. Diem refused even to consult about nation-wide elections; and the North started to infiltrate trained guerrillas and cadres into the South. Both carried out reprisals in their own 'zones' against supporters or sympathizers of the other: the North against Catholics, rich farmers and 'bourgeois' elements; the South against ex-partisans of the Vietminh, whether Communist or nationalist, against the dissident sects (Cao Dai and Hoa Hao), and eventually against any form of organized opposition.

Given the propriety of the US commitment to an existing South Vietnam—which under the Republicans, contrary to their Laos policy, was indeed both cautious and limited—the question was how best to carry it out. For the Americans faced three major obstacles to the creation of a viable South. These were, and are: the difficulty in dealing with an unpopular but obstinate client régime; the lack of unity in the region; and the strength of the Vietminh (Vietcong). The apparent success of Ngo Dinh Diem in smashing the opposition to his rule in 1955-56 and in consolidating his power served to obscure the fragmentation of South Vietnam. But the Americans, in the early years of the régime, were at least aware of its fragility.

President Eisenhower's letter to Prime Minister (later President) Diem in October 1954, marked the first formal US commitment to South Vietnam. It has since been much cited, though not in detail, particularly during and after the crisis of 1964-65. This was when the Democratic Administration sought to represent American armed intervention in Vietnam as flowing from the same commitment as that undertaken by Eisenhower ten years before—see, for example, Dean Rusk's statement of April 25, 1964[129]—and as consistent with the 'pledge' made by 'three Presidents'—according to President Johnson's State of the Union address in January 1965[130] and subsequent remarks.

Eisenhower's message was not so much a 'pledge' as a declaration of intent. His 'commitment' to aid South Vietnam was both cautious and conditional—on the Saigon Government carrying out 'needed reforms'. The motives for US assistance were, of course, similar. As Eisenhower put it, it sprang from America's 'grave concern' for the future of a country 'temporarily divided', weakened by war and 'faced with enemies without and by their subversive collaborators within'. The US, he wrote, would therefore 'examine'—

'how an intelligent programme of American aid . . . can serve to assist Vietnam . . . in developing and maintaining a strong viable state, capable of resisting attempted subversion or aggression through military means. The Government of the United States expects that this aid will be met by performance on the part of the Government of Vietnam in undertaking needed reforms. . . . Such a government would, I hope, be so responsive to the nationalist aspirations of its people, so enlightened in purpose and effective in performance, that it will be respected both at home and abroad and discourage any who might wish to impose a foreign ideology on your free people.'[131]

This was a valid 'hope', but when the Diem régime turned out to be neither responsive, nor enlightened nor effective—though it was not until the eve of its downfall that Washington would fully admit this—what was the United States to do?

The answer is suggested in President Eisenhower's view of the 'international facts of life': that if 'aggression or subversion' should win against the weaker free nations the Communists would 'step by step' overcome other 'once-free' areas. Then the danger, even to the strongest, would be 'increasingly menacing'. This 'truth' he—and his successors—applied to South Vietnam:

'Strategically, South Vietnam's capture by the Communists would bring their power several hundred miles into a hitherto free region. The remaining countries in South East Asia would be menaced by a great flanking movement. The freedom of twelve million people would be lost immediately and that of 150 million others in adacent lands would be seriously endangered. The loss of South Vietnam could set in motion a crumbling process that could, as it progressed, have grave consequences for us and for freedom.'[132]*

This strategic-ideological concept had dominated US Government

* President Johnson quoted this passage word for word in his 'San Antonio' speech of September 29, 1967 (*Department of State Bulletin*, October 23, 1967).

policy towards the Far East at least since the Korean war. What was once considered an anti-colonial struggle—even if Communist-led—became part of a holding operation by 'free nations' against 'aggression', to quote President Truman in 1952.[133] And the final about-turn was revealed in Dulles's statement of September 1953, that the 'Communist-dominated armies in Indo-China have no shadow of a claim to be regarded as the champions of an independence movement'.[134]

US obsession with the global threat of Communism had as its natural counterpart a conviction of the righteousness of the anti-Communist cause. But it was to create serious difficulties for Washington with regard to the post-1954 situation in Vietnam. First of all it inhibited the Administration from pressing for effective action and 'needed reforms' by the Diem régime. For the US Government either failed to realize or consistently under-estimated both the extent of popular opposition to the 'free' régime and the inroads being made by the Vietcong. Second, in the much-publicized belief that South Vietnam (led by Diem) was indispensable to America's security, the US forfeited any real leverage over the régime. The latter took every advantage of this weakness; it not only begged for US aid but insisted on its full right to use (or abuse) it as it wished.[135] And finally, taking on an ever-growing commitment, the US found itself bogged down in a deteriorating situation, unable to extricate itself—both before and after the fall of Diem—for fear of the alarming consequences it had itself conjured up; and in due course obliged to intervene in far greater strength in order to 'underwrite' the entire structure.

This was the 'brink' from which the Americans had recoiled in China nearly twenty years before. As Secretary of State George Marshall had then pointed out:

'Direct armed intervention in the internal affairs of China runs counter to traditional American policy towards China and would be contrary to the clearly expressed intent of congress which indicated that American aid to China under the $25,000,000 grants did not involve the use of United States combat troops nor United States personnel in command of Chinese troops. . . .

The United States Government must be exceedingly careful that it does not become committed to a policy involving the absorption of its resources to an unpredictable extent. . . . To achieve the objective of reducing the Chinese Communists to a completely negligible factor in China in the immediate future, it would be necessary for the United States virtually to take over the Chinese Government and administer its economic, military and governmental affairs. . . . It would be impossible to estimate the final cost of a course of action of such magnitude. . . . It would involve the United States Government in a continuing commitment from which it would practically be impossible to withdraw, and it would very probably involve grave consequences to this action by making China an arena of international conflict. . . .'[136]

How is it—besides the difference of time (attitudes only three years after a major war may vary considerably from those twenty years after)—that America could stand aside from the 'loss' of China, a country of very great importance, and yet feel impelled to intervene, presumably aware of the probable consequences of such a step (as expressed by Marshall), in Vietnam? There seems no convincing answer to this question. But it is worth pointing out that the US administration was well informed of the weakness and failings of the Nationalist régime in China, whereas it suffered severely from ignorance and wishful thinking about Vietnam. Secondly, the climax in China came barely two or three years after the end of the Pacific war; but this stage was not reached in South Vietnam for some eight or ten years after independence. A more gradual deterioration was marked by a more gradual—and hence more insidious US involvement. Instead of facing a desperate plunge into unknown waters, which could be resisted, the Americans in Vietnam were already half immersed and perhaps felt themselves getting accustomed to the swirling currents around them.

The US reacted to the threat of North Vietnamese invasion after 1954 by building up conventional forces in the South, and it ignored the unrest in the countryside. So consistently did it follow this policy that by April 1962, when the Vietcong was controlling large areas of the Mekong delta and the Central Highlands, the head of the US Military Advisory Assistance Group, General O'Daniel, reported that because the South Vietnamese 'units are trained for fighting conventional armed forces', they 'find it quite a problem to bring the Communist Vietminh to battle'.[137]

Until almost the end of this period optimism abounded. According to a South Vietnamese Government handout in 1957, the 'Vietminh authorities have disintegrated and been rendered powerless'.[138] When President Diem visited Washington in May 1957, a joint statement declared that a chaotic situation had been transformed into one of progress and stability, while 'internal security had been effectively established'.[139] A year later, the South Vietnamese Foreign Minister, Vu Van Mao (who was to resign in 1963 in protest against the régime's repression of the Buddhists) reaffirmed that the 'Government had the threat of internal Communist subversion under control'.[140] After President Eisenhower had reached the 'inescapable conclusion' in April 1959, that 'some help' was required for the US 'in sustaining the morale, the economic progress and the military strength necessary to its [South Vietnam's] continued existence in freedom',[141] the US deputy military chief in Vietnam, Major-General Myers, blandly asserted that 'the Vietminh guerrillas . . . were gradually nibbled away until they ceased to be a major menace to the Government'. Two territorial regiments reinforced occasionally by one or two regular regiments he considered would be able to cope with their depredations.[142]

As late as October 1960—though admittedly the US was then engaged in tackling Laos—Eisenhower found it 'refreshing' to observe 'how clearly the Government and the citizens of Vietnam have faced the fact that the greatest danger to their independence was Communism'. But 'You and your countrymen,' he wrote to President Diem, 'have used your strength well in accepting the double challenge of building your country and resisting Communism.'[143] So serious had the situation actually become that the new US Secretary of State, Dean Rusk, was obliged to warn in May 1961, that guerrilla raids, armed attacks and terrorism had reached an 'unprecedented level'. In 1960, he declared, over 3,000 local officials, soldiers and civilians had been killed or kidnapped. The Vietcong, he said, was attacking isolated garrisons and new townships, ambushing roads and canals, destroying bridges and sabotaging public works and lines of communication. There had been 'urgent' discussion in Washington, and the US would give 'every possible help' to Vietnam.[144]

In December 1961 President Diem himself appealed to President Kennedy for further help. 'The level of their [Communist] attacks is already such,' he wrote, 'that our forces are stretched to the utmost. . . . The forces of international Communism now arrayed against us are more than we can meet with the resources at hand.'[145] A senior State Department official later admitted that 'to be frank, the war was being lost fast in the fall of 1961'. He said there was a real threat that the Vietcong might 'liberate' and hold a remote area in Vietnam, possibly as a 'seat of government' which Communist countries could recognize and aid.[146] Another senior American, deputy director of the 'Vietnam Working Group' in 1963, reported that in the first half of 1962 the Vietcong had launched over 3,000 armed attacks, including a number in battalion strength.[147] Units of such size—up to 500 men—could overwhelm any locally defended village or isolated military post with impunity. And for the first time Vietcong units of a thousand or more troops went into action, overrunning district—and even a provincial capital—in the Central Highlands, the northern provinces and near Saigon. The Vietcong in 1962 numbered over 60,000 armed men, with 100,000 peasants actively supporting their campaign.

The crisis appeared so threatening that Vice-President Lyndon Johnson, visiting Saigon in May 1961, was said to have raised the possibility of sending American troops to Vietnam; but, according to Scigliano, 'this offer was rejected by President Diem on the grounds it would be contrary to the Geneva Agreements and would provide strong propaganda to the Communists'.[148] However General Maxwell Taylor's further investigation for President Kennedy in October 1961 bore the seeds of American intervention—and the bombing of the North. Publicly General Taylor recommended a bigger American role in training and advising the Vietnamese army and administration. As a result, the US Military Assistance Advisory Group was greatly enlarged, a new Military Assistance Command was established under General Harkins and the first US helicopters and fighter bombers arrived in Vietnam.

General Taylor is also said to have proposed—though this was not made public—the commitment of an American military 'task force' of perhaps 10,000 men to maintain 'perimeter security'; and if the South Vietnamese army were hard pressed it could act as an emergency reserve. But according to Schlesinger, the President rejected this proposal.[149] No doubt his reasoning was similar to that of the State Department's Deputy Under-Secretary for Political Affairs, U. Alexis Johnson (later Deputy-Ambassador, under Taylor, in Saigon). He pointed out in 1962 that in every case where Communist insurgency had been defeated 'it has been primarily by the forces of nationalism within the country'. Johnson concluded: 'We can assist and advise, as we are doing in South Vietnam, but we do not and should not wage "American wars" against insurgent forces.'[150]

A further recommendation in Taylor's 1961 report—according to Schlesinger's account—was to stop the infiltration of troops and supplies from North Vietnam, which Taylor believed would otherwise jeopardize in the South both the proposed programme of civil reforms (which it was envisaged that Diem would carry out) and the increased military effort. Taylor reportedly advocated a contingency policy of retaliation against North Vietnam, graded to match the intensity of Hanoi's aid to the Vietcong. This, too, was rejected[151]—at the time. Infiltration from the North in 1961 and for several years to come was far from being a major factor.

The Director of Intelligence and Research in the State Department, Roger Hilsman, analysed in September 1962 the relative importance of the two major supply lines—internal and external—used by the guerrillas in South Vietnam. The infiltration routes from the North were used chiefly to provide the Vietcong with trained officers, non-commissioned officers and 'specialized equipment'. The main supply line was the network of internal jungle trails connecting the thousands of South Vietnamese hamlets. 'It is from these villages,' Hilsman reported, 'that the Communists get food, recruits and raw materials with which to manufacture arms and ammunition.' Food, of course, had to come from the South. As for weapons, an examination of those captured from the Vietcong showed that they were either arms left over from French colonial days, or home-made guns, mines and grenades, or weapons seized from the South Vietnamese forces. 'By hitting army, security and police units suddenly and in superior force, the guerrillas are able to assure themselves a local supply of arms and ammunition and reduce their dependence on long supply lines from the north'; these, Hilsman suggested, should in any case be vulnerable to interdiction, at various points within South Vietnam, by the South Vietnamese forces.[152]

This is not to suggest that infiltration from the North was simply a myth. In December 1961 the US State Department published its 'White paper', *A Threat to the Peace: North Viet-Nam's Effort to conquer South Viet-Nam*, which documented some individual case histories of agents and 'military personnel' who had been captured in the South after infiltration from the North. But the publication did not attempt to estimate the total numbers involved. In its own words, it was a 'study of *Vietcong activities* in South Vietnam and of the elaborate organization in the North that *supports* these activities'.[153] The SEATO Council of Ministers, meeting in March 1961, expressed the same point of view by referring to the 'efforts of an armed minority [in South Vietnam] again [as in Laos] supported from outside. . . .'[154] Rusk himself, in answer to a question whether the Communists were opening up a 'new theatre' in Vietnam since the war in Laos was closing, explained that the 'most active' part of the Communist efforts in South Vietnam occurred not in the north of the country—near the Communist-infiltrated areas of Laos—'but in the south, the far south, in the Saigon area'.[155] (Two years later it was evident that the greatest successes of the insurgents were in the Mekong delta—the most heavily populated region of South Vietnam—where entire provinces were virtually under Vietcong control.) Rusk added that a 'considerable number' of personnel and some supplies were being infiltrated from the North. But he also agreed that the quality of society in South Vietnam, the mobilization of energies and the satisfaction of the people had a 'great deal' to do with security and the ability to withstand assault, penetration and subversion from 'outside'.[156]

Hilsman and some of his colleagues were aware that *local con-*

ditions were a sufficient explanation of the guerrilla resurgence in South Vietnam (as of the Huk resurgence in the Philippines, which is far apart from any Communist country). But this was not understood—or if understood, not admitted—in the higher reaches of the State Department and the Pentagon. Increasingly preoccupied with 'aggression' from the North* they failed to observe the marked deterioration of the situation in the South. Indeed, as a result of the temporary stimulus of US assistance, 'optimism' resumed its sway. This was most strikingly revealed in the White House statement of policy on Vietnam of October 2, 1963, shortly before the collapse of the Diem régime: 'Secretary McNamara and General Taylor reported their judgement [after a further investigation of the situation in South Vietnam] that the major part of the US military task can be completed by the end of 1965, although there may be a continuing requirement for a limited number of US training personnel.'[157]

It must be admitted that the US faced great difficulty in obtaining accurate information about the situation in Vietnam, and especially in the countryside. No US military advisers operated below divisional level before 1962 and, in the words of an American aid official working in the field, 'thus had tended to be remote from the village security problems'.[158] General Taylor himself recalled that 'President Diem had originally opposed the presence of Americans outside of Saigon, but we eventually broke down his resistance'. When a 'large number of Americans' began to be established in the provinces and districts—as a result of the American army build-up from 700 to some 10,000 advisers by the end of 1962—'we began to improve the quality of our information'. Writing in 1966, Taylor candidly admitted this 'lesson' of Vietnam:

'We must have good information on the internal situation in countries in which we have a present or potential interest. This kind of information was sorely lacking in the early days of our involvement in Vietnam. . . . I am not talking about military information about the enemy but rather that bearing on the internal conditions in South Vietnam itself. When I visited Saigon in the fall of 1961 to survey the conditions there at the directive of President Kennedy, I became progressively impressed with the fact that the data upon which our

* Every time things went badly in Vietnam, President Kennedy told Hilsman early in 1962, there would be more reports about the increased use of the Ho Chi Minh trails: 'No matter what goes wrong or whose fault it really is, the argument will be that the Communists have stepped up their infiltration and we can't win unless we hit the north. Those trails are a built-in excuse for failure, and a built-in argument for escalation.' Roger Hilsman, *To Move a Nation* (Doubleday, 1967), p. 439.

government had been basing its plans in Washington were of little value. . . . I found that the information needed at home frequently did not exist, or if it existed, its reliability was highly suspect. Often when American officials, prodded by Washington, pressed their [Vietnamese] counterparts for information, they received either inaccurate data hastily put together to meet the American requirement or data doctored to cover up an embarrassing situation from the prying Americans. As a result, in Washington we were often solemnly drawing graphs and preparing reports and recommendations that had very little relation to the actual conditions in the country.'[159]

Wishful thinking—the belief so often expressed that the 'corner has been turned'—added to the lack of experience of Americans on the spot (largely because of the one-year tours of duty, prescribed for reasons of morale) has continued to make this a problem. As late as November 1967—six years after Taylor's first report—General Westmoreland, the US Commander in Vietnam, and Ambassador Ellsworth Bunker were reported to be 'privately critical of past US intelligence estimates made by an American officer who has been transferred to another post' and to be 'confident' in the estimates they were now getting of America's 'steady progress'.[160] General Westmoreland announced in Washington on November 22, 1967, that a 'new phase' in the war would begin in 1968 with US efforts to bring South Vietnamese armed forces to 'combat effectiveness' and that some time thereafter the 'Communist infra-structure will be cut up and near collapse'.

The interlinked problem of American unawareness and Vietnamese Government ineffectiveness ruined the first serious attempt to get to grips with the political, social and military deterioration in the Vietnamese countryside. This was the application of 'counter-insurgency' measures—a doctrine re-formulated in the Kennedy era as America's response to the 'unconventional' challenge of Khruschev's 'wars of national liberation' and of Mao's 'people's wars'. Counter-insurgency experts argued, reasonably enough, that only after understanding the conditions which enabled guerrilla, 'shadow' or 'internal' wars to arise in developing countries would it be possible to undertake the positive military and political measures required. In practice, these boiled down to the best way to prevent supplies of food, arms and recruits from swelling the insurgent force.

A classic exposition of the theory and intended practice of counter-insurgency appeared in Hilsman's 'A Report on South Vietnam' of September 1962.[161] Isolation of rural communities from the central government through lack of communications and difficulties of terrain, 'but more importantly . . . in a psychological and political sense'. Hilsman explained, was the usual setting for guerrilla warfare, as in South Vietnam. One result of such isolation, often over hundreds of years, was that villagers were 'turned in' on themselves; 'they appear rarely to have strong political convictions one way or the other'. Another was insecurity. Cut off from contact with government officials, villagers usually had no choice but to 'go along with' the armed guerrillas; it was not surprising in these circumstances that villagers would give or sell rice and that some of the young men would be recruited 'with promises of adventure and good things to come'.

The counter-measures needed were therefore interlinked: a military presence to provide security and a 'social new deal' to win village support. 'The principle is that in fighting guerrillas, military operations must be so conducted as to achieve political ends.' The aim was to create a system in which 'information about the needs of the villagers can flow upward and government services can flow downwards'. But to do this, the military must move away from cumbersome, conventional military operations designed to take and hold territory, which failed to counter the political motivation of guerrilla tactics. For the guerrillas' objectives were not to take territory but to 'win recruits and alienate the people from their government'. As Hilsman explained:

'The guerrilla's purpose is well served when large military formations sweep the countryside, for this tends to make life difficult for the villagers and hence to make the villagers turn against their government. [This remains a major criticism of current US military operations.] Thus, for political reasons the military tactics used against guerrillas should be those of the guerrilla himself—small roving units constantly patrolling and ambushing. Finally, these tactics should be designed to cut the lines of communication between the guerrilla and the thousands of villages to which he goes for food and recruits.'

'Strategic hamlets', based on British experience in Malaya, would be the answer. For the army itself could not garrison all the outlying villages (over 2,500 in South Vietnam—subdivided into some 16,000 hamlets); while if the latter were not protected they would be obliged, from fear of retaliation, to provide food and shelter for the guerrillas. And 'without protection the villager is afraid to pass on information about the Communist guerrillas to the government'. The prime purpose of properly armed and fortified 'strategic hamlets' was to enable the villagers to defend themselves. A second was to control the movement of people and supplies. Strategic hamlets would form a 'hedgehog of defended villages' interdicting the network of local supply routes used by the Vietcong. As Hilsman saw it:

'The barbed wire and curfews deny the guerrilla easy access to the villages. If the guerrillas need rice, they must attack a defended village. Thus the whole war is turned round. Instead of the government forces chasing the Communists and falling into ambush, the Communists must attack the villages and fall into ambush themselves.'

The concept was brilliant; the execution muddled; the conditions unsuitable; and the result, after an initial upsurge, was disastrous.

The Americans considered the strategic hamlet programme the 'heart of the war effort in Vietnam'.[162] As the Deputy Director of the 'Vietnam Working Group' in Washington described it in August 1963—at the height of the Buddhist crisis—'it is also the first time in Vietnamese history that the national government has been effectively "plugged in" to hamlet-level society'. Schools, dispensaries, clinics, agricultural extension work and cheap credit 'are provided'; access roads and irrigation works 'also come from the government'. This he concluded, was an 'economic and political stake which they [the villagers] will want to defend'.[163] Morale in the countryside was up, affirmed the deputy Secretary of State for Political Affairs in April 1963; 'to date about half the population—nearly seven million people—live in about 5,000 strategic hamlets. . . . Perhaps the most important result is the intangible knitting together of Government and people'. . . .[164] 'Both the Vietnamese and we recognize,' declared Dean Rusk, 'that this is a political and social struggle as well as a military conflict. . . . We are confident that they [the South Vietnamese Government] are on the right track.'[165] In April 1963, according to Rusk, 'the "strategic hamlet" programme is producing excellent results'.[166]

On the contrary the Vietnamese Government and particularly the 'master mind' of the programme, Ngo Dinh Nhu, had different ends in view. They intended the strategic hamlet not just as a base for launching attacks against the guerrillas but as a 'control device' to facilitate Government manipulation of the rural Vietnamese. Douglas Pike comments: 'One can search in vain through governmental directives and the speeches of Diem and his brothers for a listing of the benefits or rights that the rural Vietnamese could expect within the strategic hamlet.'[167] Nhu's attitude was expressed to strategic hamlet cadres in October 1962 where he told them that 'participation [in combat] is considered a citizen's duty'. 'Do not rely on foreign aid,' he added, 'but on your own internal means. . . . Try to improve your own virtue and behaviour.'[168] The then Public Affairs Officer at the US Embassy reports that Nhu was adamant against any slogan implying material benefits for the peasants.[169] General Duong Van Minh confirmed on November 8, 1963, after the overthrow of the Diem régime; 'Nhu used strategic hamlets for political rather than pacification purposes. That is why the people in the villages suffered very much.'

Diem himself referred to the 'irresistible movement' of the strategic hamlet programme, which had 'already gone far beyond the original tactical objective'. He saw it as laying the foundations for the 'Personalist revolution' in the countryside 'bringing the certainty of victory for the Just Cause'.[170] Because of the powerful insistence on the programme by their leaders, subordinate officials could not afford to lag behind. An American provincial representative reported that 'the Division commander [in Danang], eager to please Diem, accelerated the schedule for completion to a work span of two and one-half months instead of six months, as previously programmed'.[171] Diem declared in his speech to the National Assembly on October 7, 1963, that 'in the construction of the strategic hamlets, we have held firm to the criterion of speed rather than solidity' and expected that 'at the end of 1963, almost all the hamlets planned will have been built'. But he also admitted to an Australian correspondent that the reason he favoured speedy completion was that building slowly gave the Communists too great an opportunity to mobilize the people to destroy the hamlets; this, as Osborne comments, indicates the extent of government control in rural areas.[172]

In complete contrast to the methodical, carefully planned and well-organized resettlement of half a million Chinese squatters in Malaya during the Emergency, the feverish construction of strategic hamlets for some ten million Vietnamese was pushed ahead regardless of practical considerations. The 'Inter-Ministerial Committee for Strategic Hamlets' was not set up until February 1962, seven months after the first official references to the programme.[173] The British adviser, Robert Thompson, who had had great experience of security operations in Malaya, warned President Diem against going ahead too fast, as it would create a grave risk of over-extending the forces available to protect the hamlets.[174] But, he reported later, strategic hamlets were set up haphazardly, there was no solid nucleus in any one area, military operations were not co-ordinated to support them, particularly in the Mekong delta, and no real effort was made to eliminate Vietcong agents and supporters or to impose proper controls. Whereas it had taken the British, under far more favourable conditions, over three years to resettle half a million Chinese squatters in some 500 defended villages, the Vietnamese authorities had rushed through the 'construction' of 8,000 strategic hamlets—with a population of nearly ten out of a total of fourteen millions—in under two years, and most of these in less than one year.[175]

Abuses and disorganization flourished. In Quang Nam province in Central Vietnam, for example, the Vietcong chose the newly completed hamlets as special targets, because they had co-operated with the Government. 'Often there were no fences, no weapons, and no radios to call for help as the Vietcong arrived. It became obvious later that these delays [in supplying equipment], often involving months of waiting, gave the Vietcong ample time to establish "agreements" with the villagers not to oppose their propaganda or their calls for taxes and recruitment.' And as the situation worsened 'evidence of embezzlement of pacification funds by the Province Chief [a militant Catholic officer from Hanoi, without civil experience, in a predominantly Buddhist area] and several District Chiefs was discovered. . . .'[176] An informal paper written by the US economic mission in Saigon—'Some comments on the Counter-Insurgency Programme of Vietnam and USOM [US Operations Mission]'—reported in 1964:

'From the very inception of the Strategic Hamlet programme it was apparent that many of these [provincial Vietnamese] officials did not fully understand the concept, and were so frightened by the pressures from the President [Diem] and his brother that they would employ any measures from forced labour and confiscation to false reporting, to achieve the quantitative goals set. . . .'[177]

After the overthrow of Diem, the new Military Revolutionary Council decided on December 2, 1963, to call a temporary halt to the strategic hamlet programme. The Council ordered province chiefs to stop forcing peasants to move into hamlets and stop insisting that they contribute financially.[178] As an American correspondent pointed out, villagers in the Mekong delta region (a contrast to the compact villages of Central Vietnam) were widely scattered and all too often the pressure to bring them into strategic hamlets meant removing them from their land and homes. 'By and large the population of the delta had been on the fence, but the very act of relocation turned thousands of peasants against the Government.'[179] There the Vietcong, who were usually local Southerners—as opposed to the ex-Northern and Central Vietnamese predominant in the Diem administration[180]—were able to infiltrate insecurely established hamlets, often through the help of an embittered peasantry. Defence Secretary McNamara confirmed that because of the administrative disruption and 'loss of physical security' in the countryside, 'many over-extended hamlets have been overrun or severely damaged'.[181] Despite the ambitious 'paper' plans of 1964, the programme in many areas was in a state of collapse.

(2) *Credibility*

United States' policy towards Vietnam continued to be an uneasy mixture of occasional outbursts of realism— at times of crisis when the deteriorating situation could no longer be ignored—against a general background of indiscriminate optimism. Thus after the two-day visit to South Vietnam of Defence Secretary McNamara, C.I.A. Director McCone, Major-General Krulak, 'Special Assistant for Counterinsurgency and Special Activities, Joint Chiefs of Staff'—an 'optimistic' supporter of the strategic hamlet programme[182]—and others in December 1963, the White House reported that the mission had reviewed 'in great detail' the 1964 operation plans of the South Vietnamese and US military advisers and 'we have every reason to believe they will be successful'.[183] Secretary McNamara and General Taylor, then Chairman of the Joint Chiefs of Staff, went on a five-day 'inspection trip' in March 1964. 'There have unquestionably been setbacks,' they admitted on their return to Washington, but 'General Khanh and his Government [Khanh had ousted General Minh two months before] are acting vigorously and effectively. They have produced a sound central plan for the prosecution of the war. . . .' Further American assistance was needed, they recommended, but with 'continued vigorous leadership' the 'situation can be significantly improved in the coming months'.[184]

McNamara in his first major statement on 'US Policy in Vietnam', eulogized Khanh:

'Today the Government of General Khanh is vigorously rebuilding the machinery of administration and reshaping plans to carry the war to the Vietcong. He is an able and energetic leader. He has demonstrated his grasp of the basic elements—political, economic and psychological as well as military—required to defeat the Vietcong. He is planning a programme of economic and social advances for the welfare of his people. He has brought into support of the Government representatives of key groups previously excluded. He and his colleagues have developed plans for the systematic liberation of areas now submissive to Vietcong duress and for mobilization of all available Vietnamese resources in the defence of the homeland.'[185]

This was in March 1964. By August the *New York Times* correspondent in Saigon was reporting that the early progress made in 'pacification'—the concept now in vogue—was being threatened by

Vietcong terrorism and its deadly practice of ambushes. Many Americans working in the provinces doubted if Vietnamese officials in the countryside either understood or cared about the tedious business of pacification—an American programme in which they showed little confidence.[186] Khanh himself was ousted as 'President' at the end of August—he had been appointed a few days before under his own new Constitution—following violent demonstrations by students and Buddhists. After nine more months of mounting confusion—of demonstrations, riots, frequent changes of government, *coups* and abortive *coups*—Air Vice-Marshal Ky, the new Prime Minister, pointed in June 1965 to the effects of the 'crisis in leadership':

'The administrative machinery has been impaired and parts of it dismantled. . . . In many rural areas, the collapse of administrative agencies has frustrated the government's effective control and the fighting efficiency of the armed forces. . . . In view of these circumstances, it is only natural that the economic and financial systems should also be in a state of collapse. The uncertainty prevailing has provoked alarm among the people. . . . Inflation has caused prices to spiral constantly and the cost of living to soar. . . . Similarly tragic is the picture of the social, educational and cultural fields. . . . The social evils which already existed at the time we were born still appear rampant, unchanged, and compounded with new ones. . . . Pupils and students rely on their parents for help, but the latter are helpless because of the miserable state of a highly divided society. . . .'

As for the war:

'That the Vietcong have succeeded in bringing into the Republic of Vietnam such a large force as they have today has mainly been due to errors, errors which became increasingly serious, committed under the old [Diem] régime. But the biggest failure has been the lack of appropriate and timely tactics to prevent the conquest through Communist wars of subversion. . . . Under successive governments, the errors of the past, far from being corrected, were compounded by new errors. This crisis of tactics has brought about the result that the Vietcong have now succeeded in staging co-ordinated attacks in which they have been able to deploy several regiments against areas defended by only one or a few of our battalions. . . .'[187]

At the same time General Thieu, Chairman of the newly formed 'Council for the Leadership of the Nation', revealed that 'at the moment half of Vietnamese territory is controlled and morally dominated by the Vietcong'. Direct general elections were impossible. The security of the towns was being sabotaged, with large scale military operations not far away. . . .'[188] So in March 1965 the first American combat units were sent to Vietnam. In May there were over 40,000 US troops, in June over 50,000. The bombing of North Vietnam started in February 1965. Yet in April President Johnson was still speaking of 'calculated action' rather than sudden escalation against the North; of building up South Vietnamese ground forces to cope with the Vietcong, rather than bringing in US combat units. . . .[189] 'The South Vietnamese Government has not asked for international ground forces to support their effort in South Vietnam.' The South Vietnamese felt this is 'not what is needed', said Dean Rusk.[190]

'Instead of entering the war directly,' observed in 1963 a perceptive American historian who had worked in Vietnam, 'the United States backed into it.'[191] He continued: 'What American officials failed to grasp in 1959 was that Communist political activity and terrorism were the visible signs of a deteriorating security situation. American miscalculation of the Communist threat continued well into 1961'[192]— and into 1963, 1965 and 1967.

It was not for lack of warning. Nguyen Thai, for over five years director of the official news agency *Vietnam Press,* resigned in 1961 to draw 'urgent' attention to the 'desperate situation' in South Vietnam. He wrote:

'. . . the Ngo Dinh Diem régime has been unable to rally any popular support. Even its early supporters can no longer tolerate the climate of corruption, hypocrisy and inefficiency created by the various cliques of sycophants who try to exploit the régime before its collapse. . . .

Thus in South Vietnam today, a well trained, well equipped Vietnamese army and a relatively large administration cannot effectively fight Communist political subversion. . . . Instead they are making a massive effort to hide the truth about South Vietnam, misleading even the Americans into thinking there is no political alternative to the present situation.'[193]

Washington's commitment to the 'indispensable' anti-Communist leader was reinforced with optimism— first about Diem, then Khanh, then Ky. Thus Admiral Felt, Commander-in-Chief, US Forces in the Pacific, declared on July 14, 1963, that the war in Vietnam was going very well: 'The Vietcong are definitely on the run.' Senior American officials in Saigon were reported two months later as saying that the war could be won in nine months, that the border with North Vietnam was 95 per cent closed and 'Vietcong guerrillas are being starved out.'[194] General Harkins, the American Commander in

Vietnam, added in November 1963: 'Victory in the sense it would apply to this kind of war is just months away and the reduction of American advisers can begin any time now.'[195] Yet, as the *New York Times* correspondent in Saigon reported a month later, November had been disastrous for the South Vietnamese Government. Casualties and loss of weapons were higher than in any previous period. For a long time, he wrote, the Vietcong had been building up guerrilla capabilities, especially in the Mekong delta, and if no change took place the area would be swallowed up in six months.[196]

While the Vietcong was gaining control of the delta almost by default—President Diem believed it reflected badly on his régime if his army suffered casualities*—US officials were claiming that the 'tide has now turned . . . the Communist threat has been stopped and is beginning to be rolled back'.[197] Rusk himself argued early in 1963 that 'government forces clearly have the initiative in most areas of the country', that 'defections from the Vietcong have grown rapidly' and that the ratio of arms captured to those lost had 'shifted dramatically in favour of the government troops'.[198] If so, this was a temporary phenomenon. However no attempt was made (until much later) to rectify this assessment and so a misleading impression remained. In fact—according to US official estimates published in 1966—desertions from the Vietcong amounted to over 11,000 in 1963, 5,400 in 1964 and just over 11,000 in 1965.[199] But this should be compared to 36,000 who deserted from government forces in 1963,[200] 72,000 in 1964[201] and 96,000 in 1965[202]. As for weapons losses the trend against the government had set in as early as 1962. In 1963 the Vietcong—according to US Defence Department figures lost 5,400 weapons while government forces lost 8,500. In 1964 the guerrillas lost 4,900 to the government's 13,700.[203] By late 1964 it was estimated that the Vietcong completely controlled one-third of South Vietnam's over 200 administrative districts and 'contested' —government-controlled by day, Vietcong at night—most of the rest.[204] Hanoi-trained infiltrators actually formed quite a small element of total Vietcong strength— in late 1964 there were some 34,000 Vietcong regulars with some 90,000 regional and local guerrillas—thus about 15 per cent at most.[205] They were facing about 400,000 South Vietnamese troops, half of them regulars.

McNamara fitfully recognized, as in his March 1964 policy speech, that the 'large indigenous support that the Vietcong receives means that solutions must be as political and economic as military. Indeed there can be no such thing as a purely "military" solution to the war

* Diem frequently fired commanders reporting unpleasant news or who had too many casualties. (Mecklin, p. 10. And see the consequences in Halberstam, p. 141.)

in South Vietnam'. But there is little to show that the State Department was (and is?) thinking in these terms. Rusk's public statements consistently minimized adverse political—and military—developments, but exaggerated the 'optimistic' ones. To Rusk in April 1963, the four 'national elections' held by the Diem régime (which most observers agree were rigged) and the elected hamlet councils and proposed village council elections (Diem himself had abolished these in 1956) 'show steady movement towards a constitutional system resting upon public consent'. The war in Vietnam, he concluded, was 'a battle to the end between freedom and coercion'.[206]

The official impression of the South Vietnamese régime presented to Americans was, as Vice-President Johnson put it in May 1961, that of 'dedicated leadership' by the President, recently re-elected by the 'overwhelming majority' of his countrymen (he received over 99 per cent of the votes in one Communist-dominated province[207]) 'in the vanguard of those leaders who stand for freedom on the periphery of the Communist Empire'.[208] The protests of the opposition in South Vietnam were ignored. Yet a year before Johnson's visit to Saigon, a highly respectable group of Vietnamese including eleven ex-Ministers and four former senior officials—one of whom was to become Head of State and two to become Prime Minister after the fall of Diem—had 'beseeched' the President to remedy the situation, lest the people 'burst forth in irresistible waves of hatred' to sweep away the 'ignominies and injustices which surround and oppress them'. As the 'Manifesto' of April 26, 1960, declared:

'The people do not know a better life or more freedom. . . . A Constitution has been established in form only; a national assembly exists whose deliberations always fall into line with the government; anti-democratic elections—all those are methods and "comedies" copied from the dictatorial Communist régimes . . . continuous arrests fill the jails and prisons. . . . Public opinion and the press are reduced to silence. . . . Political parties and religious sects have been eliminated. . . . Effective power is . . . concentrated in fact in the hands of an irresponsible member of the [Ngo] "family", from whom emanates all orders. . . . Favouritism based on family or [the régime's] party connections should be banished; the selling of influence, corruption and abuse of power must be punished. . . .'[209]

This statement appeared in the American press. It was not allowed to be published in South Vietnam. After the fall of Diem, the chairman of the Military Revolutionary Council, General Minh, spoke of the realities of 'free' Vietnam:

'No one can deny that this [Diem] administration gradually led to the unavoidable consequences of all dictatorial régimes: the suppression of individual freedoms, the destruction of nationalist opposition forces and the development of abuse and exploitation. At the same time they fooled world public opinion by pretending to be supported by the masses. Through the so-called people's organizations, associations and services, which were similar to fascist organizations, they established an intelligence and secret police network in the service of their administration. . . . The loss of the people's confidence and the division they deliberately created between the Army and the people led to extremely dangerous consequences. During the last six months, lies and the barbarous repression of monks, students and Buddhist laymen marked the last phase of their corruption. . . .'[210]

How could Washington have ignored or evaded such issues for so long? Was it 'operating in a world of illusion', as the US Embassy in Saigon was said to be in 1962-63?[211] As one of its senior officials later wrote, much of what the American newsmen took to be 'lies' about the political and military situation in Vietnam was exactly what the Mission genuinely believed.[212] But after the 1963 upheaval did the US Administration still not understand what was happening in South Vietnam? Did it know and try to hide this information? Or was it simply hoping against hope that things would get better—and thus could keep putting off painful decisions? The tentative answer—in the absence of such published policy documentation as has appeared, for instance, in *United States Relations with China*—seems to be that Washington could not have been unaware that the military and political position was deteriorating; the Administration tried to conceal the gravity of the situation; but this was more a reflection of helplessness than of deliberate bad faith.

Even so, some of the State Department appraisals strain credibility. Do you share Ambassador Lodge's 'qualified optimism', Rusk was asked at his News Conference on July 1, 1964? 'Yes, I must say that I do,' he replied. 'I am one of those people in town who read every day the complete and detailed operational report that comes in every day from South Vietnam—reports that cover the military operations, the political and psychological situation. And I must say, as I read those reports on a day-by-day basis, I find myself wondering about the morale of the Vietcong.' The Vietcong, in Rusk's view, was facing a 'very serious problem' in terms of losses, disruption and morale.[213] Be this as it may, the US Government decided that month to increase its forces in Vietnam by about 30 per cent. Why was there not a 'full and public explanation' of the new US build-up', Rusk was asked at the end of July? Because it was 'primarily a matter for the

Department of Defence', came the reply, and in any case there was 'not much magic' in theoretical numbers and strength tables.[214]

Three weeks later, a 'working paper' on Vietnam by an official of the Central Intelligence Agency, which had leaked to the Press, was published. It was dated June 8, 1964, and had received the 'general approval' of the 'Board of National Estimates' of the C.I.A. These were its conclusions:

'The guerrilla war in South Vietnam is in its fifth year and no end appears in sight. The Vietcong in the South, dependent largely upon their own resources but under the direction and control of the Communist régime in the North, are pressing their offensive more vigorously than ever. . . .

The counter-guerrilla effort continues to flounder, partly because of the inherent difficulty of the problem and partly because Diem's successors have not yet demonstrated the leadership and inspiration necessary.

There remains serious doubt that victory can be won, and the situation remains very fragile. If large-scale United States' support continues and if further political deterioration within South Vietnam is prevented, at least a prolonged stalemate can be attained.

There is also a chance that political evolution within the country and developments upon the world scene could lead to some kind of negotiated settlement based upon neutralism.'[215]

A critical month elapsed between Rusk's news conferences at the end of July and the end of August 1964—there were also crises in the Congo and in Cyprus and the Democratic Party was nominating Johnson for the Presidency. During that month the *New York Times* reported, chiefly from Vietnam:

Aug. 1: Vietcong strike at a village only four miles from Saigon.
Aug. 2: North Vietnamese attack U.S.S. Maddox in Tonkin Gulf.
Aug. 4: US retaliation against North Vietnam.
Aug. 7: Khanh orders State of Emergency; "temporary suspension" of "all laws and regulations", as necessary.
Aug. 16: Khanh appointed President (General Minh removed as Head of State) under new Constitution voted by Military Revolutionary Council. "War Cabinet" to be announced. Senior American officials informed.
Aug. 17: Vietcong battalion inflicts over 100 casualties on Government troops ambushed in Mekong delta.
Aug. 18: Cyrus Vance, US Deputy Defence Secretary: Khanh's "broad new powers" should improve governmental

organization and make for greater unity of effort in pacification.

Aug. 20: South Vietnamese troops ambushed in delta, 200 killed or missing.

Aug. 21: Student demonstration against Khanh's "military dictatorship".

Aug. 23: Students demand end of emergency restrictions; Buddhists demand religious freedom, removal of "anti-Buddhist" elements in the régime.

Aug. 24: US State Department reaffirms support for Khanh; anything of a "divisive nature" is not in the interest of the South Vietnamese Government or people.

Aug. 25: Khanh yields to pressure, pledges to liberalize régime, revise Constitution and step down after election of new Head of State. "Power struggle" reportedly under way in Saigon as US officials look on "in apparent helplessness". Military Revolutionary Council votes to withdraw Constitution. US Embassy in Saigon "hopes" this will lead to greater unity in the country and more effective prosecution of the war against the Vietcong.

Aug. 26: Military commanders fail to agree on new Head of State. Khanh: "Situation is very serious."

Aug. 27: "Provisional leadership" of Khanh (Prime Minister), Khiem (Khanh's rival) and Minh (victim of Khanh's first *coup*).

Aug. 27: Khanh, suffering "physical and mental breakdown", leaves Saigon: Acting Prime Minister Oanh. Washington "relatively optimistic" that new appointment will end tensions.

This was the depressing situation that confronted Rusk when he met the Press on August 30, 1964.[216] Yet the US policy, he told the meeting, was 'utterly simple': for the past ten years it was assistance —'large assistance'—to the government and people of South Vietnam, who were defending themselves against aggression from the North represented by 'guerrillas called the Vietcong'. As for recent events in Saigon, 'nothing behind the scenes' from the US Embassy suggested anything different from what was in the extensive newspaper reports. He elaborated: 'What has been happening there has been an attempt to work out on a long-range basis some changes in the constitutional situation, along the lines that General Khanh has been thinking about and working on for some time.' As for the nine-day President, 'General Khanh is taking a few days' rest. Just how long we don't know.' (Khanh returned to Saigon on September

4, foiled a *coup* by two 'disgruntled' generals on September 13, and handed over to a civilian government in November, which lasted three months.)

The explicit assumptions of the Administration were, first, that the political situation was not a 'main issue' in South Vietnam and second, that even if there was political confusion it was not affecting the conduct of military operations. Both assumptions were wrong. But Rusk saw it in a different light. The 'fundamental' point to him was that no group other than the Vietcong wanted to turn to Hanoi. Therefore the differences among religious groups and 'rivalries of one sort or another' among the South Vietnamese 'ought to be put aside until the main issue against the Vietcong has been resolved'. The US Government was urging a 'moratorium on lesser matters' until the 'great national victory over the Vietcong can be achieved'. Among these 'lesser matters', according to Rusk, were the 'differences of view' as to 'how Government ought to be organized' and who ought to hold particular positions in it.

These matters were surely of very great importance to the Vietnamese, who had suffered under former governments, even if less important to the Americans, who had not. It is impossible to explain how the insurgency was able to develop so strongly without regard to the insufficiencies of the Diem and successive règimes. The strength of the guerrillas reflects the weakness of the government. Thus the popularity of the one—in the absence of a democratic, or at least more representative 'third force', which an authoritarian règime could not permit to emerge—was directly related to the unpopularity of the other. For the Vietnamese it was 'performance' that counted: 'performance' was of course the criterion for granting US assistance in 1954—a point that was ignored in later presentations of the case for commitment. The Vietnamese peasant in particular wanted more land, less taxation, relief from official abuses: this was what the Vietcong both promised and performed. The argument that 'there is no popular wave of interest in the political solutions that are offered by Hanoi, no desire to pick up Communism as a way of life', which Rusk found 'one of the most encouraging elements of the situation' in July 1964,[217] is simply beside the point. Communism was not being offered by the Vietcong.

The Administration's second assumption followed from the first: that political disunity—being a 'lesser matter'—did not affect military security. That this was not so had been evident at least from 1963, if not before. General Minh had spoken of the 'deep influence' of Diemist repression of the Buddhists on the countryside: 'We know it, because we all have relatives in the villages.' And he rightly concluded that 'we must first win the support of the people before we can win against the Communists'. This did not prevent Rusk from claiming on August 30, 1964: 'This [political confusion] does not seem to affect what is going on in the field against the guerrillas. . . . These problems in Saigon have not yet affected the operations against the Vietcong in the field.' He said there were two thousand 'small unit' actions every day looking for the Vietcong and twenty-five to thirty battalion-sized operations every day.[218] But Sir Robert Thompson has pointed out that the ratio of 'contacts' with the Vietcong to government operations launched was 'lamentable'. In a typical month of 1964 only 451 contacts resulted from 60,000 small unit operations.[219]

Military, if not political, optimism remained an article of faith for the Administration. On September 10, 1964, Rusk not only reaffirmed that 'events have not interfered with the prosecution of the war against the Vietcong' but maintained that the army's problem was to 'find and fix' the guerrillas 'because the Vietcong habitually does not attack the armed forces of South Vietnam'.[220] At a 'high level review' of the Vietnam situation the day before, Ambassador Maxwell Taylor 'was able to report [to the President] continued progress in the field in the Vietnamese Army's fight against the Communist Vietcong'.[221] General Westmoreland, newly appointed head of the US Military Assistance Command in Vietnam, felt there was a 'general upward trend'.[222] Events in Saigon, added Rusk a few days later, 'have not brought about dislocation and changes in the provinces' where 'considerable headway' had been made in the last few months.[223]

There were no further official statements on Vietnam for nearly two months—during the US Presidential campaign. But on December 1, 1964 a White House statement sounded the first gloomy notes. It reported that 'security problems' had increased 'over the past few months' in the northern provinces, 'with uneven progress elsewhere'. As for the economy, 'increased interdiction of the communication routes by the Vietcong is interfering to some extent with commerce. . . .' And there was 'accumulated evidence' of 'increased North Vietnamese support of the Vietcong'. Therefore the US would 'consult urgently' with the South Vietnamese Government to 'improve the situation in all its aspects'.[224]

On December 20, 1964, the High National Council of Vietnam—the 'fabric of legal government', as Taylor pointed out—was purged by ambitious young generals, headed by Ky and Thi. Rusk now conceded that unity was a 'primary requirement' for a solution in Vietnam. 'Unity,' he said, 'would be worth many, many divisions.'[225] 'The political situation today is critical,' confirmed William Bundy, Assistant Secretary of State for Far Eastern Affairs towards the end of January 1965; resolution of this crisis was 'central to turning the war around and restoring an independent and secure South Vietnam'.[226]

But America had come to the end of the road with a policy of advice and assistance. The drastic change for the worse in Vietnam, both militarily and politically, forced a drastic change in American policy. For as William Bundy stated in May 1966, if the United States had not massively intervened in 1965 'the vicious arithmetic of guerrilla warfare would have brought victory to the Vietcong and their North Vietnamese masters'.[227] Thus force of necessity compelled Washington to reverse its longstanding opposition to engagement in a war on the Asian mainland. For, as Eisenhower had pointed out, involvement in all-out war in Indo-China 'would be no greater tragedy' for the United States.[228]

Four 'options' had been variously canvassed during 1964: US withdrawal (advocated by certain critics of the Administration); neutralization of South Vietnam (de Gaulle's proposition); military action against North Vietnam (foreshadowed by the Tonkin Gulf attacks); and continued support for Saigon against the Vietcong. Washington rejected outright the first two: withdrawal would mean virtual abandonment of South East Asia to the Communists,[229] while neutralization could only be an 'interim device' prior to a Communist takeover.[230] Throughout the year the possibility of 'expanding the war' to North Vietnam—the third option—had been conveyed, 'if the Communists persist in their course of aggression', as Rusk put it.[231] But the Administration's basic policy—expressed as late as January 1965—was that the 'root of the problem' was in South Vietnam.[232] 'The fact is that only the Vietnamese can win this war,' it was argued before. 'It is the struggle for the loyalty of a whole people. . . . We can help the Vietnamese but we can't do their fighting for them.'[233] Action against the North 'would only be a supplement to, not a substitute for, progress within South Vietnam's own borders', McNamara reaffirmed in 1964.[234] The 'central problem' of pacification was in South Vietnam, agreed Rusk, 'and no miracle in the north is going to suddenly transform or eliminate the problem in South Vietnam'.[235]

It was only when faced with the imminent collapse of South Vietnamese authority*—and with it of a decade of 'helping' Saigon

* How bad the situation was early in 1965 was revealed by the Chairman of the US Joint Chiefs of Staff, General Earle Wheeler, two years later. Reporting from north to south: 'In the I Corps area, the Vietcong had moved into the coastal lowlands and were beginning to isolate Da Nang and Hue. In the II Corps region, the Vietcong and North Vietnamese units moved with total freedom and were on the verge of overrunning several provincial capitals. In

to win its war—that the US sought a 'miracle' in the North. Rather than 'underwrite' the struggle in the South, Washington counted on the threat of aerial destruction to force North Vietnam—since it 'directed' the Vietcong—to call off the war. Since threats had no effect the US had to step up the pressure. The Tonkin Gulf incidents had already produced the required blank cheque in the form of a Joint Congressional Resolution authorizing the President, as Commander-in-Chief, 'to take all necessary steps, including the use of armed force, to assist any member or protocol State [e.g. South Vietnam] of the South East Asia Collective Defence Treaty requiring assistance in defence of its freedom'.[236] Plans for a 'limited air war' against North Vietnam, prepared in 1964, were put into effect in February 1965. (Ironically the first strike, unrelated to previous Vietcong 'provocation', had to be postponed because of the uncertain situation in Saigon following an attempted military *coup*.)

When force, even though rapidly intensified, had no effect on Hanoi—and no lasting effect, after the initial elation, in the South—President Johnson tried inducement. Previously Washington had insisted that negotiations were out of the question until 'Communist aggression' had ceased: 'We are not going to negotiate to reward aggression,' according to Rusk.[237] But in his Baltimore speech of April 7, 1965, Johnson appealed for 'unconditional discussions' to lead to a 'peaceful settlement';[238] and even 'neutralization' was later considered possible, though not by Saigon which had labelled it a crime.[239] However it was too late. Just as the Americans had turned down a negotiated settlement in 1964,[240] when they believed they still had the upper hand, so the North Vietnamese and the Vietcong spurned Johnson's offers in 1965. The Americans, who rejected withdrawal—the only terms really offered by the Communists—were forced back to their fourth option; and with the Saigon régime crumbling there was no way out but armed intervention. America's response, and with it the character of the war, had changed.

PEACE—AND THE TET OFFENSIVE

For the first time in nearly two years, early in 1968, the Vietcong went over to the offensive. A force of between 100,000 and 120,000 men was secretly organized—half of them in fighting units—which struck a devastating and surprise blow to thirty-eight (out of forty-four) provincial capitals and some sixty district towns hitherto virtu-

III and IV corps [around Saigon and the Mekong delta, respectively] the Vietcong were moving unimpeded between war zones C and D, their sanctuaries, and the critical delta areas. . . .' Speech on January 17, 1967 (*Department of State Bulletin*, February 6, 1967.)

ally untouched by war. Less than one-third of these armed men were regular North Vietnamese troops.[241] Thus Joseph Alsop, himself a 'hard-liner', challenged the old 'aggression from the North' theory when he pointed out: 'The great bulk of the attacking troops were true Vietcong in the old sense—local units composed of Southerners. . . .'[242]

If as General Westmoreland, US Commander in Vietnam since 1964, reiterated, 'this whole campaign is a go-for-broke proposition' and the enemy 'has put forth a maximum effort',[243] and, as President Johnson claimed, the offensive was intended as a 'general uprising' to 'overthrow the constitutional government in Saigon',[244] then clearly once the Vietcong had been driven out of Saigon, Hue and the highland and delta towns, its 'desperate' final effort had failed. It had shot its bolt. In this belief, 'reports brimming with confidence and satisfaction over the outcome of that [first] stage of the offensive have been sent to the White House both by General William C. Westmoreland . . . and Ambassador Ellsworth Bunker [in Saigon]'.[245] After the 'second wave' of Vietcong mortar and rocket attacks on cities and bases, in mid-February 1968, President Johnson and his senior advisers publicly doubted that the Vietcong could soon mount another offensive on a nation-wide scale. General Walt, the US Marines' Deputy Commander, believed that the enemy's failure to take-over the citices amounted to a 'real defeat', while W. W. Rostow, the President's Special Assistant, told reporters that the South Vietnamese army had given such a good account of itself in the Tet offensive that it was 'riding high', full of pride and confidence that it could defend the cities.[246]

Only ten days later, General Wheeler, Chairman of the US Joint Chiefs of Staff, brought back from Saigon General Westmoreland's request for another 200,000 men—a 40 per cent increase in US forces—needed if he was to 'regain the initiative' from the Vietcong and the North Vietnamese.[247] General Wheeler, in contrast to the optimistic statements expressed before and after the Tet offensive—for example in Ambassador Bunker's 'Report on Vietnam', 'today the initiative is ours'[248]—admitted on his return from Saigon: 'I think the initiative now lies on both sides. In certain areas where the North Vietnamese and Vietcong have sizeable uncommitted forces, of course they can move. They have tactical flexibility. In other areas, particularly in areas where they have been repulsed, I would say that General Westmoreland's forces have the initiative.'[249] This was a very different story from General Westmoreland's own 'Progress Report on the War in Vietnam' (delivered in Washington in November 1967). This anticipated 'Phase III' of the war, 'when the end begins to come into view', as starting in 1968 with the employment

of 'US and free-world forces to destroy North Vietnamese forays while we assist the Vietnamese to reorganize for territorial security . . . [and] help the Government of Vietnam single out and destroy the Communist shadow government'. Allied forces were said to have completed Phase II (mid-1966 to end 1967) when they: 'Drove the enemy divisions back to sanctuary or into hiding. . . . Raised enemy losses beyond his input capacity. . . . Discovered and thwarted the enemy's battle plans before they could be executed.'[250] So if, as Alsop says of the Tet offensive, 'the enemy's plan went horribly wrong'—expecting a general uprising and disintegration of the South Vietnamese army[251]—so, it seems, did Westmoreland's.

The verdict had actually been given three years before by Major General Edward Lansdale, former adviser to Presidents Magsaysay and Diem, in his article, 'Vietnam: Do we understand Revolution?': 'The harsh fact . . . is that, despite the use of overwhelming amounts of men, money and material, despite the quantity of well-meant American advice and despite the impressive statistics of casualties inflicted on the Vietcong, the Communist subversive insurgents have grown steadily stronger, in numbers and in size of units, and still retain the initiative to wreak their will in the very areas of Vietnam where Vietnamese and American efforts have been most concentrated.'[252]

General Westmoreland's recall—announced on March 22, 1968—and President Johnson's decision nine days later not to stand again for the Presidency, only confirm this verdict. US policy had reached a dead-end in Vietnam. The addition of only 24,000 troops to level off at 550,000, the limitation of bombing of North Vietnam and Johnson's plea to Hanoi to join in peace talks, mark a turning point in the war. For Johnson it is the last chance. He is staking his future—with some possibility of success now that the military balance has once more (as in 1964) evened out—on a negotiated settlement.* The question is whether Hanoi and the Vietcong consider the change in US policy to be a fatal sign of weakness which they can ruthlessly exploit or—under pressure from the Russians and perhaps with only verbal opposition from the Chinese—they are prepared to compromise, as Washington at last is, in the belief that the alternative

* There is 'considerable evidence' that the N.L.F. leaders seriously considered taking part in an authentic coalition government in 1962, in 1963, and again in mid-1964 when it 'put forth feelers for a proposal for what appeared to be an authentic coalition government' [of Left-Wing, Right-Wing and Neutralists similar to the Laos arrangement]. Interestingly, part of the 1964 settlement was to 'involve de facto partition of South Vietnam, with the N.L.F. having exclusive control over the five southern provinces adjacent to the Cambodian border. . . .' Douglas Pike, *Viet Cong* (M.I.T., 1966), pp. 359-61.

of continued hardship and destruction would be worse.

Hanoi's attitude to negotiations may be gauged from a confidential report by General Nguyen Van Vinh, head of the Lao Dong (North Vietnam Communist Party) Reunification Department in April 1966—recorded in the notebook of a Vietcong cadre, captured in Ninh Thuan province on January 28, 1967:

'. . . Fighting continues until the emergence of a situation where both sides are fighting indecisively. Then, a situation where fighting and negotiations are conducted simultaneously may arise. . . . At present there are three viewpoints with regard to war and peace:

The Americans find it necessary to negotiate, but negotiate from a strong position. . . .

A number of countries want us to enter negotiations, any form of negotiations—so that a big war does not break out and this war can be ended—regardless of the interests of Vietnam. Some other countries wonder whether we can defeat the Americans, and if not, we should enter into negotiations. (Most of these countries are nationalist countries in Asia, Africa and Latin America). . . .

China holds the view that conditions for negotiations are not yet ripe, not until a few years from now and, even worse, seven [several?] years from now. In the meantime we should continue fighting to bog down the enemy. . . .

Our policy: to continue fighting until a certain time when we can fight and negotiate at the same time. . . .'[253]

Johnson's about-turn from intensification to de-escalation is in recognition that the military conflict has indeed reached a stalemate—'both sides are fighting indecisively'—although the pacification struggle—'the heart of the matter' as Cabot Lodge has rightly said—has suffered a shattering reverse. This was probably the real aim of the Tet offensive: (1) to destroy the confidence of the townspeople in government protection, (2) to divert government forces from the countryside into maintaining permanent garrisons in the towns, (3) by the threat of renewed attacks to aggravate popular insecurity, and (4) to make the most of the freedom of movement in the countryside to consolidate and enlarge Vietcong control of the villages. To reverse this situation, as Westmoreland desired, would require the mobilization of an additional 200,000 US soldiers—at a cost of $20,000 to $40,000 a man*—over and above the

* An estimated $40,000 each soldier for the first US combat troops in Vietnam, but nearer $20,000 each for their successors, since much of the basic construction and equipment has been provided. Testimony of US Director of Budget, Charles Zwick, before the Senate Finance Committee (*International Herald Tribune*, March 14, 1968).

present half million troops and the current $30 billion annual budget: a virtual impossibility in election year. But even these drastic measures were far from certain to 'regain the initiative'. For the one obvious fact—ever since the American build-up in 1965—was that the North Vietnamese were prepared and able to match every increase in US strength; not in numbers, but in effective capacity to tie down American units. Already the heavy losses suffered during the Tet offensive have been made up, first, by increased infiltration from North Vietnam—a further 20,000 or 30,000 in the two months since the end of January 1968[254]—and second, by the greater scope for recruitment open to the Vietcong in presently undefended rural areas. Above all, the North Vietnamese have ample reserves of manpower to draw on to maintain a 'reasonable ratio' of strength to whatever level of forces the US may decide on.[255]

As for pacification, it had been lagging well behind plans and expectations, even before the Tet offensive. The main reason for this is that the US military command is still fighting a conventional war: Westmoreland's strategy of 'attrition' gives priority to massive sweeps to 'search and destroy' the enemy main force units rather than to attempt to 'clear and hold' newly secured areas. Second, and following from the first, the US military seriously under-estimated the village-based strength and organization of the Vietcong. This was a failure of intelligence on a large scale and over a long period of time, culminating in the evident 'massive failure of intelligence' to discover the extent of the enemy's preparations for the Tet offensive. The puzzlement of Americans in face of an unconventional war is well brought out by a 'senior US officer responsible for policy making' in Vietnam, interviewed in July 1967: 'We keep on destroying them [the Vietcong] yet they always come back. And in the meantime nothing changes in the enemy position among the population. . . . We hoped at one time [the Manila Conference, October 1966] that the Vietnamese Army would handle the guerrillas and thereby destroy the military arm of the Communist political organization. That was part of our misconception. Few realized the depth and scope of this threat. I didn't think that the threat was as bad, or that Saigon, for example, was as close to being strangled, or that the enemy was so deeply embedded in the fabric of the country. . . .'[256] Yet shortly after Ambassador Bunker's arrival in Saigon in May 1967, the pacification programme was actually removed from civilian responsibility—'pressure' which the State Department had resisted during 1966—and placed under General Westmoreland's command.[257]

The South Vietnamese leaders recognized at the Manila Conference that the 'tactics of search and destroy, so often employed by allied forces in the past, had been shown to be inadequate without follow-up civic action and reconstruction. This search-and-destroy type of action left the Vietcong in the area to engage in sabotage after the military forces had moved on. . . .'[258] Australian troops amply confirmed from their experience in Phuoc Thuy province (as the British had found out in Malaya): that continual small operations, harassment, constant patrolling and systematic searches for guerrillas and supplies were far more effective than major search-and-destroy operations; the latter were generally rejected as 'very costly in manpower and casualties, and unproductive, given the Communist troops' capacity for dispersion and evasion'.[259] A recent example was the 'biggest combined operation of the war' launched by over 50,000 US and South Vietnamese troops six weeks after the Tet offensive. The aim was to destroy two divisions of Vietcong and North Vietnamese menacing Saigon—fresh units uncommitted in the Tet fighting. But after a few days, according to intelligence reports, the Vietcong eluded pursuit and withdrew to their old war zones 'C' and 'D' to the north west of Saigon.[260]

US search-and-destroy missions have evidently inflicted heavy casualties on the North Vietnamese and Vietcong (17,000 killed in 1964, 35,000 in 1965, 55,000 in 1966 and 88,000 in 1967, according to probably inflated US estimates).[261] But it is no less evident that Communist strategy is to accept these losses as the price of luring the Americans away from populated regions (which thus remain not properly pacified) into the remote and rugged country near Laos, Cambodia and the demilitarized zone (where, into the bargain, the North Vietnamese and Vietcong are able to regroup in comparative safety). Thus the threat to Khe Sanh—helped by ominous hints of another Dien Bien Phu—drew off forty of the ninety US combat battalions in South Vietnam, before the Tet offensive, into the five northern provinces of I Corps.[262] Alsop, vigorously backing Westmoreland's plea for more troops, reported in March 1968 that nearly half the forces at the general's disposal were still concentrated in I Corps area (which had previously been 'quiet') with the result that II Corps (the Central Highlands), where there had previously been 'great progress', was now 'stripped of troops to a potentially dangerous degree'. Further, Vietcong and North Vietnamese units in III Corps (around Saigon), which had been lurking in safety near Cambodia for over a year, had taken the opportunity to 'infiltrate' close to Saigon, where they were more exposed to risk but also in a better position to threaten the capital.[263] It was to eradicate this threat that the 'biggest combined operation of the war' was launched, in vain. Thus, US forces are becoming ever more thinly stretched—just as the French were against Giap who is still the North Vietnamese commander—in an effort to cope with every potential threat, which may be only 'diversionary'—Giap's great skill was in creating the semblance of a major offensive—but which cannot be ignored in case it turns out to be the reality. Yet as there are insufficient US forces, according to Westmoreland, to deal effectively with the military threat, which is the major priority, so there are all the fewer troops available for pacification.

The Tet offensive had a 'serious' effect on pacification efforts in thirteen provinces—particularly in I Corps and the delta region—a 'moderate' effect in sixteen provinces and a 'light' effect in the remaining fifteen, according to the Americans.[264] Eighteen of the fifty-five South Vietnamese battalions assigned to pacification duties had to be withdrawn to help defend provincial and district towns; and half the 'Revolutionary Development' (pacification) teams in the rural areas were also withdrawn both to help defend the towns and to organize relief work.[265] Because of the continuing threat of another offensive, it is uncertain how many of these have returned. But even before the Tet offensive, pacification was 'in deep trouble', according to a classified report prepared by the Institute for Defence Analysis under contract to the US Defence Department.[266] Indeed, Maxwell Taylor considered results were 'not satisfactory' in January 1967 while McNamara added in July that progress 'has been very slow'.[267] Insecurity grew worse after that date. The Vietcong reportedly killed more than 3,000 civilians in 1967, twice the number killed the year before. And the number killed in December 1967 (584) was more than in any other month of that year.[268] (This worsening trend in security was also reflected in a decrease in the number of defectors from the Vietcong: 18,000 in the first half of 1967 to 9,600 in the second half.[269]) Thus, even before the Tet offensive, the deterioration in rural areas cast doubt on the optimistic official reports that more than two-thirds of the 17 million people of South Vietnam were under government control (compared with about half in 1965)[270]

The official US analysis of these proportions indicates how misleading is the notion of 'relative security' on which the assumption of government control is based. It is obtained by 'evaluating' rural hamlets according to five levels of security— from 'A', 'secure with high development', down to 'E', 'insecure with no development'—while the sixth level (nearly 3 million people) is under Vietcong control. Categories 'A' to 'C'—altogether 8¼ million villagers—in addition to 3½ million townspeople* (including refugees) make up the

* 'The Hamlet Evaluation System is only used to measure Government of Vietnam control in the countryside. The large urban areas are, of course, under the Government's control.' *Foreign Policy Briefs,* US Information Service, Washington, January 1, 1968.

grand total of 67 per cent of the people of South Vietnam.[271] However, by examining the official definition of these categories it is clear that part at least of these villagers—'graded' three months before the Tet offensive—lived in 'contested' rather than 'secure' hamlets, while up to a million or more of those reported to be in 'contested' areas lived more under Vietcong control.

Thus category 'E', comprising 330,000 villagers, is defined as indicating a 'government presence, usually military', but 'the Vietcong are active there, too . . . there is VC *political and subversive* activity; their *infrastructure* is operating; friendly security is inadequate; government of Vietnam officials are present *only in daytime;* and health, education and welfare programmes are non-existent'.[272] This to all intents and purposes amounts to Vietcong control, even if it also indicates 'accommodation' by local officials. Category 'D' (over two million villagers) 'is a little better. Vietcong military activities have been reduced, and *external* VC forces have been cut back by about 25 per cent. Local participation in hamlet management has begun, the medical teams are visiting *periodically*, and there is a beginning of education and welfare activity. Also, a certain amount of economic development is taking place. However, there is still VC *activity in the hamlet at night* and there is VC *terrorism and taxation.*'[273] The later, of course, is the heart of the matter, revealing the continued existence—and functioning—of the Vietcong political and supply structure.

In category 'C' (over four million villagers, i.e. half the 'relatively secure' rural population) Vietcong *military* control has been broken, '*most* of the hamlet's infrastructure identified and no *overt* VC incidents motified', officials remain overnight, primary education is carried out in permanent classrooms and full-time medical facilities are available; but even there 'continuing VC taxation is suspected'. In strategic terms this area has been 'cleared', but not yet firmly 'held'. Finally, the 'B' category (nearly 3½ million people) is 'still more secure' and in 'A' (650,000) 'everything is going right'.[274] From the official explanation that emerged in October 1967 the situation was as follows:

Vietcong control—2¾ million villagers in nearly 4,000 hamlets.
Government control [A,B,C]—8¼ million villagers in over 5,000 hamlets.
Contested [D,E]—2½ million villagers in some 2,700 hamlets.

Adding the urban population this gave the figure of 67 per cent under government control. But considering the *definition* of these categories, the situation at the end of 1967 was more like this (assuming, which is open to doubt, that the evaluations were correct):

Vietcong control [E+VC]—3 million villagers in 5,000 hamlets.
Government control [A,B]—4 million villagers in 2,000 hamlets.
Contested [C,D]—6 million villagers in 5,400 hamlets.

This left the government in control of 44 per cent of the total population, 38 per cent being contested.*

Now the confidence of a large proportion of the villagers formerly under government control or in 'contested' areas would have been badly shaken by the post-Tet withdrawal of one-third of the South Vietnamese military and one-half of the pacification teams—even if most of them subsequently returned. Nor is the present uncertainty about the US commitment likely to reassure the rural population. The situation, from Saigon's point of view, is almost certainly worse than it was in September 1966 when Robert Komer, sponsor of the 'Hamlet Evaluation System', estimated there were proportionately 4¼ million villagers under the Vietcong, less than 5 million under government control (excluding the urban population) and some 3½ million in contested areas.[275]

Even in 1967, according to an American specialist, 'the only province [out of 44] to enjoy wide-scale security is An Giang, where the militantly anti-N.L.F. Hoa Hao sect was already maintaining local defence and police functions. . . .'[276] (The Hoa Hao was alienated from Diem but rallied to Khanh in 1964.) The importance of popular commitment—in this case to a religious group which is felt to represent the interests of the local people—could not be better demonstrated. In the absence of such commitment, pacification depends, as in Binh Dinh province, on 'exceptional local leadership' by government officials and on the 'availability of large, permanently assigned military screening forces'.[277] As Robert Komer explained in September 1966:

'Insecurity, poverty, low health standards, lack of opportunity, social injustice and land inequities, have enabled the Vietcong to exploit a rural feeling of alienation from the government. The Revolutionary

* The present situation is much more fluid than it was during the Vietminh war, when distinct 'liberated zones' were established, especially in northern and central Vietnam. 'The essential feature of the Vietcong adaptation of the revolutionary method was that they did not set up a zone apart from government territory this time; as a result, supporting them entailed no definite and irrevocable act like taking to the hills to "join the resistance".' The rank and file mostly carried on their everyday existence, performing only certain services, as directed by the cadres. The Vietcong 'enmeshed itself into the economic and political life of the government and of the community it proposed progressively to take over'. Duncanson, *Government and Revolution in Vietnam,* pp. 295, 297.

Development programme must change all that—or else ultimately be judged a failure like its predecessors.'[278]

But the 'first pre-requisite' of pacification, he pointed out, was 'adequate local security and elimination of the remaining Vietcong threat, after main enemy military forces have been driven from an area'. And the reason the forerunners of 'Revolutionary Development' failed was primarily 'because the Vietcong/North Vietnamese Army destroyed the Government of Vietnam's ability to provide essential local security'.[279]

In August 1965 a 'dynamic new Minister', Major-General Nguyen Duc Thang, was put in charge of pacification. 'Thang's incorruptibility and enthusiasm' won high praise from the Americans.[280] But this rather exceptional ability only served to highlight the basic weaknesses of the programme—personal and family aggrandizement, local rivalries, 'inept or corrupt leadership', and conflict of loyalties between immediate superiors and Corps Commanders[281]—when General Thang resigned in January 1968 as Army Deputy Chief of Staff in charge of pacification and local security forces. The General had apparently given up hope that the government would take the necessary 'vigorous and prompt action to stem corruption, and nepotism, reward competence and set an austere, responsible example of duty and dedication'. Progress in rural pacification would only be 'illusory',* he considered, until the local population came to believe that the government was serious in attacking corruption and other social ills.[282]

The Saigon Government's inability or unwillingness to respond to popular needs is again revealed in President Johnson's momentous March 31, 1968, announcement, when he spoke of 'further efforts' required by the South Vietnamese authorities:

'—to move back into the countryside;
—to increase their taxes;
—to select the very best men they have for civil and military responsibility;
—to achieve a new unity within their constitutional government;
—and to include in the national effort all those groups who wish to preserve South Vietnam's control over its own destiny.'[283]

* General Thang—appointed Commander of IV Corps (Mekong delta region) following the Tet offensive—expressed little faith in the statistical approach to progress in pacification (Komer's Hamlet Evaluation System). A correct assessment by computers depended on asking the right questions and providing the right data: 'You must be careful about input.' Thang was replaced as IV Corps Commander in June 1968—in the purge by President Thieu of Vice-President Ky's supporters.

These—particularly the last—have never yet been achieved by any South Vietnamese régime: and this alone makes it unlikely that the present system—or whatever emerges from a settlement reflecting the realities of power—will have much control over the objective for which so harsh and fruitless a struggle has been fought—the destiny of South Vietnam.

REFERENCE NOTES TO CHAPTER IV

1. Colonel Napoleon D. Valeriano and Lt. Colonel Charles T. R. Bohannan, *Counter-Guerrilla Operations: The Philippine Experience* (Praeger, 1962), p. 48.
2. Cited in *ibid.*, p. 107.
3. Ian Morrison, 'Aspects of the Racial Problem in Malaya', *Pacific Affairs*, September 1949.
4. Lucian W. Pye, *Guerrilla Communism in Malaya: its social and political meaning* (Princeton Univ. Press, 1956), p. 49.
5. Richard Clutterbuck. *The Long, Long War: The Emergency in Malaya 1948-1960* (Cassell, 1967), p. 69.
6. Cited in Milton E. Osborne, *Strategic Hamlets in South Vietnam: a Survey and a Comparison* (Cornell Univ., Data Paper 55, Southeast Asia Program, 1965), p. 12.
7. Clutterbuck, *op. cit.*, p. 51.
8. *Ibid.*, pp. 55-6.
9. Harry Miller, *Menace in Malaya* (Harrup, 1954), p. 139.
10. Clutterbuck, *op. cit.*, p. 44.
11. Osborne, *op. cit.*, p. 16.
12. Clutterbuck, *op. cit.*, p. 61.
13. Published by Malayan Government on May 12, 1949, cited in Osborne, *op. cit.*, p. 15 (italics added).
14. Examples in Clutterbuck, *op. cit.*, pp. 96-9.
15. Sir Robert Thompson, *Defeating Communist Insurgency: Experiences from Malaya and Vietnam* (Chatto & Windus, 1966). p. 146.
16. *Ibid.*, p. 85.
17. *Ibid.*, p. 60.
18. Valeriano and Bohannan, *op. cit.*, pp. 33-4.
19. F. Sionil Jose, 'Land is the Philippines' Public Problem No. 1', *Asia Magazine*, March 11, 1962.
20. Alvin H. Scaff, *The Philippines' Answer to Communism* (Stanford Univ. Press, 1955), see note 7, p. 148.
21. *Ibid.*, p. 25.
22. Valeriano and Bohannan, *op. cit.*, p. 23.
23. Scaff, *op. cit.*, p. 28.
24. Jesus M. Vargas, 'Communism in Decline: The Huk Campaign', published by the South East Asia Treaty Organisation [1958].
25. Carlos P. Romulo and Marvin M. Gray, *The Magsaysay Story* (Pocket Books ed. 1957), p. 85.
26. *Ibid.*, p. 92.
27. *Ibid.*, p. 93.
28. *Ibid.*, pp. 112-3.

29. *Loc. cit.*
30. *Ibid.*, p. 119.
31. 'Upsurge of the Anti-Imperialist Movement in the Philippines', *World Marxist Review* (Prague), November 1965.
32. Vargas, *op. cit.*
33. Clutterbuck, *op. cit.*, p. 63.
34. *Ibid.*, p. 64.
35. *Ibid.*, p. 70.
36. 8,000 guerrillas in *ibid.*, pp. 80, 87; over 10,000 in Thompson, *op. cit.*, p. 44.
37. Official US figures estimated in 1966, cited in Roger Hilsman, *To Move a Nation* (Doubleday, 1967), table on p. 529.
38. Thompson, *op. cit.*, p. 57. Foreword to Clutterbuck, *op. cit.*
39. *Thompson,* op. cit., pp. 55-6.
40. Clutterbuck, *op. cit.*, pp. 87-8.
41. *Ibid.*, p. 118.
42. *Ibid.*, pp. 116-18.
43. Miller, *op. cit.*, p. 203.
44. 'Self-criticism' adopted September 1966, reportedly published in *Indonesian Tribune* of January 1967, excerpts printed in *Peking Review*, July 21, 1967.
45. *Loc. cit.*
46. *Loc. cit.*
47. Cited by Suharjo 'Indonesia's Communist Party and the Peasantry', *World Marxist Review* (Prague), July 1965.
48. Donald Hindley, *The Communist Party of Indonesia 1951-1963* (Univ. of California Press, 1964), p. 180.
49. Editorial of *Red Flag,* theoretical journal of the Chinese Communist Party, reprinted in *Peking Review,* July 14, 1967. The P.K.I. 'Statement' was reportedly issued on August 17, 1966.
50. Abdul Haris Nasution, *Fundamentals of Guerrilla Warfare: And the Indonesian Defence System Past and Future* (Information Service of Indonesian Armed Forces, Government Printing Office, Djakarta, [1960?]; Author's foreword May 1953), p. 14. Also reprinted Praeger, 1965.
51. *Ibid.*, p. 46.
52. *Ibid.*, p. 34.
53. *Ibid.*, p. 23.
54. *Ibid.*, p. 25.
55. *Ibid.*, p. 46.
56. *Ibid.*, pp. 185-7.
57. *Ibid.*, map on p. 198.
58. *Ibid.*, p. 12.
59. *Ibid.*, p. 47.
60. *Ibid.*, pp. 78-9.
61. *Ibid.*, p. 15.
62. *Ibid.*, p. 20.
63. David Galula, *Counter-Insurgency Warfare: Theory and Practice* (Pall Mall, 1964), p. 98.
64. *Documents on American Foreign Relations, 1952* [henceforth D.A.F.R.] for Council on Foreign Relations (Harper Bros., New York, 1953), p. 284.
65. [US] *Department of State Bulletin* [henceforth D.S.B.] (Washington), August 7, 1961.

66. D.S.B., July 24, 1967.
67. D.A.F.R., 1953, p. 81.
68. D.S.B., November 5, 1956.
69. Walter S. Robertson, Assistant Secretary of State for Far Eastern Affairs, D.S.B., April 30, 1956.
70. *Ibid.*
71. D.S.B., November 7, 1955.
72. D.S.B., April 12, 1954.
73. D.A.F.R., 1954, pp. 8-9.
74. Acheson, February 8, 1949. D.A.F.R. XI (1949) (Princeton Univ. Press), p. 589.
75. Dulles, January 27, 1953. D.S.B., February 9, 1953.
76. D.S.B., August 22, 1955.
77. Truman, September 1, 1950. D.A.F.R. XII (1950) (Princeton Univ. Press), p. 10.
78. Truman, State of the Union. D.A.F.R. XII, p. 1.
79. Acheson, November 29, 1950. D.A.F.R. XII, p. 13.
80. Truman, December 15, 1950. D.A.F.R. XII, p. 16.
81. *Ibid.*, p. 18.
82. D.A.F.R. XII, p. 214.
83. Acheson, December 30, 1951. D.A.F.R. XIII (1951) (Princeton Univ. Press), p. 13.
84. *Ibid.*,
85. D.A.F.R. XII, p. 17.
86. D.A.F.R. 1954 (Harper Bros.), pp. 9-10.
87. 'Threat of a Red Asia', March 29, 1954. D.S.B. April 12, 1954.
88. 'Security in the Pacific', June 11, 1954. D.S.B. June 28, 1954.
89. D.A.F.R. 1952, p. 83.
90. Eisenhower (then Supreme Allied Commander, Europe) April 2, 1952. D.A.F.R. 1952, p. 140.
91. Stevenson, Sept. 9, 1952. D.A.F.R. 1952, p. 96.
92. Dulles, Radio and T.V. address, January 27, 1953. D.S.B. February 9, 1953.
93. D.A.F.R. 1950, p. 61.
94. Dulles, April 23, 1951. D.A.F.R. XIII, pp. 462-3.
95. D.A.F.R. 1953, p. 83.
96. Acheson, June 29, 1951. D.A.F.R. XIII, pp. 6-9.
97. Eisenhower, April 4, 1959. D.S.B. April 27, 1959.
98. Dulles, November 29, 1954. D.A.F.R. 1954, p. 20.
99. Dulles, June 30, 1954. D.A.F.R. 1954, pp. 416, 418.
100. Acheson, January 12, 1950. D.A.F.R. XII, pp. 432-3.
101. Arthur J. Dommen, *Conflict in Laos: The Politics of Neutralisation* (Praeger/Pall Mall, 1964), p. 96.
102. Souvanna Phouma, interviewed in Phnom Penh, *New York Times*, January 20, 1961.
103. *New York Times*, August 30, 1959.
104. Robertson, September 21, 1959. D.S.B. October 12, 1959.
105. On September 5, 1959. D.S.B. September 21, 1959.
106. Alsop, *New York Herald Tribune*, September 3, 1959.
107. *Ibid.*, September 6, 1959.
108. Phoui, August 22, 1959. *Lao Presse*, August 26, 1959.
109. Dommen, *op. cit.*, p. 109.
110. *Ibid.*, pp. 110-11.

111. Cited in Sisouk na Champassak, *Storm over Laos: A Contemporary History* (Praeger, 1961), appendix.
112. On September 15, 1959. D.S.B. October 5, 1959.
113. D.S.B. September 28, 1959.
114. Dommen, *op. cit.*, pp. 98-9.
115. *Ibid.*, p. 102.
116. *Ibid.*, p. 103.
117. Kong Lae, reported by Vientiane radio, August 10, 1960.
118. Dommen, *op. cit.*, p. 154.
119. *Ibid.*, p. 158.
120. *Ibid.*, p. 160.
121. *Ibid.*, p. 167.
122. *Ibid.*, p. 179.
123. On January 7, 1961. D.S.B. January 23, 1961.
124. *Ibid.* (emphasis added.)
125. Kennedy, March 23, 1961. D.S.B. April 17, 1961.
126. Kennedy, radio and TV address, June 6, 1961. D.S.B. June 26, 1961.
127. Marguerite Higgins in *New York Herald Tribune*.
128. Agreement on Cessation of Hostilities in Vietnam and Final Declaration of the Geneva Conference. D.A.F.R. 1954, pp. 283, 287, 313.
129. D.S.B. May 11, 1964.
130. D.S.B. January 25, 1965.
131. Eisenhower's letter to Diem, delivered October 23, 1964. D.A.F.R. 1954, pp. 366-7.
132. Eisenhower, April 4, 1959. D.S.B. April 27, 1959.
133. Truman, March 6, 1952. D.A.F.R. 1952, p. 33.
134. Dulles, September 17, 1953. D.A.F.R. 1953, pp. 38-9.
135. Robert Scigliano, *South Vietnam: Nation under Stress* (Boston, Houghton Mifflin Co., 1964), p. 209.
136. Marshall's reply to US Embassy, Nanking, October 1948. *United States Relations with China* (Washington, 1959), pp. 280-1.
137. Bernard Fall, *The Two Viet-Nams* (Praeger, 1964), p. 325.
138. *Ibid.*, p. 324.
139. May 11, 1957.
140. Washington, November 18, 1958.
141. D.S.B. April 27, 1959.
142. Fall, *op. cit.*, p. 327.
143. Eisenhower's message to Diem on fifth anniversary of Republic, October 22, 1960. D.S.B. November 14, 1960.
144. Rusk, May 4, 1961. D.S.B. May 22, 1961.
145. D.S.B. January 1, 1962.
146. U. Alexis Johnson, Political Under-Secretary of State, April 8, 1963. D.S.B. April 29, 1963.
147. Theodore Heavner, August 25, 1963. D.S.B. September 9, 1963.
148. Scigliano, *op. cit.*, p. 150.
149. Arthur M. Schlesinger, Jr., *The Bitter Heritage: Vietnam and American Democracy, 1941-1966* (Deutsch, 1967), p. 29.
150. U. A. Johnson, September 15, 1962. D.S.B. October 1, 1962.
151. Schlesinger, *op. cit.*, p. 29. Confirmed by William Bundy, August 15, 1967. D.S.B. September 4, 1967.
152. Roger Hilsman, 'A Report on South Vietnam', September 18, 1962. D.S.B. October 8, 1962.

153. *A Threat to the Peace . . .* (Washington, December 1961), p. 1 (emphasis added).
154. SEATO Council, Bangkok. D.S.B. March 30, 1961.
155. Rusk, May 4, 1961. D.S.B. May 22, 1961.
156. *Ibid.*
157. White House Statement, October 2, 1963. D.S.B. October 21, 1963.
158. William A. Nighswonger, *Rural Pacification in Vietnam* (Praeger, 1966), p. 54.
159. Maxwell D. Taylor, *Responsibility and Response* (N.Y., Harper and Row, 1967), pp. 56-7.
160. James Reston of *New York Times* (reported, *Canberra Times,* November 24, 1967).
161. Hilsman, D.S.B. October 8, 1962.
162. Heavner, August 25, 1963. D.S.B. September 9, 1963.
163. *Ibid.*
164. U. A. Johnson, April 8, 1963. D.S.B. April 29, 1963.
165. Rusk, February 13, 1963. D.S.B. March 4, 1963.
166. Rusk, April 22, 1963. D.S.B. May 13, 1963.
167. Douglas Pike, *Viet Cong: The Organisation and Techniques of the National Liberation Front of South Vietnam* (Cambridge, Mass., M.I.T. Press, 1966), pp. 65-6.
168. *Ibid.,* p. 67.
169. John Mecklin, *Mission in Torment: An Intimate Account of the U.S. Role in Vietnam* (Doubleday, 1965), p. 36.
170. Milton Osborne, *Strategic Hamlets in South Vienam* (Cornell Univ. Data Paper 55, 1965), p. 32.
171. Nighswonger, *op. cit.,* p. 98.
172. Osborne, *op. cit.,* p. 39.
173. *Ibid.,* p. 27.
174. Sir Robert Thompson, *Defeating Communist Insurgency: Experiences from Malaya and Vietnam* (Chatto and Windus, 1965), p. 134.
175. *Ibid.,* p. 141.
176. Nighswonger, *op. cit.,* pp. 102-3, 78.
177. Cited in Osborne, *op. cit.,* p. 35.
178. *New York Times,* December 4, 1963.
179. David Halberstam, *The Making of a Quagmire* (Bodley Head, 1964), p. 185.
180. Scigliano, *op. cit.,* pp. 51-3.
181. McNamara, March 26, 1964. D.S.B. April 13, 1964.
182. Halberstam, *op. cit.,* pp. 176, 254.
183. White House Statement, December 21, 1963. D.S.B. January 13, 1964.
184. White House Statement, March 17, 1964. D.S.B. April 6, 1964.
185. McNamara, March 26, 1964. D.S.B. April 13, 1964.
186. Peter Grose, *New York Times,* August 12, 1964.
187. Nguyen Cao Ky, presenting the new 'Council for the Leadership of the Nation', Saigon, June 19, 1965.
188. Nguyen Van Thieu, June 24, 1965.
189. *New York Times,* April 25, 1965.
190. Rusk, March 7, 1965. D.S.B. March 29, 1965.
191. Scigliano, *op. cit.,* p. 150.
192. *Ibid.,* pp. 214-15.
193. Nguyen Thai, *Is South Vietnam Viable?* (Manila, Carmelo and Bauermann, 1962. p. xi.

194. Marcus Ruskin and Bernard Fall (eds.), *The Viet-Nam Reader* (N.Y., Vintage Press, 1965), pp. 391-2.
195. *Loc. cit.*
196. *New York Times,* December 16, 1963.
197. Heavner, D.S.B. September 9, 1963.
198. Rusk, News Conference, March 8, 1963. D.S.B. March 25, 1963.
199. US official estimate, November 1966 (*Canberra Times,* January 6, 1967).
200. Wesley Fishel, *Asian Survey* (Univ. of California), January 1966.
201. A.P., November 23, 1965.
202. *Canberra Times,* January 6, 1967.
203. I. F. Stone, March 8, 1965 (*Viet-Nam Reader*, p. 156).
204. Malcolm Browne, *The New Face of War: A Report on a Communist Guerrilla Campaign* (Cassell, 1965), p. 147.
205. *Ibid.,* p. 146. Hilsman, *To Move a Nation,* p. 529.
206. Rusk, April 22, 1963. D.S.B. May 13, 1963.
207. Scigliano, *op. cit.,* p. 97.
208. L. B. Johnson, May 13, 1961. D.S.B. June 19, 1961.
209. *Viet-Nam Reader,* pp. 116-23; also Fall, *The Two Viet-Nams,* appendix.
210. Duong Van Minh, January 2, 1964.
211. Mecklin, *op. cit.,* p. 100.
212. *Loc. cit.*
213. Rusk, D.S.B. July 20, 1964.
214. Rusk, News Conference, July 31, 1964. D.S.B. August 17, 1964.
215. Willard Mathias, reported in *New York Times,* August 23, 1964.
216. Rusk, D.S.B. September, 21, 1964.
217. Rusk, D.S.B. July 20, 1964.
218. Rusk, D.S.B. September 21, 1964.
219. Thompson, *op. cit.,* p. 88.
220. Rusk, D.S.B. September 28, 1964.
221. D.S.B. September 28, 1964.
222. *Loc. cit.*
223. Rusk, September 14, 1964. D.S.B. October 5, 1964.
224. D.S.B. December 21, 1964.
225. Rusk, News Conference, December 23, 1964. D.S.B. January 11, 1965.
226. W. Bundy, January 23, 1965. D.S.B. February 8, 1965.
227. W. Bundy, D.S.B. June 20, 1966.
228. Eisenhower, February 10, 1954.
229. W. Bundy, September 29, 1964. D.S.B. October 19, 1964.
230. McNamara, March 26, 1964. D.S.B. April 13, 1964.
231. Rusk, D.S.B. June 8, 1964.
232. W. Bundy, D.S.B. February 8, 1965.
233. Heavner, August 25, 1963. D.S.B. September 9, 1963.
234. McNamara, March 26, 1964.
235. Rusk, February 27, 1964. D.S.B. March 16, 1964.
236. Joint Congressional Resolution (unanimous vote House of Representatives, Senate 88-2), August 7, 1964. D.S.B. August 24, 1964.
237. Rusk, March 7, 1965.
238. L. B. Johnson, D.S.B. April 26, 1965.
239. Decree Law, outlawing propaganda in favour of Communism and neutralism, February 1, 1964.
240. L. B. Johnson, April 20, 1964.
241. 'Vietnam Allies Take Stock', *Canberra Times,* February 21, 1968.

242. Joseph Alsop, 'General Giap's Costly Assault', *International Herald Tribune,* February 8, 1968.
243. General Westmoreland, February 1, 1968 (*I.H. Tribune,* February 2, 1968), reaffirmed in interview with Associated Press, February 26, 1968.
244. L. B. Johnson, February 2, 1968 (*I.H. Tribune,* February 3-4, 1968).
245. Murrey Marder, Washington (*I.H. Tribune,* February 12, 1968).
246. *I.H. Tribune,* February 20, 1968.
247. Hedrick Smith, Neil Sheehan, *New York Times* (I.H. Tribune, March 11, 1968).
248. New York, November 17, 1967. (D.S.B. December 11, 1967).
249. Washington, February 29, 1968.
250. Address to National Press Club, Washington, November 21, 1967. (D.S.B. December 11, 1967).
251. *I.H. Tribune,* February 20, 1968.
252. *Foreign Affairs,* October 1964.
253. 'Viet Cong Documents on the War', *Communist Affairs* (Univ. of Southern California), November-December 1967.
254. *I.H. Tribune,* March 9-10, 1968.
255. C.I.A. assessment reported *I.H. Tribune,* March 11 and 25, 1968.
256. Peter Arnett, Associated Press (*Bangkok World,* July 24, 1967).
257. John C. Donnell, 'Pacification Reassessed', *Asian Survey* ('Vietnam: A Special Issue'), August 1967
258. Harold Holt, late Prime Minister of Australia, commenting on the Manila Conference (*Canberra Times,* October 28, 1966).
259. *Bulletin,* Sydney, October 21, 1967.
260. *Canberra Times,* March 16 and 21, 1968.
261. R. Hilsman, *op. cit.,* p. 529; Gen. Westmoreland (D.S.B. May 15, 1967); L. B. Johnson (D.S.B. April 3, 1967); McNamara, (*The Times,* February 13, 1968).
262. *I.H. Tribune,* March 25, 1968.
263. Joseph Alsop, 'The Argument for More Troops', *I.H. Tribune,* March 7, 1968.
264. *The Times,* February 26, 1968.
265. *Loc. cit.;* also M. Marder and Chalmers Roberts, *Washington Post* (*Australian,* March 1, 1968); R. Evans and R. Novak, *I. H. Tribune,* March 14, 1968.
266. Report for period September 1966-April 1967, cited by R. Schweiker (*Canberra Times,* March 26, 1968).
267. Taylor, January 30, 1967; McNamara, July 12, 1967.
268. Robert Komer, Ambassador in charge of pacification (*Saigon Daily News,* January 6, 1968).
269. Neil Sheehan, *I.H. Tribune,* March 22, 1968.
270. Ellsworth Bunker, 'Report on Vietnam' (D.S.B. December 11, 1967).
271. 'New Hamlet Evaluation System', *Foreign Policy Briefs,* US Information Service, Washington, January 1, 1968.
272. *Loc. cit.*(italics added).
273. *Loc. cit.* (italics added).
274. *Loc. cit.* (italics added).
275. 'The Other War in Vietnam—A Progress Report', Robert Komer, then Special Assistant to the President, September 13, 1966 (D.S.B. October 10, 1966).
276. Donnell, *op. cit.*
277. *Ibid.*

278. Komer, 'The Other War in Vietnam . . .'.
279. *Ibid.*
280. Donnell, *op. cit.*
281. *Ibid.*
282. *New York Times* news service, Saigon, January 27, 1968.
283. President Johnson's 'de-escalation' speech, announcing that he would not seek re-election as President.

ANNOTATED BIBLIOGRAPHY

CHINA

Brandt, Conrad, Schwarz, Benjamin and Fairbank, John K. *A Documentary History of Chinese Communism.* Harvard U.P., 1952. Translalations from original documents with commentary.

Ch'en, Jerome. *Mao and the Chinese Revolution.* Oxford U.P., 1965. Good detailed study of Mao up to 1949.

Fairbank, John K. *The United States and China.* Viking, 1962. Lucid and informative general survey, particularly useful on China.

Feis, Herbert. *The China Tangle.* Princeton U.P., 1953. American policy towards China during the Second World War.

FitzGerald, C. P. *The Birth of Communist China.* Penguin, 1964. Praeger, 1966. Revised ed. of *Revolution in China.* Cresset, 1952. Masterly account of traditional and contemporary forces in China.

Isaacs, Harold R. *The Tragedy of the Chinese Revolution.* Stanford U.P., rev. ed. 1961. Bitter description of Stalinist betrayal of the Chinese Communist Party in the 1920s.

Johnson, Chalmers A. *Peasant Nationalism and Communist Power: The Emergence of Revolutionary China, 1937-1945.* Stanford U.P., 1962. Pioneering study of Chinese Communist Party during the war against Japan, making full use of captured Japanese documents.

Lin, Piao. 'Long Live the Victory of People's War', *Peking Review,* September 3, 1965. Summary of Chinese Communist experience in the war against Japan and the Kuomintang with (intended) lessons for struggling insurgents elsewhere.

Mao Tse-tung. *Selected Works of Mao Tse-tung.* Foreign Languages Press, Peking, 1965. Brilliant and lively analyses of the 'concrete conditions' in China and the revolutionary opportunities for peasant-based guerrilla fighters. Particularly important for the study of insurgency are the earlier pieces, notably '... Investigation of the Peasant Movement in Hunan', 'A Single Spark can start a Prairie Fire', 'Problems of Strategy in China's Revolutionary War', 'Problems of Strategy in Guerrilla War against Japan' and 'On Protracted War'.

North, Robert C. *Moscow and Chinese Communists.* Stanford U.P., 1953. Clear and useful account of Russia's 'China tangle'.

Schwarz, Benjamin. *Chinese Communism and the Rise of Mao.* Harvard U.P., 1951. Illuminating, thoroughly documented study of Mao's early years, in opposition to the official party line.

Smedley, Agnes. *The Great Road: The Life and Times of Chu Teh.* Monthly Review Press, 1956. Recounted by Chu himself before 'Liberation': A good picture of the old warrier—war lord, KMT chief and inspired Communist military leader.

Snow, Edgar. *Red Star over China.* Gollancz, 1937. Grove Press, 1961 (paperback ed.). Celebrated report of a visit to the 'Red' areas including interviews with Mao and other Communist leaders.

Tang, Tsou. *America's Failure in China, 1941-56.* Chicago U.P., 1963.

Excellent and detailed account of conditions in China and US attitudes; though it is doubtful if any other policy by the *Americans* (than that of seeking a compromise settlement) could have 'saved' the Nationalist régime.

US Department of State. *United States Relations with China: With Special Reference to the Period 1944-1949*. Washington, 1949. US 'White Paper', quoting extensively from policy statements and Embassy despatches, issued shortly before the collapse of the Kuomintang.

INDO-CHINA

Devillers, Philippe. *Histoire du Viet-Nam de 1940 à 1952*. Eds. du Seuil, 1952. Detailed, sympathetic study by former Press Attaché to General Leclerc. Essential reading.

Fall, Bernard B. *Le Viet-Minh: La République Démocratique du Viet-Nam 1945-1960*. Lib. Armand Colin, 1960. Valuable account of the Vietminh régime. *Street without Joy: Indochina at War, 1946-54*. Stackpole Co., 1961. Realistic picture of campaigns based on French military files.

Hammer, Ellen. *The Struggle for Indochina 1940-1955*. Stanford U.P., new ed. 1966. A lively narrative; critical of French official policy and of the Bao Dai régime (with good reason).

Ho Chi Minh. *Selected Works*. Foreign Languages Publishing House, Hanoi, 1961. No theoretical brilliance, but practical guidance issued to party and Vietminh members by a professional revolutionary and ardent nationalist.

Lancaster, Donald. *The Emancipation of French Indochina*. Oxford U.P., 1961. Fascinating history, expressed in rolling periods and Gibbonian irony (ends with Diem's establishment of the Republic).

Le Thanh Khoi. *Le Viet-Nam: Histoire et Civilisation*. Eds. de Minuit, 1955. Standard account by a Vietnamese historian.

Mus, Paul. *Viet-Nam: Sociologie d'une Guerre*. Eds. du Seuil, 1952. By a distinguished scholar of Vietnamese culture; rather opaquely written but shows penetrating and sympathetic insight into French and Vietnamese attitudes and circumstances. Essential to an understanding of the Vietminh (and hence the present) period.

Ngo-Van-Chieu. *Journal d'un Combattant Viet-Minh*. Eds. du Seuil, 1955. How it all began—the story of one man's war.

Tanham, George K. *Communist Revolutionary Warfare: The Vietminh in Indochina*. Praeger, 1967. Brief but well-informed analysis by a RAND specialist.

Truong Chinh. *The Resistance will Win*. Foreign Languages Publishing House, Hanoi, 1960. An early work (written in 1947) by North Vietnam's foremost theorist and later doctrinaire organizer of 'land reform'; shows a realistic grasp of problems.

Vo Nguyen Giap. *People's War, People's Army*. For. Lang. Pub. House, Hanoi, 1961. Praeger, 1962. A classic of revolutionary warfare by the

'Trotsky' of Vietnamese Communism (rival of Truong Chinh) who still directs military strategy in North and South.

VIETNAM (SOUTH)

Browne, Malcolm. *The New Face of War: A Report on a Communist Guerrilla Campaign.* Cassell, 1965. A sceptical look at US reliance on gadgetry in Vietnam.

Burchett, Wilfrid G. *Vietnam: Inside Story of the Guerrilla War.* International Publishers, 1965. Valuable report on 'liberated zones' around Saigon and in the Central Highlands marred by too much propaganda.

Duncanson, Dennis J. *Government and Revolution in Vietnam.* Oxford U.P., 1968. The most remarkable book to have emerged from the second Vietnam war, matching—though in a different field—Paul Mus's work (see above) in insight and understanding: the fruit of administrative experience, knowledge of Chinese, and six years (as member of the British Advisory Mission) in Vietnam. Conservative in temper—a common trait among administrators—the author cannot bring himself to admit the part played by idealism (nationalism, Communism) and economic grievances in the growth of Vietminh and subsequently of the Vietcong; and he attributes the obvious failings of the Saigon régimes—brilliantly dissected—chiefly to the corrupting influence of American aid and to administrative ignorance and malpractice.

Fall, Bernard B. *The Two Viet-Nams: a Political and Military Analysis.* Praeger, 1963 and subseq. eds. A clear and comprehensive picture, understandably critical of both régimes. The author's foresight has been abundantly justified by events.

Gettleman, Marvin E. (ed.). *Viet Nam: History, Documents and Opinions on a Major World Crisis.* Fawcett Premier, 1965. Useful compilation of articles, speeches and excerpts from books—tends to be critical of Saigon régime(s) and of US policy but is not unduly selective: presents various points of view.

Halberstam, David. *The Making of a Quagmire.* Random House and Bodley Head, 1965. By the *New York Times*' correspondent in Saigon whose acute—and accurate—reporting roused the ire of Mme Nhu and the US State Department.

Hickey, Gerald Cannon. *Village in Vietnam.* Yale U.P., 1964. An American anthropologist's report on the customs, religious observances, economic activities and social life of villagers in a Mekong delta community.

Knoebl, Kuno. *Victor Charlie: The Face of War in Viet-Nam.* Praeger and Pall Mall, 1967. Vigorous report by a European journalist, in the firing line with both sides.

Mecklin, John. *Mission in Torment: An Intimate Account of the U.S. Role in Vietnam.* Doubleday, 1965. By the Public Affairs Officer at the US Embassy in Saigon, caught between official 'optimism' and a critical Press.

Nighswonger, William A. *Rural Pacification in Vietnam.* Praeger, 1966.

Personal experience of the impediments to pacification, especially the strategic hamlet programme, by a former US official in the provinces.

Nguyen, Kien. *Le Sud-Vietnam depuis Dien-Bien-Phu.* Francois Maspero, 1963. By a Vietnamese exile in Paris, opposed to Diem, favouring the NLF.

Nguyen Thai. *Is South Vietnam Viable?* Carmelo & Bauermann, Manila, 1962. Despairing plea for reform by disillusioned ex-official of the 'family' régime. A rare account of the working of 'Diemocracy' from within.

Osborne, Milton. *Strategic Hamlets in South Vietnam: a Survey and a Comparison* [with Malaya]. Cornell Data Paper, 1965. The comparison is convincing.

Pike, Douglas. *Viet Cong: The Organisation and Techniques of the National Liberation Front of South Vietnam.* M.I.T. Press, 1966. A massive survey by an experienced and well-informed US information official using extensive (captured) documentary material. Basically up to 1964, it tends to overlook the reasons for Vietcong successes in 1965. But the evidence is invaluable.

Raskin, Marcus and Fall, Bernard (eds.). *The Viet-Nam Reader: Articles and Documents on American Foreign Policy and the Viet-Nam Crisis.* Random House, 1965. A well-selected compilation.

Scigliano, Robert. *South Vietnam: Nation under Stress.* Houghton Mifflin, 1964. Critical but penetrating analysis of the Diem régime.

Shaplen, Robert. *The Lost Revolution: Vietnam 1945-1965.* Harper & Row, 1965; Deutsch, 1966. Harper, 1965, pap. Persuasive and well-written lament for opportunities lost by the régimes and by the US.

Tanham, George K., and others. *War Without Guns: American Civilians in Rural Vietnam.* Praeger, 1965. Personal reports from the Mekong delta, the tribal Highlands and Central Vietnam with a stimulating introduction and conclusion by Tanham.

Thompson, Sir Robert. *Defeating Communist Insurgency: Experiences from Malaya and Vietnam.* Chatto & Windus, and Praeger, 1966. The author was head of the British Advisory Mission to Vietnam and acted as adviser to President Diem on the strategic hamlet programme. A first-rate study of the techniques of counter-insurgency. Emphasis on the village subversive organization rather than the guerrilla recommended: on patient, methodical, co-ordinated action, not 'crash programmes'.

Warner, Denis. *The Last Confucian* [Diem]: *Vietnam, South East Asia and the West.* Angus & Robertson, 1964. Fluent, thoughtful and perceptive reporting by a veteran correspondent.

BURMA

Cady, J. F. *A History of Modern Burma.* Cornell U.P., 1958. A good account of developments from British rule to Independence.

Tinker, Hugh. *The Union of Burma.* Oxford U.P., 1957 and subseq. eds. Authoritative analysis—political, diplomatic, economic and military (insurgencies).

CAMBODIA

Leifer, Michael. *Cambodia: The Search for Security.* Praeger and Pall Mall, 1967. Well-informed and sympathetic study of the Prince and his policies.

INDONESIA

Brackman, Arnold C. *Indonesian Communism: a History.* Praeger, 1963. Readable and clear narrative by an American correspondent.

Grant, Bruce. *Indonesia.* Melbourne U.P., 1964. Penguin, 1967 (paperback ed.). A useful survey.

Hindley, Donald. *The Communist Party of Indonesia 1951-1963.* Univ. of California, 1964. Authoritative analysis of PKI problems and policies under Aidit's leadership.

Kahin, George McT. *Nationalism and Revolution in Indonesia.* Cornell U.P., 1952. Admirable study of the independence struggle.

Kroef, Justus van der. *The Communist Party of Indonesia: Its History, Program and Tactics.* Univ. of Brit. Columbia, 1965. Much useful material, thought not too well organized. (With hindsight) takes too alarmist a view of the threat from the PKI.

Nasution, A. H. *Fundamentals of Guerilla Warfare: and the Indonesian Defence System Past and Future.* Djakarta (1960?). Also Praeger facsimile ed., 1965. Theory and practice from the point of view of a guerrilla (and later a counter-guerrilla) commander bears out the essential need for popular support.

LAOS

Dommen, Arthur J. *Conflict in Laos: The Politics of Neutralisation.* Praeger, 1964. An experienced American reporter's critical—but not unduly so—survey of US policy and activities (clandestine and otherwise) in Laos during the Eisenhower era and after.

Sisouk Na Champassak. *Storm over Laos: A Contemporary History.* Praeger, 1961. Written by a prominent member of the Right-wing 'Young Turks', but a not unfair impression of personalities and events; the author is now Minister of Finance in Prince Souvanna Phouma's Government.

Toye, Hugh. *Laos: Buffer State or Battleground.* Oxford U.P., 1968. An absorbing historical picture of Laos, divided between tribal peoples in the mountains (now supporting the Pathet Lao) and the Lao rice-cultivators in the lowlands (mainstay of the Government). Up to 1965.

MALAYA

Clutterbuck, Richard. *The Long, Long War: The Emergency in Malaya 1948-1960.* Praeger, 1966, and Cassell, 1967. Clear and convincing account of early British failures (the conventional military approach) followed by well-deserved successes in tackling intelligently the crux of the matter—the Communist political and supply organization in the villages.

Hanrahan, Gene Z. *The Communist Struggle in Malaya.* Inst. of Pacific

Rels., 1954. Valuable historical study of the strategy and tactics of the Malayan Communist Party (to 1953).

Miller, Harry. *Menace in Malaya.* Harrap, 1954. Lively and effective account of the Emergency by an experienced *Straits Times*' reporter.

Osborne, Milton. *Strategic Hamlets in South Vietnam: a Survey and a Comparison* [with the Malayan 'New Villages']. Cornell, 1965. (See under Vietnam.)

Purcell, Victor. *Malaya: Communist or Free?* Gollancz, 1954. Notable report on the Emergency by a former Malayan Civil Servant specializing in Chinese affairs; opposed to General Templer's 'Coercive' policy.

Pye, Lucian W. *Guerrilla Communism in Malaya: Its Social and Political Meaning.* Princeton U.P., 1956. Case studies of 'Surrendered Enemy Personnel' preceded by a brilliant analysis of revolutionary Communism and its applicability to Malayan conditions.

Thompson, Sir R. *Defeating Communist Insurgency: Experiences from Malaya and Vietnam.* Chatto & Windus, and Praeger, 1965. A former Malayan Civil Servant, latterly Secretary for Defence (until 1961), stresses the importance of co-ordinated civil-police-military operations, a unified plan, sound administration and good intelligence—this was developed in Malaya, but not in South Vietnam (see also under Vietnam).

PHILIPPINES

Romulo, Carlos P. & Gray, Marvin M. *The Magsaysay Story.* Pocket Books, 1957. Colourful account of a decisive leader.

Scaff, Alvin H. *The Philippines' Answer to Communism.* Stanford U. P., 1955. Brief survey of the Huk revolt, the Army's civic action programme, including the EDCOR scheme, and points from interviews with ex-Huks.

Valeriano, Napoleon D. & Bohannan, Charles T. R. *Counter-Guerrilla Operations: The Philippines Experience.* Praeger, 1962. Useful study, emphasizing the importance of the political aspects of insurgency and counter-measures; but not quite the authoritative work which the subject requires.

Vargus, Jesus M. *Communism in Decline: The Huk Campaign.* SEATO (1958). An effective, concise report by the Armed Forces Chief of Staff under Magsaysay, later Secretary of Defence.

THAILAND

Darling, Frank. *The United States and Thailand.* Cornell U.P., 1965. A former C.I.A. official picks on the weaknesses of US support for military-controlled régimes, but his accusations are exaggerated.

Neuchterlein, Donald E. *Thailand and the Struggle for Southeast Asia.* Cornell U.P. 1965. A counter to Darling. Sympathetic view of Thai foreign policy, particularly during the Laotian crisis. Sounds a remarkably Dullesian note.

Wilson, David A. *Politics in Thailand.* Cornell U.P., 1962. First thorough account by a Western writer, using Thai sources, of the contemporary scene.

US POLICY

Documents on American Foreign Relations. Harper, formerly Princeton U.P., for Council on Foreign Relations. Annual selection of important speeches and official reports.

Fifield, Russell. *Southeast Asia in United States Policy*. Praeger, 1963. Useful but not very inspired. Good bibliography.

Hilsman, Roger. *To Move a Nation: The Politics of Foreign Policy in the Administration of John F. Kennedy*. Doubleday, 1967. Valuable source of information on US policy towards Laos and Vietnam—attitudes of President, State Department and Pentagon—by the former Director of Intelligence and Research, and Assistant Secretary for Far Eastern Affairs at the State Department, who resigned (was dismissed?) early in 1964. Challenges the conventional military approach to insurgency.

Kahin, George McT. & Lewis, John W. *The United States in Vietnam: An Analysis in Depth of the History of America's Involvement in Vietnam*. Delta Books, 1967. Useful survey, not particularly 'deep' (impossible in such short space), by an authority on Indonesia and on China respectively. Critical, objectively presented.

Taylor, Maxwell D. *Responsibility and Response*. Harper & Row, 1967. Two lectures by the former Chairman of the Joint Chiefs of Staff and ex-Ambassador to Saigon, an advocate of bombing the North. Discusses question of US intervention and commitments; points out difficulties in accurate assessment of the situation (as in Vietnam).

US Department of State. *Aggression from the North: The Record of North Viet-Nam's Campaign to Conquer South Viet-Nam*. Washington, 1965. The 'massive evidence of North Vietnamese agression' published, not very convincingly, to justify US bombing of the North. *A Threat to the Peace: North Viet-Nam's Effort to Conquer South Viet-Nam*. Washington, 1961. Issued to explain the need for increased US assistance to the Government of South Vietnam; useful account of Vietcong organization and guerrilla activities. *Department of State Bulletin*. Texts of foreign policy statements, speeches, interviews, news conferences by the President, Secretary of State, etc.

COMMUNISM AND INSURGENCY

Brimmell, J. H. *Communism in Southeast Asia: A Political Analysis*. Oxford U.P., 1959. Still one of the best surveys of this period, particularly on the 1948 uprisings.

Galula, David. *Counter-Insurgency Warfare: Theory and Practice*. Praeger and Pall Mall, 1964. Brilliant and lucid discussion with examples from Algeria, Indo-China, Greece and Vietnam.

Kennedy, D. E. *The Security of Southern Asia*. Chatto & Windus, and Praeger, 1965. An excellent exposition of the problems of defence ranging from India to Japan

McLane, Charles B. *Soviet Strategies in Southeast Asia: An Exploration of Eastern Policy under Lenin and Stalin.* Princeton U.P., 1966. Detailed study by a Soviet specialist making good use of Russian sources.

Sun Tsu (trans. Samuel B. Griffith). *The Art of War.* Oxford U.P., 1963. More than 2,000 years old, but relevant today (much quoted by Mao Tse-tung). Thus: 'Know the enemy, know your self; your victory will never be endangered' and 'those skilled in war avoid the enemy when his spirit is keen and attack him when it is sluggish. . . .'

Trinquier, Roger. *Modern Warfare*, Praeger, 1964. Rather fanatical approach to insurgency, especially in the use of informers and population control, but good advice on pacification.

PERIODICALS

Asia Survey (California); *China Quarterly* (London); *Far Eastern Economic Review* (Hong Kong); *Foreign Affairs* (New York); *International Affairs* (London); *Journal of Asian Studies* (Ann Arbor); *Pacific Affairs* (Vancouver); *Peking Review*; *Summary of World Broadcasts* (*Far East*)—B.B.C. Caversham; *World Marxist Review* (Prague).

INDEX